The Exchange University

Edited by Adrienne S. Chan and Donald Fisher

The Exchange University
Corporatization of Academic Culture

UBCPress · Vancouver · Toronto

16 15 14 13 12 11 10 09 08 5 4 3 2 1

Printed in Canada with vegetable-based inks on FSC-certified ancient-forest-free paper (100% post-consumer recycled) that is processed chlorine- and acid-free.

Library and Archives Canada Cataloguing in Publication

The exchange university : corporatization of academic culture / Adrienne S. Chan and Donald Fisher, eds.

Includes bibliographical references and index.
ISBN 978-0-7748-1569-7 (bound); ISBN 978-0-7748-1570-3 (pbk.)

1. Education, Higher – Economic aspects – Canada. 2. Universities and colleges – Canada – Finance. 3. Business and education – Canada. 4. Academic spin-outs – Canada. 5. Education, Higher – Research – Economic aspects – Canada. 6. Higher education and state – Canada. I. Fisher, Donald II. Chan, Adrienne

LC67.68.C3E93 2008 338.4'337871 C2008-904296-4

Canada

UBC Press gratefully acknowledges the financial support for our publishing program of the Government of Canada through the Book Publishing Industry Development Program (BPIDP), and of the Canada Council for the Arts, and the British Columbia Arts Council.

This book has been published with the help of a grant from the Canadian Federation for the Humanities and Social Sciences, through the Aid to Scholarly Publications Programme, using funds provided by the Social Sciences and Humanities Research Council of Canada, and with the help of the K.D. Srivastava Fund.

UBC Press
The University of British Columbia
2029 West Mall
Vancouver, BC V6T 1Z2
604-822-5959 / Fax: 604-822-6083
www.ubcpress.ca

FSC
Mixed Sources
Cert no. SW-COC-001271
www.fsc.org
© 1996 Forest Stewardship Council

Contents

Illustrations

Figures

Tables

Abbreviations

ATOP	Access to Opportunities
AUCC	Association of Universities and Colleges of Canada
AUTM	Association of University Technology Managers
CAPS	Coalition to Advance the Protection of Sports Logos
CASAE	Canadian Association for the Study of Adult Education
CAUBO	Canadian Association of University Business Officers
CFI	Canada Foundation for Innovation
CIHR	Canadian Institutes of Health Research
CIO	chief information officer
COU	Council of Ontario Universities
CRC	Canada Research Chair
CSSE	Canadian Society for the Study of Education
CSSHE	Canadian Society for the Study of Higher Education
CUA	Committee on University Affairs
CURA	Community-University Research Alliance
DOC	Department of Commerce
FCAR	Formation des chercheurs et l'aide à la recherche
FFRDC	Federally Funded Research and Development Centers
GATT	General Agreement on Tariffs and Trade
GNP	gross national product
IECA	Independent Educational Consultants Association
IHETS	Indiana Higher Education Telecommunication System
ILO	industry liaison office
INE	Initiatives for the New Economy
IP	intellectual property
IPO	initial public offering

IPR	intellectual property regime
IT	information technology
MCNC	Media Center North Carolina
MCRI	Major Collaborative Research Initiative
NAFTA	North American Free Trade Agreement
NCE	Networks of Centres of Excellence
NCES	National Center for Education Statistics
NDP	New Democratic Party
NIH	National Institues of Health
NRC	National Research Council
NSB	National Science Board
NSERC	Natural Sciences and Engineering Research Council
NSF	National Science Foundation
OCE	Ontario Centres of Excellence
OCUA	Ontario Council on University Affairs
OECD	Organization for Economic Co-operation and Development
OFSTED	Office for Standards in Education, Children's Service, and Care
PEQAB	Post-Secondary Education Quality Assessment Board
PI	performance indicators
RAE	Research Assessment Exercise
R&D	research and development
SRG	Standard Research Grant
SSHRCC	Social Sciences and Humanities Research Council of Canada
URIF	University Research Incentive Fund

Preface

In May 2003, academics gathered at the Dalhousie University in Halifax, Nova Scotia, for the annual meeting of the Congress of Humanities and Social Sciences/Canadian Federation for the Humanities and Social Sciences, with various educational societies meeting over a period of days. An all-day symposium was organized by the Centre for Policy Studies in Higher Education and Training, University of British Columbia. With the support of the congress and the federation, we were able to draw national attention to our symposium. The day also had the co-sponsorship of the Canadian Society for the Study of Education (CSSE), the Canadian Association for the Study of Adult Education (CASAE), and the Canadian Society for the Study of Higher Education (CSSHE).

The session we organized began with a keynote address delivered by Dr. Sheila Slaughter, University of Arizona, co-author with Gary Rhoades of *Academic Capitalism and the New Economy: Markets, State, and Higher Education* (2004). The address was followed by a series of paper presentations from scholars across Canada, the United Kingdom, and Argentina.

Approximately fifty people attended the whole day, with interested scholars attending during various portions of the day. Attendees at the colloquium overwhelmingly indicated the importance and timeliness of the dialogue that was generated through the paper presentations. Animated discussion occurred throughout the day. Some of the discussion focused on questions such as the following:

- What can be done to stem the tide of academic capitalism and increasing commercialization in universities?
- How are the relationships between universities and the government changing, given the tendencies for government to be more directive and "interventionist"?
- How has academic culture changed given the pressures of marketization and commercialization?

- How has the emphasis on hiring more contingent faculty affected issues related to governance and equality of opportunity for women and minorities?

Although the authors of this volume make no claims to "answer" these questions, it is our intention to pursue them further. An outcome of the colloquium was the expressed interest of all presenters to pursue the possibility of producing an edited volume of the paper presentations. This book is a result of this interest and collaboration. The editors wish to thank all the contributors for their willingness to edit and revise portions of their original papers.

The Exchange University

Introduction: The Exchange University

Adrienne S. Chan and Donald Fisher

Historically, higher education in Canada has been a public enterprise. While this is still the case, the boundary separating public and private sectors in provincial systems of higher education has become more complex and more porous since the 1990s. The boundary changes documented in this book have occurred primarily as a response to declining federal transfers, the dominance of market ideology, and the emergence of the knowledge economy. Furthermore, given that the constitutional responsibility for education has been assigned to the provinces, it is not surprising that changes in the ideological perspectives of provincial governments have had a substantial impact on higher education policy (Fisher et al., 2006). In succession, we have seen the election of free-market, neoliberal governments in Ontario (1995-2003), British Columbia (2001-), and Quebec (2003-).

Through legislation and other policy instruments, governments have created quasi-markets that encourage institutional competition within the public sector and between the public and private sectors. By the same means, universities have been encouraged to become centres for capital accumulation through the commercialization of research, an increase in technology transfer and the production of intellectual property, and a weakening of the boundary between the academy and industry. The relationships between the academy and industry now constitute a new academic culture for universities.

Academic culture has been described as the interconnection between teaching, learning, and research and the beliefs associated with these three forms of academic practice (Ringer, 1992). The culture of the academy is highly influenced by external influences, internal directives, and social, political, and educational agendas (Becher and Trowler, 2001; Clark, 1987; Elzinga, 1985; Neave and van Vught, 1991; Shils, 1997; Tierney, 1991). An elaboration of these specific influences will be presented within the chapters of this book. It provides examples of research and investigation into university practice and life and into what the university has become in the twenty-first century. The changes in the academy as outlined are informed by four structural trends that served as sensitizing concepts: globalization, commodification of knowledge and the knowledge economy, science policy, and federal funding and linkages across the boundaries separating the academy, industry, and the state. Through these examples, this book provides a view of changes within the university and the emergence of the "exchange university" – where exchange is linked to commodity production and capitalist production in the education system.

Background

Universities are clearly expected to perform within an environment of globalization and within the relationship of higher education to the knowledge economy (AUCC, 1999; Currie and Newson, 1998; Slaughter and Leslie, 1997). Slaughter and Leslie (1997) make a direct link between globalization, the marketplace, and the development of academic capitalism. In their study of four countries (Australia, Canada, the United Kingdom, and the United States), they found that "tertiary education policies in all countries moved toward science and technology policies that emphasized academic capitalism at the expense of basic or fundamental research, toward curricula policy that concentrated moneys in science and technology and fields close to the market" (p. 55).

A specific example in Canada was the Science Council of Canada (1988), an advisory body to the federal government. The council stated that priority should be placed on knowledge as part of the world economy and that the prosperity of Canada depends on an integrated relationship between the university and the marketplace. The council thus set the stage for a series of statements by federal and provincial governments that were part of a growing emphasis on science, technology, innovation, relationships with industry, and their place in the global economy. Canadian universities have been compelled to come to grips with the world economy and globalization. Globalization manifests itself in universities through the interrelationships of economic and political agendas, which influence both educational reform and policy responses and reactions (Morrow and Torres, 2000).

Commodification of knowledge production also evokes the question of whether universities, particularly in science disciplines, are subservient to the economy. The place of science in the knowledge economy is evidenced by research funding in the science disciplines, funding that has increased even during periods when research funding was reduced overall (Parizeau, 2001). The distinction between "pure" and "applied" research breaks down, as research can be both useful and fundamental (Fisher, Atkinson-Grosjean, and House, 2001). Pure basic research, pure applied research, research directed toward particular phenomena, or user-inspired basic research may co-exist within a model of scientific research (Stokes, 1997).

In 1999, a report on the commercialization of university research (Advisory Council on Science and Technology, 1999) was released. It emphasized innovation, intellectual property, and commercialization of knowledge as priorities for Canadian universities. Relationships with industry were emphasized – universities and industry have had a long-standing relationship, particularly in the natural and applied sciences. Since the late 1980s, the provision of matching grants for research support provided by the private sector has been one of a number of policy instruments designed to shift universities toward conducting more "industrially relevant" research activities such as intellectual property and technology transfer policies.

The federal government has explicitly expressed the importance of Canada's role in the knowledge economy through the Networks of Centres of Excellence (NCE) program; the Canada Research Chair program (CRC); the transformation of the Medical Research Council into the Canadian Institutes of Health Research (CIHR), which entailed a massive increase in the research budget; the creation of the Canada Foundation for Innovation (CFI); and the increase in funding to the other two research councils, the Natural Sciences and Engineering Research Council (NSERC) and the Social Sciences and Humanities Research Council of Canada (SSHRCC). The CFI received an additional $500 million in 2003 for a total of $3.15 billion to strengthen the capacity (infrastructure) of universities and research institutions. CIHR received $562 million in 2002-3, an increase of $75 million over the previous year. Together with federal and provincial policies, the Canadian funding councils have played a direct role in shaping the research priorities of institutions and influencing the professoriate's research agendas.

The NCE was established in 1989 as part of a program of initiatives in science and technology. This has been one of the most significant changes in Canada's science policy since the National Research Council (NRC) was established in 1916 (Fisher, Atkinson-Grosjean, and House, 2001). The federal government established the CRC in 1999 to provide funding for 2,000 chairs between 2000 and 2005. The program was established to increase research activity in the universities through the creation of specific chair positions at two levels: senior faculty/scholars and promising new scholars. The criteria for choosing recipients for chairs have meant that 80 percent will be in disciplines and fields under the umbrellas of natural, applied, and medical sciences. Furthermore, the current distribution map of these chairs shows a dramatic trend in favour of men. Polster (2002) suggests that the CFI and CRC are part of a wider perspective that influences academic research in a trend toward innovation in a globalized knowledge economy. All these programs and initiatives indicate the government's increased interest in knowledge production and the potential for the government to influence university research priorities.

Theoretical Framework

This book presents some common theoretical viewpoints. Contributors acknowledge that there are alternatives suggesting that globalization, capitalism, and corporatization make an important contribution to university life. Concurrently, accountability has become a watchword for university administrators in a time of reduced public resources. We suggest that the social demand that once directed growth of the postsecondary education system is gradually giving way to a new, economically driven imperative that places importance on highly developed human capital, science, and technology to support Canada's needs for economic restructuring and greater international competitiveness. This economic imperative has been amplified by limitations on public expenditures and emergence of the accountability movement. While institutions must be accountable to the public, there are growing doubts regarding public institutions and an increasing value placed on the efficiency of free-market forces.

If privatization was the symbol of the tension between the public and the private sectors during the 1980s, then marketization and the corollary of commodification took over that role in the 1990s. In particular, the university has been described as the centre of the drive toward the "commodification" of higher education (Rooney and Hearn, 2000), while Etzkowitz, Webster, and Healey (1998) invoke the image of the "triple helix" to describe the revolution that has occurred with intertwining of the interests of the state, the market, and higher education. Bok (2003) draws attention to the "commercialization" of higher education, while Noble (1976, 2001), looking at an extended period of time, pushes us to think about education as a mode of production. For Clark (1998), the new model for our universities is characterized by "entrepreneurship," while Marginson and Considine (2000) use the label "enterprise" university. At the heart of the changes is "marketization" of liberal democratic societies and necessarily of higher education (Slaughter and Leslie, 1997). We have begun to label the change as one that produces the "exchange university."

Simon Marginson and Sheila Slaughter are two authors who have led the way in helping us to understand and explain the impact of capital and market ideology on our higher education systems. In *Markets in Education* (1997), Marginson places the changes we observe in a larger political-economic context. Drawing on the work of Marx and Braudel, we are reminded of the power of capital to universalize commodity production and market forms. For Marginson, "market relations are a normalizing system in which everything and everyone has a price, and all difference, all the heterogeneous kinds of value are reworked as standardized exchange values, strung out on a standard grid according to the different quantities of money they represent" (1997, p. 30). The knowledge society is then understood as an extension of capitalist production, consumption, and exchange into education. Knowledge, and by extension education, become commodities valued for their "exchange" value rather than their "use" value. For Marginson, all markets in education are "quasi-markets" involving a mix of use and exchange values and a mix of both public and private interests. He divides production in education markets into two types of goods: student goods (e.g., credentials) and knowledge goods (e.g., patents). Furthermore, he divides production in education markets into simple commodity production and fully capitalist production. In the latter, exchange values dominate; the examples Marginson gives are full-fee courses, commercial research, and much private training – again leading to the notion of the exchange university.

Slaughter and Leslie (1997) build on the earlier work done by Slaughter and Rhoades (1996) to map the rise of what they call "academic capitalism." This concept defines "the reality of the nascent environment of public research universities, an environment full of contradictions, in which faculty and professional staff expend their human capital stocks increasingly in competitive situations ... University employees are employed simultaneously by the public sector and are increasingly autonomous from it. They are academics who act as capitalists from within the public sector; they are state-subsidized entrepreneurs" (1997, p. 9). The concept is useful because it captures how commercialization and marketization overlap to change the power relations within universities. It provides a basis for understanding how academic culture is changing as these entrepreneurs move their institutions closer to the market.

Slaughter and Rhoades (2004 and Chapter 1 in this volume) take us further in describing the "academic capitalist knowledge/learning regime." In documenting the dominance of this regime, the authors provide us with a way to understand changes in the territory that connects the public and the private sectors in higher education, between the state, higher education, and the market. For Slaughter and Rhoades, academic capitalism is not privatization but a redefinition of public space and of appropriate activity in that space. As the configuration of state resources changes and public universities and colleges are pushed to seek alternative sources of funding, our conception of "public" is blurred and altered. As the boundaries between state, higher education, and the market change (Fisher, Atkinson-Grosjean, and House, 2001), our attention is drawn to the boundary workers (Fisher and Atkinson-Grosjean, 2002) who create new "circuits of knowledge" as they promote market behaviours. The focus is on both the restratification of institutions and the restructuring of faculty work. We see, rather than the removal of public subsidies, a shift in particular toward students, who are faced with higher fees. To understand the rise of academic capitalist knowledge learning regimes, we must focus on policies that concern patents, copyright, expansion of distance education, and the concentration of student markets, both domestic and international (see Chapter 3 in this volume).

The dominant policy paradigm in Canada over our period of study has been accountability. This movement has rejected the idea that the state is primarily responsible for the public good function of education. Critics have called for less taxation, less government interference, more public choice, more deregulation and privatization, and more accountability to taxpayers by the government and its subsidiaries (Dale, 1997; and Chapter 4 in this volume): "This new state abandons its role as direct economic agent (producer of goods and services) and as a regulator of economic life (minimum wages, maximum prices, protectionism, subsidies, etc.), becoming instead a subsidiary agent whose main function is to guarantee a social and economic environment propitious for capital accumulation ... It also implies the withdrawal of state from the commitment to universal provision of public services such as education, health, housing and social security, which are now becoming increasingly regulated by market dynamics" (Schugurensky, 1999, p. 285).

In a neoliberal framework, public choice, marketization, and privatization of education are prevalent themes, emphasizing stronger links between industry training needs and the postsecondary sector. These changes manifest themselves in education and other public services in two major ways. First, there is reluctance to use public funds to fund public services; second, public institutions are to engage in market behaviour in order to fund more of their services. This shift creates changes to organizational forms, managerial practices, and institutional cultures (Deem, 2001). Policy changes are accompanied by downloading more financial responsibility onto postsecondary institutions and are characterized by less state funding and an increased emphasis on business practices (Currie, 1998). Clark (1998) states that themes of efficiency, effectiveness, excellence, and continuous quality improvement are examples of thinking that prevail within the entrepreneurial university.

Governments strategically promote increased efficiency and innovation using education markets (Dill, 1997a; Slaughter and Leslie, 1997): "Long perceived as a unique characteristic of the US system of higher education, experiments with market competition in academic labor markets, institutional finance, student support, and the allocation of research funds are now evident in the higher education policy of many different nations" (Dill, 1997b, p. 167). In a neoliberal environment, institutions are often granted more autonomy from central government but are then forced to go into the market, where they must seek sponsorship. In order to gain sponsorship, they must adapt to new methods and systems. Under resource dependency, the rules are subject to change according to the interdependency established.

The social controls that accompany government funding differ from the social controls established in a market environment. In the latter, the behaviours that result include academic capitalism and institutional entrepreneurship (Clark, 1998; Marginson, 1997; Slaughter and Leslie, 1997; and Chapter 6 in this volume).

On the supply side, if the public sector is unable to respond and adapt its curriculum accordingly, other providers of higher education are poised to do so. The private sector views the provision of educational services as a viable business opportunity, in both the international and the domestic student markets, and shows a competitive presence in the education industry. This is evident in the prominent role that private education companies are playing on the stock exchange and the proliferation of new publicly traded companies. If the public system responds with market-oriented behaviour, there will still be increased competition from the private sector for students due to the profit potential. Examples include international student programs in English as a second language, business, and computer studies, which are attractive to the private sector. These programs have the highest probability of returning a profit due to low capitalization costs (Cantor, 2000). The private sector can selectively pick programs to deliver based on areas projected to provide the best profit margins (Cantor, 2000; Collis, 2001). But the public system is expected to provide a broad range of programs, regardless of profit, to their communities; if an entrepreneurial approach is what is required in order to meet budget demands, the question is at what cost?

Marginson (1997) and Slaughter and Leslie (1997) believe that globalization creates conditions where nation-state educational policies converge in areas including access, curricula, research, and autonomy for faculty and institutions. Existing institutional structures, values, and beliefs erode as higher education develops to meet a specific economic agenda, such as emphasis on international activity (Currie, 1998; Dudley, 1998; Frost and Taylor, 2001; Slaughter, 1998). For example, Knight (1999) points out that the purpose of international education has already shifted in the academy. It began as a way of providing aid to developing nations, then evolved to a position of mutual benefit, and is now a commodity to trade in a globalized world. In contrast, Clark (1998) states that, while a shift in organizational structures, values, and attitudes may occur, there can be a positive outcome that is evident through institutional renewal and an enhanced funding base. Cantor (2000) believes that it is necessary for the public system to become more entrepreneurial given increased competition for the provision of educational services and diminished government funding. He insists that the system needs to explore alternative options given the political and economic climate.

Educational markets affect institutional governance models, and the main model has become increasingly corporatized and managerial (Currie, 1998;

Fisher and Rubenson, 1998; Marginson, 2000; Pietrykowski, 2001; Schugurensky, 2000; Slaughter, 1998). Faculty have less input into the decision-making process of the institution because decisions are made by an executive core of administrators who increasingly depend on directors and managers of non-academic units for advice and guidance on institutional matters. Financial systems are more complex in quasi-market and entrepreneurial-based environments, with increased accountability requirements, reporting obligations, and budgeting processes. Determining what makes business sense, in assessing various projects and their potential to make a financial contribution to the institution, requires business knowledge. Under these conditions, it is likely that senior administrators will continue to seek business expertise in dealing with institutional matters (Evans, 2005).

Research and Academic Culture

The business ethos in universities is influencing their culture, so that the focus is on a particular type of research and research intensity. In order to understand how universities are responding to the market economy, we examined the top twelve research-intensive Canadian universities' rankings from 1999 to 2004. Some important trends in research were revealed. Universities were examined for sponsored research income by source; level of participation in the Canada Research Chairs program; and level of participation in the Networks of Centres of Excellence program.

The twelve (English-speaking) universities identified showed a marked increase in sponsored research income from 1999 to 2000 and from 2003 to 2004. The rank indicated is based on research intensity.[1] Sponsored research income included grants from federal sources (e.g., funding councils, specific funding envelopes), provincial sources, municipal sources, industry, and private contributions. The presence of an industry liaison office (ILO) and a technology transfer office, revenue from royalties, and licensed income were indicators of the investment climate arising out of universities and research organizations established within universities. Table I.1 shows the increase by dollars (in US funds and in constant dollars) and by percentage.

The twelve universities examined participate in the Canada Research Chairs program and the Networks of Centres of Excellence. Announced in 2000 by the government of Canada, a fund of $900 million was established to support the CRC program in Canadian universities between 2000 and 2005. This program enables universities and affiliated research institutes and hospitals to work toward achieving the highest levels of research excellence and *"to become world-class research centres in the global, knowledge-based economy"* (Canada Research Chairs, 2001, www.chairs.gc.ca). The NCE is part of a federal program of initiatives in science and technology. There are twenty-one networks (2004-5) and partnerships with seventy-nine universities. Of the twelve universities considered, there was a participation rate of anywhere

Table I.1

Sponsored research income comparison

Institution	Rank 2004	Rank 2003	($000s) 1999	($000s) 2000	% Change	($000s) 2003	($000s) 2004	% Change
Toronto	1	1	306,519	371,119	21.4	534,356	623,995	16.8
McGill	2	4	198,899	234,340	17.8	342,690	543,497	58.6
Montreal	3	2	253,099	206,224	22.7	394,426	446,247	13.1
UBC	4	3	139,102	165,992	19.3	349,101	363,337	4.1
Alberta	5	6	174,296	206,667	18.6	272,853	360,009	31.9
Calgary	7	9	107,843	134,507	24.7	165,622	251,379	51.8
McMaster	8	7	85,899	106,892	24.4	218,183	246,173	12.8
Ottawa	10	8	89,373	114,612	28.2	186,174	190,343	2.2
Queen's	11	10	68,854	83,217	20.9	159,136	174,762	9.8
Manitoba	12	12	67,717	76,016	12.3	130,029	126,493	-2.7
Saskatchewan	15	13	51,068	71,849	40.7	116,789	107,598	-7.9
Dalhousie	16	16	45,107	77,130	71.3	79,479	92,898	16.9
Memorial	23	22	27,872	33,896	21.9	42,780	50,300	17.6

[a] The University of Montreal is not English speaking but included here because it ranked number two and three in years 2003 and 2004 respectively.

[b] Saskatchewan, Dalhousie, and Memorial were included for a broader geographic comparison. Quebec is not represented except for McGill, but note that the University of Montreal and Laval University are consistently within the top ten research universities.

Source: Re$earch Infosource (2001).

Table I.2

Networks of Centres of Excellence and Canada Research Chairs

Institution	Participation in NCEs (2001)	CRCs: Actuals for years 1-3 (2000-3)
Toronto	17	148
McGill	18	98
Alberta	18	71
UBC	21	87
Calgary	12	39
Ottawa	13	32
McMaster	16	41
Queen's	13	32
Dalhousie	14	32
Manitoba	14	31
Saskatchewan	10	24
Memorial	7	16

Sources: Networks of Centres of Excellence website (www.nce.gc.ca) and Canada Research Chairs website (www.chairs.gc.ca).

from seven to twenty-one of the networks. Table I.2 indicates the level of participation for the universities in the NCE as partners and the number of chairs through the CRC program.

Table I.3

Federal contributions to total sponsored research expenditures in Canadian universities (1981-82 to 2001-2) in constant dollars (2002-3)

Year	Federal source	Sponsored research total	Percent
1981-82	722,410,815	1,151,117,912	63
1991-92	1,006,450,151	1,960,081,015	51
2001-2	1,734,089,175	3,854,750,438	45

Note: Income by fund and by type. All universities for various years.
Source: Canadian Association of University Business Officers (CAUBO).

With the exception of the University of Saskatchewan, all universities have been the headquarters for at least one NCE. Participation in both of these programs indicates a commitment by universities to enhance and build research capacity and research strength.

Table I.3 provides a comparison of federal contributions to total sponsored research expenditures in Canadian universities. In constant dollars (2002-3), the federal contribution to the total sponsored research expenditure decreased from 63 percent ($722 million) in 1981-82 to 51 percent ($1,006 million) in 1991-92 and to 45 percent ($1,734 million) in 2001-2. This is a drop of almost 20 percent in twenty years. Even though the federal proportion is decreasing, real funding increase (after discounting inflation) from the 1971-72 level is 28 percent in 1981-82, 39 percent in 1991-92, and 71 percent in 2001-2. The apparent proportional federal decrease is due to federal funding not keeping up with the real increase in the overall sponsored research revenue of universities.

Since matching funds policies were introduced in Canada, universities have been forced to examine their role in the "knowledge economy" and the weighting they give to science, technology, and "innovation" (de la Mothe and Pacquet, 1999). In some instances, granting councils have been required to earmark funding for university-industry collaborations. Universities and industry have had a long-standing relationship, particularly in the natural and applied sciences. This has led to significant commodification in research areas such as biotechnology (Dickson, 1984). The Canada Foundation for Innovation is an example where emphasis in federal research funding as a whole has been on the natural, applied, and health sciences. Between 1998-99 and 2004-5, the federal government added a total of $9.13 billion in new research funding. Of this total, only $1.02 billion or 11.2 percent funded research in the humanities and social sciences (Statistics Canada, 2006). Additionally, Canadian funding councils have encouraged collaboration through joint funding, with some research envelopes requiring partnerships between the university and industry. This has also resulted in other commercial activities, such as the establishment of "spin-off" companies and use of patents.

One of our interests is examining the relationship between research culture and the diffusion of knowledge within the context of the knowledge economy and how this economy has become more embedded in academic discourses. Gibbons and his colleagues have juxtaposed two ideal types of knowledge production (Gibbons et al., 1994; Nowotny, Scott, and Gibbons, 2001; Scott, 2000). In Mode 1, traditional forms of academic research produced knowledge through hierarchically structured, relatively stable means. This knowledge was furthered by academic interests, evaluated by peer review, and diffused through publications, conferences, and training. Mode 2 is an emergent form of knowledge production that is heterarchically structured, transdisciplinary, project-centred, shaped by various interests, and evaluated in terms of effectiveness by peers, non-peers, and sponsors of projects. Diffusion of knowledge under Mode 2 depends on the commercial value of that knowledge, whereby a business may not wish to diffuse knowledge if that knowledge gives it a competitive advantage. Mode 2 represents a progressive industrial research culture, although it may be present in noncommercial cultures as well. Both Mode 1 and Mode 2 are present in university research, but the latter represents a commercialization of knowledge that was not present fifteen years ago in the academy. Higher education is strongly implicated in the market language of the production, distribution, and utilization of knowledge.

Organization of the Book

The authors contribute to educational theorizing and policy debates in at least three areas: academic capitalism, global competitiveness, and relationships with industry. The chapters in this book provide insight into emerging discourses within the framework of a knowledge economy and increased market-like behaviours in universities. Partnerships between faculty and industry and corporations have been highly valorized by both the state and the university. The question is what the appropriate role for the academy in these partnerships should be. Resistance to such collaboration stems from the fear expressed by many academics that academic capitalism is taking over as private corporations increasingly influence the university. Many of the authors here describe state policy agendas in the context of the historical and current political economies. The policy environment for higher education has changed dramatically to favour not only the market but also the natural, applied, and health sciences. Thus, there is concern regarding the role and influence of the state at both the micro and the macro levels of the university. *The Exchange University* provides an insider view of the tensions and debates occurring in universities and the changing role of faculty and university administrators in the intellectual life of their universities. Faculty and administrators articulate their concerns with the changing academic culture and the process of knowledge creation. Pressures to perform in a competitive research environment and to meet state and institutional objectives to contribute to the global economy have had a clear impact on research and teaching. In conclusion, we consider the future of the university as an institution of higher learning and the preservation of the goal of broad-based education.

The book has nine chapters and a conclusion. We begin with a chapter by Sheila Slaughter and Gary Rhoades.[2] Earlier work by Slaughter and Leslie (1997) has provided many academics with a backdrop for considering academic capitalism, commodification of universities, and transnationalism of the knowledge economy. The chapter here, "The Academic Capitalist Knowledge/Learning Regime," expands the theory of academic capitalism by incorporating the key concepts "regime" and "circuits of knowledge." Circuits of knowledge include policy, patenting, and copyrighting. The state and public space are redefined to include an engagement with privatization, commercialization, deregulation, and reregulation. Universities and colleges have become the foundation of the new economy in an "academic capitalist knowledge/learning regime."

Academic capitalist knowledge/learning regimes reconsider knowledge in a number of ways: knowledge as a commodity, knowledge as privately held, income from knowledge, students as consumers, and the balance between public and private sectors. Universities have become far more involved in market behaviours such as for-profit activities, patenting, royalty and licensing agreements, intellectual property, spin-off companies, and university-industry partnerships. This has led to the co-existence of different knowledge regimes within universities, including a tension between disciplines that receive funding and profits and those not engaged in funding and revenue activities.

Chapter 2, "Academic Culture and the Research-Intensive University: The Impact of Commercialism and Scientism" (Chan and Fisher), considers the internal factors, external factors, and internal responses that have shaped changes in academic culture. The chapter highlights the findings of fieldwork and documentary evidence in one of Canada's research intensive universities, the University of Ottawa. Emergent themes reveal concerns regarding the changing nature of research and collegiality and the increasing problematic of the commodification of knowledge and education. Tensions regarding university values, institutional priorities, and a compelling managerial agenda have provoked serious debate among faculty, administrators, and members of university governance structures. The emergence of cultural divisions is evident through the discourses of faculty and administrators concerning the values of a knowledge economy, the emphasis on science compared to broader learning and educational imperatives, and the place of the academy within an overriding, competitive, global knowledge economy. Changes in academic culture were based on the University of Ottawa's motivation and determination to become a research intensive university.

Chapter 3, "The New Production of Researchers" by Brigitte Gemme and Yves Gingras, examines graduate education and the increasing presence of graduates and graduate students in sectors such as industry and public service, a trend promoted by federal and provincial innovation policies. This trend, and growing pressure to turn professors into "innovators," calls for transformations in graduate education. Most importantly, it is expected that graduate students will spend more time and energy on problems and issues raised by the so-called demands of society, which means mostly demands from industry in the case of the natural, applied, and health sciences and from government and NGOs in the case of the social sciences and humanities.

Involving graduate students with non-university organizations has implications for students themselves, the university, and the future of the new professoriate. Findings suggest that, although variable between sectors and programs of study, new requirements for research are being imposed on students, while other requirements may remain fairly constant.

Paul Axelrod in Chapter 4, "Public Policy in Ontario Higher Education: From Frost to Harris," provides an overview of university-government relations in Ontario from 1945 to the present. He considers what has occurred during this period with the growing incorporation of higher education into provincial and national policy agendas tied largely to economic concerns. From the early 1970s to the mid-1990s, the economic environment in which higher education policy evolved was turbulent and uncertain, though the structure of university-government relations in Ontario changed relatively little, and universities retained much of their historic institutional autonomy.

Following the election of the Mike Harris Conservatives in 1995, the government asserted its authority over universities in increasingly direct ways while simultaneously opening the door to private providers of post-secondary education. Both strategies were designed to integrate higher education into the marketplace and to ensure that universities (and colleges) would be instrumental components of the government's economic action plans. This approach, reinforced by federal government initiatives, had important implications for university governance and for the institutions' curricular and research programs.

Linda Muzzin examines in Chapter 5, "How Fares Equity in an Era of Academic Capitalism? The Role of Contingent Faculty," the emerging trend to have contingent faculty. As part of economic globalization, universities in Canada in the past twenty years have engaged in significant restructuring, introducing a way of thinking that Broadbent, Dietrich, and Roberts (1997) have called "accounting logic." One restructuring strategy has involved increased use of contingent faculty, paralleling the trend in health and welfare sectors. Sessional and contractual teaching is undertaken not only by students eventually intending to apply for tenure-stream faculty positions but also by a cadre of last-hired, first-fired academic labourers who maintain work in other sectors in order to earn a living. Using a national study of contingent faculty and current or former administrators in professional education as well as in the social sciences, Muzzin examines how the use of contingent labour in Canadian academia undermines attempts to address issues of gender and racial equity (Muzzin et al., 1999).

In Chapter 6, "Reclaiming Our Centre: Toward a Robust Defence of Academic Autonomy,"[3] Jan Newson and Claire Polster show how academic autonomy is being infringed upon. They critique how academics have responded – both individually and collectively – to these infringements. Specifically, they argue that the ways in which academics have defended against erosion of their autonomy actually advances the process. This paradox is attributed to academics' impoverished conception of professional autonomy. The authors argue for a more robust conception and practice of academic autonomy as a means of remedying the situation.

Jo-Anne Dillabough and Sandra Acker examine in Chapter 7, "'Gender at Work' in Teacher Education: History, Society, and Global Reform,"[4] the "crises of meaning," "crisis of politics," and "regulatory state" (Bourdieu, 1999; Hood and Scott, 2000) as well as the links to "work" and "working life" and the impact of global economic, cultural, and political reforms on the ethical consciousness of the university. Of particular concern is the part played by gender in mediating the effects of such regulatory controls and their impact on the construction of female work in professions that "institutionalize women's labours."

Dillabough and Acker discuss how such "crises" or forms of state regulation are evident in the daily lives of *women workers* in one professional discipline in the university – teacher education. A particular interest stems from concern about the constitution of cultural fields known as "research culture" and "academic accountability," how such fields are imbued with masculine inflections in higher education, and the effects of these fields on women teacher educators' work in times of substantial change and restructuring. Interview data are highlighted from three different studies of women teacher educators in the United Kingdom and Canada.

In Chapter 8, "The Political Economy of Legal Scholarship: A Case Study of the University of British Columbia Law School," Theresa Shanahan considers the academic discipline of law within the framework of contemporary political economy. Law is an unusual case in the contemporary higher education environment because it does not have a strong tradition of academic scholarship in Canadian universities. Emergent themes from this study at UBC suggest that law professors' scholarship is largely unfunded, requiring and generating little money. Legal research is an unprofitable enterprise that has little commercial value and does not bring products to market (i.e., through innovation or technology transfer). Most legal scholarship does not conform to patterns of other disciplines across the university either in the social sciences and humanities or in the natural, applied, or health sciences in how it is conducted or in the nature and extent of funding.

Jennifer Sumner in Chapter 9, "Keeping the Commons in Academic Culture: Protecting the Knowledge Commons from the Enclosure of the Knowledge Economy," focuses on universities as sites of inquiry, examining the commodification of knowledge in the age of corporate globalization. She provides examples of resistance to this enclosure of the commons and explores the commodification of knowledge in higher education, emphasizing how universities, using a deliberate policy of underfunding, are being forced into alliances with corporate "partners." These alliances produce changes that faculty must engage with, such as profit-driven research, selective funding, a highly corporatized campus, and an exponential increase in commodification of knowledge. Sumner suggests that we need to build new relations of knowledge production, both in the academy and in society at large, through a "reaching-out" process. Finally, she suggests that faculty work together to build the knowledge commons by forming knowledge collectives.

In the Conclusion, we consider some thematic issues raised in earlier chapters, focusing on significant questions with regard to the influence of commercialization and marketization. We also return to the theoretical frames that guided the collective efforts of the various contributors to the book, with particular reference to the work of Slaughter and Rhoades (2004 and Chapter 1). We highlight the effects and consequences of the adoption by Canadian universities of the academic capitalist knowledge/learning regime and draw attention to the changing shape of the boundary territory that connects Canadian public universities to the private sector, showing how much academic culture has changed in Canada since the 1990s.

Notes

1 Research intensity refers to sponsored research income per full-time faculty position (Re$earch Infosource, 2001).
2 This chapter is a revised version of the Conclusion in Slaughter and Rhoades (2004).
3 Originally published in *Science Studies, 14*(1) (2001), 55-75; reprinted with permission.
4 Revised version of Dillabough and Acker (2002); permission granted to use in this book.

References

Advisory Council on Science and Technology. (1999). *Public investments in university research: Reaping the benefits*. Report of the Expert Panel on the Commercialization of University Research. Ottawa: Government of Canada.

AUCC. (1999). *Trends: The Canadian university in profile.* Ottawa: Publications and Communications Division.

Becher, T., and Trowler, P.R. (2001). *Academic tribes and territories*. London: Society for Research into Higher Education and Open University Press.

Bok, D. (2003). *Universities in the marketplace: The commercialization of higher education.* Princeton: Princeton University Press.

Bourdieu, P. (1999). *The tyranny of the market.* London: Routledge.

Broadbent, J., Dietrich, M., and Roberts, J. (1997). *The end of the professions? The restructuring of professional work.* London: Routledge.

Canada Research Chairs. (2001). www.chairs.gc.ca.

Cantor, J. (2000). *Higher education outside of the academy*. ASHE-ERIC Higher Education Report *27*(7). San Francisco: Jossey-Bass.

Clark, B.R. (1987). *The academic life.* Princeton: Princeton University Press.

–. (1998). *Creating entrepreneurial universities: Organizational pathways of transformation.* Oxford: IAU Press and Pergamon.

Collis, D. (2001). "When industries change" revisited: New scenarios for higher education. In M. Devlin and J. Meyerson (Eds.), *Forum futures: Exploring the future of higher education* (pp. 103-26). Forum Strategy Series. San Francisco: Jossey-Bass.

Currie, J. (1998). Globalization practices and the professoriate in Anglo-Pacific and North American universities. *Comparative Education Review, 42*(1), 15-29.

Currie, J., and Newson, J. (1998). (Eds.) *Universities and globalization: Critical perspectives.* Thousand Oaks, CA: Sage.

Dale, R. (1997). The state and governance of education: An analysis of the restructuring of the state-education relationship. In A. Halsey, H. Lauder, P. Brown, and A.S. Wells (Eds.), *Education, culture, economy, society* (pp. 273-82). Oxford: Oxford University Press.

de la Mothe, J., and Pacquet, G. (Eds.). (1999). *Information, innovation, and impacts*. The Netherlands: Kluwer Academic Publishing.

Deem, R. (2001). Globalisation, new managerialism, academic capitalism, and entrepreneurialism in universities: Is the local dimension still important? *Comparative Education, 37*(1), 7-20.

Dickson, D. (1984). *The new politics of science.* New York: Pantheon Books.

Dill, D. (1997a). Markets and higher education: An introduction. *Higher Education Policy, 10,* 163-66.

–. (1997b). Higher education markets and public policy. *Higher Education Policy, 10,* 167-85.

Dillabough, J., and Acker, S. (2002). Globalization, women's work, and teacher education: A cross-national analysis. *International Studies in the Sociology of Education, 12*(3), 227-60.

Dudley, J. (1998). Globalization and education policy in Australia. In J. Currie and J. Newson (Eds.), *Universities and globalization: Critical perspectives* (pp. 21-44). Thousand Oaks, CA: Sage.

Elzinga, A. (1985). Research, bureaucracy, and the drift of epistemic criteria. In B. Wittrock and A. Elzinga (Eds.), *The university research system* (pp. 191-217). Stockholm: Almqvist and Wiksell.

Etzkowitz, H., Webster, A., and Healey, P. (1998). *Capitalizing knowledge: New interactions of industry and academe.* Albany: SUNY Press.

Evans, K. (2005). *Going global within the locals: A study of international activity in the university colleges.* Unpublished doctoral dissertation, University of British Columbia, Vancouver.

Fisher, D., and Atkinson-Grosjean, J. (2002). Brokers on the boundary: Academy-industry liaison in Canadian universities. *Higher Education, 44,* 449-67.

Fisher, D., and Rubenson, K. (1998). The changing political economy: The private and public lives of Canadian universities. In J. Currie and J. Newson (Eds.), *Universities and globalization: Critical perspectives* (pp. 77-98). Thousand Oaks, CA: Sage.

Fisher, D., Rubenson, K., Shanahan, T., Trottier, C., Bernatchez, J., Clift, R., Jones, G., Lee, J., MacIvor, M., and Meredith, J. (2006). *Canadian federal policy and post-secondary education.* Vancouver: Centre for Policy Studies in Higher Education and Training.

Frost, N., and Taylor, R. (2001). Patterns of change in the university: The impact of lifelong learning and the world of work. *Studies in the Education of Adults, 33*(1), 49-60.
Gibbons, M., Limoges, C., Nowotny, H., Schwartzmann, S., Scott, P., and Trow, M. (1994). *The new production of knowledge: The dynamics of science and research in contemporary societies.* London: Sage.
Hood, C., and Scott, C. (2000). *Regulating government in a "managerial" age: Towards a cross-national perspective.* London: Centre for Analysis of Risk and Regulation at the London School of Economic and Political Science.
Knight, J. (1999). Issues and trends in internationalization: A comparative perspective. In S. Bond and P. Lemasson (Eds.), *A new world of knowledge: Canadian universities and globalization* (pp. 201-38). Ottawa: IDRC Press.
Marginson, S. (1997). *Markets in education.* St. Leonards: Allen and Unwin.
–. (2000). Rethinking academic work in the global era. *Journal of Higher Education Policy and Management, 22*(1), 23-37.
Marginson, S., and Considine, M. (2000). *The enterprise university.* Cambridge, UK: Cambridge University Press.
Morrow, R.A., and Torres, C.A. (2000). The state, globalization, and educational policy. In N.C. Burbules and C.A. Torres (Eds.), *Globalization and education: Critical Perspectives* (pp. 27-56). London: Routledge.
Muzzin, L., Boyd, M., Gregor, F., Spafford, M., Albas, C., and Nygaard, V. (1999): Gendered retrenchment: Non-tenured faculty and knowledge production. Unpublished paper.
Neave, G., and van Vught, F.A. (Eds.). (1991). *Prometheus bound.* Oxford: Pergamon Press.
Noble, D.F. (1976). *America by design: Science, technology, and the rise of corporate capitalism.* New York: Knopf.
–. (2001). *Digital diploma mills: The automation of higher education.* New York: Monthly Review Press.
Nowotny, H., Scott, P., and Gibbons, M. (2001). *Rethinking science: Knowledge and the public in an age of uncertainty.* Cambridge, UK: Polity Press.
Pietrykowski, B. (2001). Information technology and the commercialization of knowledge: Corporate universities and class dynamics in an era of technological restructuring. *Journal of Economic Issues, 35*(2), 299-307.
Polster, C. (2002). Break from the past: Impacts and implications of the Canada Foundation for Innovation and the Canada Research Chairs initiatives. *Canadian Review of Sociology and Anthropology, 39*(3), 275-99.
Re$earch Infosource. (2001). Canada's top 50 research universities. www.researchinfosource.com.
Ringer, F. (1992). *Fields of knowledge: French academic culture in comparative perspective, 1890-1920.* Cambridge, UK: Cambridge University Press.
Rooney, D., and Hearn, G. (2000). Of minds, markets, and machines: How universities might transcend the ideology of commodification. In S. Inayatullah and J. Gidley (Eds.), *The university in transformation: Global perspectives on the future of the university* (pp. 91-104). Westport, CT: Bergin and Garvey.
Science Council of Canada. (1988). Winning in a world economy: Canadian universities and economic revival. Ottawa: SCC.
Schugurensky, D. (1999). Higher education restructuring in the era of globalization. In R. Arnove and C. Torres (Eds.), *Comparative education: The dialectic of the global and the local* (pp. 283-304). Lanham: Rowman and Littlefield.
Scott, P., (Ed.). (2000). *Higher education re-formed.* London: Falmer Press.
Shils, E. (Ed.). (1997). *The calling of education.* Chicago: University of Chicago Press.
Slaughter, S. (1998). National higher education policies in a global economy. In J. Currie and J. Newson (Eds.), *Universities and globalization: Critical perspectives* (pp. 45-70). Thousand Oaks, CA: Sage.
Slaughter, S., and Leslie, L. (1997). *Academic capitalism: Politics, policies, and the entrepreneurial university.* Baltimore: Johns Hopkins University Press.

Slaughter, S., and Rhoades, G. (1996). The emergence of a competitiveness research and development policy coalition and the commercialization of academic science and technology. *Science, Technology, and Human Values, 21*(3), 303-39.

–. (2004). *Academic capitalism and the new economy: Markets, state, and higher education*. Baltimore: Johns Hopkins University Press.

Statistics Canada. (2006). *CAUT almanac 2006*. Ottawa.

Stokes, D.E. (1997). *Pasteur's quadrant: Basic science and technological innovation*. Washington,DC: Brookings Institution Press.

Tierney, W. (Ed.). (1991). *Culture and ideology in higher education*. New York: Praeger.

1
The Academic Capitalist Knowledge/ Learning Regime

Sheila Slaughter and Gary Rhoades

In the early years of the twenty-first century, the academic capitalist knowledge/learning regime is ascendant. This regime is displacing but not replacing the public good knowledge regime or the liberal learning regime. Although other knowledge regimes persist, the trend line in emphasis and investment is in academic capitalism in the new economy, as evidenced in public policy, in relations among market, state, and higher education organizations, and in the employment structure and work practices of the academy.

Many scholars acknowledge the changes to which we point, whether they refer to them as the commercialization of higher education (Bok, 2003; Noble, 2001); as entrepreneurial universities (Clark, 1998); as a triple helix that weaves together higher education, state, and market (Etzkowitz, Webster, and Healey, 1998); or as the corporatization of higher education (Soley, 1995). The contribution of our work has been to develop a theory of academic capitalism in the new economy. We track and explain how the change from one regime to another occurs; in contrast to much work in the field, we point to the active, sometimes leading, role that the academy plays in marketizing higher education rather than portray it as the victim of external, encroaching commercial interests. In this way, academics can be seen as active agents working to further marketization. In addition, we demonstrate the degree to which market behaviours have come to permeate almost all of the internal life of universities and colleges, from research to instruction, including administration. By contrast, most other work concentrates on the commercialization of research. Furthermore, we point to how academic capitalism in the new economy restructures work in universities and colleges in ways that mirror and diverge from patterns of professional employment in private enterprise. Finally, we conceptualize how higher education as an institution embodies the changing social understanding of what is "public." The idea of an academic capitalism knowledge/learning regime captures the many ways and means through which market and market-like behaviours as well as a market ethos and ideology have been incorporated into postsecondary education.

In this chapter, we offer a theoretical outline that concentrates on how the theory of academic capitalism explains the shift from earlier knowledge regimes to an academic capitalist knowledge/learning regime. Rather than focusing on the macrolevel – the growth of global markets, the rise of neoliberal states in the world – we concentrate on borders between universities and colleges and external agencies, whether located in states or markets. Attention to the borders among market, state, and institutions of higher education gives us a means to comprehend the complex networks and mechanisms that promote the academic capitalist knowledge/learning regime.

The theory of academic capitalism in the new economy sees groups of actors within universities and colleges – faculty, students, administrators, and managerial professionals – as using a variety of state resources to intersect the new economy. These groups of actors are drawn from different institutional segments and sectors of colleges and universities and do not always act together. However, their organized activity is directed toward the opportunity structures created by the new economy, which channels their efforts in similar directions. They create new circuits of knowledge that link the university to and bring it into the new economy. They form interstitial organizations that bring the corporate sector inside the university. They join organizations that intermediate among public, non-profit, and for-profit public sectors. They build expanded managerial capacity to supervise new flows of external resources, to invest in research infrastructure for the new economy, and to expand programs to market institutions, products, and services to students and other customers in the private marketplace. Their individual decisions to engage in organized activities that promote market and market-like activities consolidate the academic capitalist knowledge/learning regime.

Although market language dominates discourse about entrepreneurial universities and academic capitalism, the state continues to provide the largest share of resources for the shift in knowledge/learning regimes. Indeed, universities and colleges are not seeking to become private enterprises; rather, they wish to maintain the privileges of not-for-profit status while entering the private sector marketplace. Academic capitalism does not involve "privatization"; rather, it entails a redefinition of public space and of appropriate activity in that space. The configuration of state resources in the United States and Canada has changed, providing universities and colleges with fewer unrestricted public revenues and encouraging them to seek out and generate alternative sources of revenue. The shape of the territory that stands between the public and the private sectors is changing. These new configurations and boundaries change our conception of what "public" means.

The new configurations and boundaries also represent new circuits of knowledge, which are the harbinger of knowledge regime change. Following the new circuits of knowledge points out the segments of the economy and the state to which colleges and universities are connecting and with which they are integrated and gives us a diagram of the components of the academic capitalist knowledge/learning regime and how they are wired together.

Interstitial organizations are the leaven for change in established organizations, the means through which actors with mutual interests related to, yet not at the core of, their institution join together to express new goals and purposes for the institution. When interstitial organizations are successful, they often intersect new opportunity structures that the institution comes to see as within its purview, for example opportunities created by the rise of the new economy. The interstitial organizations that figure in the academic capitalist knowledge/learning regime were organized for the most part by professionals who are neither faculty nor administrators but interstitial personnel who possess higher degrees and whose purpose often is to manage the market dimensions of faculty work.

Like interstitial organizations, intermediating organizations (Metcalfe, 2004) intersect new environmental opportunities, in this case opportunities created by the new economy. Unlike interstitial organizations, intermediating organizations do not originate within universities and colleges and connect similar professionals at various universities and colleges. Instead, intermediating organizations are often composed of high-level administrators and span the boundaries between public, non-profit, and for-profit institutions, reshaping the boundaries that divide them, redirecting and revaluing organizational purposes. In working in such intermediating organizations, academic managers enhance the academic capitalist knowledge/learning regime by developing and facilitating market and market-like activities across public, non-profit, and for-profit institutional and sectoral boundaries.

Expanded managerial capacity is a response to the increased market and market-like activity generated by new circuits of knowledge and interstitial and intermediating organizations. The exploitation of intellectual property, the expansion of endowments, and the marketing of educational services all require staff able to compete with other institutions and organizations to capture market shares. The more the market activity, the greater the managerial staff; the more the managerial staff, the greater the institutional effort to expand markets as these professionals become an interest group seeking to expand their domains and career opportunities. In parallel to the state, these bureaucracies take on a life of their own. The rise and expansion of both the phenomenon and the role of industry-liaison offices within our universities are prime examples of this trend.

All of these processes – the creation of new circuits of knowledge, interstitial organizational emergence, intermediating organizational activity among public, non-profit, and for-profit organizations, and expanded managerial capacity – contribute to restratification among and within universities and colleges and often contribute to the restructuring of faculty work. Stratification among institutions is enhanced by their differential capacities to access segmented student markets and external revenue streams related to educational products, processes, and services. Stratification within institutions is increased by colleges' and departments' differential capacities in the same arenas, their perceived potential to intersect and capitalize on new economy student employment, research, and service markets. Restructuring of faculty work is often undertaken to maximize educational efficiencies and to enable some faculty to attend more to research and technology transfer in fields believed to have revenue-generating potential in the new economy. Such restratification of institutions and restructuring of faculty work reshape access for students. More institutional and faculty attention is directed to those student markets that can afford to pay more, and fewer opportunities are available to low-income and historically underserved students, who are less able to pay and less likely to be flowing into new economy fields of employment. Nowhere is this market orientation more obvious than in the competition for international students (Evans, 2005). As universities and colleges shift their orientation toward revenue generation through academic capitalism, they invest less in historic, democratic missions of providing increased access and upward mobility for less historically advantaged populations of students.

In the first part of this chapter, we map academic capitalism in terms of its new circuits of knowledge, interstitial organizational emergence, intermediating organizational activity, and expanded managerial capacity. In the second part of this chapter, we move to a consideration of fault lines in the structure of the new knowledge/learning/consumption regime and of alternatives within and beyond academic capitalism in the new economy. In the current context of apparent reduced public commitment to subsidizing higher education, the need for new revenues and the language of the market make the ascendance and expansion of an academic capitalist knowledge/learning regime seem inexorable. Yet the market logic embedded in academic capitalism is problematic.

Notwithstanding the connotations of academic capitalism, all of the markets we consider, ranging from markets in students to patents and start-up companies, depend heavily on state (provincial) subsidies, whether in the form of federal and state (provincial) student financial aid or federal and state subsidies for research from which university and college intellectual property is derived. Academic capitalism in the new economy involves a shift, not a reduction, in public subsidy. Moreover, despite the implications of applying market logic to universities and colleges, many, even most, institutions are not particularly successful capitalists. Academic capitalism involves institutions choosing, investing in, and betting on certain winners in the marketplace, in developing interstitial organizations, in expanding managerial capacity, and in restratifying academic fields. Two particular patterns and problems define academic capitalist institutions: they move toward similar opportunities rather than to any niche competitive advantage, and they are not particularly effective as venture capitalists, investment bankers, or investors in the (stock) market. However, their market failures tend to be underwritten by consumers (in the form of higher tuition) or by state subsidy. Furthermore, academic managers and policy makers are selling the appropriateness of market and market-like competition in higher education to the public on the grounds that academic capitalism in the new economy will make universities and colleges more self-sufficient and decrease costs to the public. This argument is prominent among industry liaison managers in Canadian universities (Fisher and Atkinson-Grosjean, 2002). Yet state allocations continue to increase, and tuition continues to escalate dramatically. Finally, making the students consumers was supposed to empower them, but institutional funds are increasingly concentrated less on teaching and more on research, public relations, and revenue-generating activity. We identify some of these fault lines in the academic capitalist knowledge/learning regime and close by exploring alternatives within and beyond academic capitalism in the new economy.

Circuits of Knowledge

Policy

The neoliberal state in the United States and Canada has concentrated funding in state agencies that are oriented to the production of economic growth, revenue generation, and private wealth, for example research funding for corporations and academe. The neoliberal state worked to build the "new" knowledge or information economy and attempted to articulate national economies with global economies. To provide funds to reshape the economy, the neoliberal state instituted processes of deregulation, commercialization, privatization, and reregulation. The benefits of the neoliberal state tended to accrue less to the broad citizenry and more to large corporations, the wealthy, and the upper middle class closely associated with the growth of the new economy.

Government policy creates a climate that encourages new circuits of knowledge that cut across the space dividing public and private territory. New circuits of knowledge, characteristic of the academic capitalist knowledge/learning regime, connect the National Institutes of Health (NIH), the National Science Foundation (NSF), and the Department of Commerce (DOC) to universities through sponsored research, frequently in partnership with corporations. Similarly, these circuits connect the national Canadian funding councils, the Canada Foundation for Innovation (CFI), to universities through sponsored research in partnership with the private sector (see Chapter 6 in this volume). The exemplar of the new circuits of knowledge in Canada is the Networks of Centres of Excellence program that has as its explicit aim the creation of alliances between universities, industry, and the state (Fisher, Atkinson-Grosjean, and House, 2001).

Federal, state (provincial), and institutional laws and policies interact in complex ways to produce knowledge/learning regimes. They do not so much dictate a new academic capitalist regime as create opportunities for academic capitalism, on which new networks of academic managers, faculty, staff, and students act. States/provinces have an array of initiatives that promote economic development. Many of these initiatives, ranging from workforce preparation of students to fostering industries that contribute to the states' economic base, feature participation of universities and colleges. Yet universities and colleges are not simply acted upon or "corporatized." Actors within participate in creating new knowledge/learning regimes by networking and partnering external actors. Segments of the administration and faculty work to shape the politico-legal climate that fosters an academic capitalist knowledge/learning regime, and they actively and ardently engage in commercialization.

Patenting

The changes in patenting policies and behaviours in universities and colleges dramatically illustrate the theory of academic capitalism. Although such changes occurred largely at research universities and in the sciences and engineering, their influence has extended beyond these realms. Moreover, changes in patenting were the precursor of changes in other forms of intellectual property, for example copyright and trademarks, that were subsequently adapted within all sectors of higher education and across a wide variety of academic fields.

The aggressive institutional pursuit of revenue generation through patents, as evidenced in institutional policies, was matched by faculties' and students' aggressive pursuit of academic capitalism. Appellate court cases and interviews with faculty and students involved in technology transfer revealed a move away from a public good model toward an academic capitalist knowledge/learning regime. Many faculty still held to some values of the public good regime, for example the importance of publishing and the corresponding value of the free flow of information, but they were willing to alter those values, sometimes delaying publication, sometimes "sanitizing" data to preserve opportunities to patent. Professors straddled two different worlds, retaining a place in the public space of the university but also assuming the role of state-subsidized entrepreneurs in the private marketplace working as consultants, officials, or even presidents of their own companies (see Chapter 2 in this volume). They were constructing new circuits of knowledge.

Patents precipitated new circuits of knowledge by connecting university actors to external actors and organizations intent on building the new/information economy. Not only are different agencies involved, but in recent years they have more directly involved representatives from business in defining research agendas and reviewing grant proposals. Companies themselves have expanded their support of academic research. Like the federal agencies, the corporations in the new circuits of knowledge are different. Rather than defence and aerospace corporations, the corporations in the new circuits of knowledge produce civilian technology: pharmaceuticals, medical substances and devices, biotechnology (NIH); information technology, telecommunications (NSF); and high-technology products for global markets (DOC). Furthermore, faculty and university administrators also create new circuits of knowledge when they start up corporations in which universities hold equity and faculty hold administrative positions. These circuits are usually connected to the broader civilian technology grid that integrates universities and colleges with the new economy.

The new circuits of knowledge affect and are reflected in faculty work. The traditional tripartite faculty role of teaching, research, and service altered during the period from 1980 to 2004. In response to surveys, faculty in the United States indicated that they preferred teaching to research until the mid-1980s, after which an increased preference for research began to emerge (Finkelstein, Seal, and Schuster, 1998). Concentrating on research allows faculty to give more time and attention to work that may result in discoveries that can be patented. In fact, the rate of faculty/university patenting has increased dramatically. Prior to 1980, about 250 patents per year were granted to universities; in 1998, the number was 3,151. "As a result, academic patents now approach 5.0 percent of all new US-owned patents, up from less than 0.5 percent two decades ago" (NSB, 2002, p. 544).[1] In addition, faculty publication patterns are more closely aligned with industry. In 1988, faculty co-authored 20.3 percent of their publications with industry. In 1998, approximately 25 percent were co-authored with industry. As the National Science Board (2002) notes, "the Federal Government has long sought to stimulate ... collaboration across sectors (e.g., industry-university ... activities)" (p. 544). Universities also sought to stimulate such collaboration. Academic institutions were at the heart of cross-sector relationships, linking private non-profits, private for-profits, the federal government, Federally Funded Research and Development Centers (FFRDCs), and institutions of higher learning.

At the same time that faculty patenting has increased and faculty are publishing more often with industry co-authors, the number of scientific and technical articles by US authors has declined. The national output across all research-producing organizations in 1999 was down by 10 percent from 1992. This trend diverged from growth in most other OECD countries during this period and is a reversal from three prior decades of consistent US publication growth. The decrease in articles produced within academia was slightly less pronounced (9 percent), but, because of the sector's high share of total output, it accounted for 64 percent of the overall decline. In academia, almost half of the decrease was in the life sciences, perhaps because they have undergone the most rapid commercialization and are the academic fields in which withholding of research results is most common (NSB, 2002).

As scientific publications declined, the number of patents referencing scientific articles increased dramatically. In the mid-1980s, patents referenced about 22,000 scientific articles, but in 1998 they referenced 310,000 (NSB, 2002). Many explanations can be offered for the rise in patent citations, from the growth of biomedical patents to changes in international patent law. However, patent citation of scientific articles points to the creation of new circuits for academic knowledge. This knowledge no longer flows primarily among scientific communities but frequently through circuits that connect it to knowledge application and the corporate world.

As universities became more involved in patenting, and as federal policy encouraged the development of organizational structures within universities to manage patenting, professionals with law and science degrees were hired in new or expanded technology transfer and/or intellectual property offices. These new professionals became "brokers on the boundary" connecting the university with the external commercial world (Fisher and Atkinson-Grosjean, 2002). Between 1980 and 1984, industry liaison offices in their current form were established at eleven key Canadian universities. By 1998, all except the smallest universities and university colleges had active offices (Fisher and Atkinson-Grosjean, 2002, p. 453). These professionals joined the Association of University Technology Managers (AUTM), an intermediating organization that operates outside universities but brings together technology transfer managers from various public and private sectors. The national association collects data on university patenting and has a journal that provides information on patenting, licensing, royalties, and start-ups. The association and the journal created a normative discourse emphasizing the contribution of intellectual property to university revenues and to the new economy and the welfare of the citizenry. Because the success of their offices depends on increased streams of revenue, technology transfer officers make every effort to expand the numbers of faculty disclosures and to patent the promising ones, linking faculty and administrators directly to corporations in the new economy. In short, AUTM illustrates how professionals other than faculty within universities and colleges respond to opportunities created by the new economy.

Yet faculty and academic units have also created interstitial organizations. Various sorts of centres and institutes in the sciences and engineering have been designed to facilitate the interaction and intersection of higher education, state, and market organizations. Such centres are in considerable part a response to a push by federal funding agencies to promote closer co-operation and partnerships between universities and business.

In spanning public, non-profit, and for-profit entities, mediating among the sectors and often reshaping their boundaries, intermediating organizations play a significant role in the postsecondary community during regime shifts. In the case of patents, another important intermediating organization (in addition to AUTM) was the Business-Higher Education Forum (Slaughter, 1990). It was made up of CEOs primarily from large corporations and research universities who met on a "principals only" basis. The explicit purpose of the forum was to increase US productivity and ability to compete in global markets for civilian technology. The forum circulated its policy documents widely, and spokespersons met regularly with members of the executive and legislative branches of government to advance their positions. A similar organization, the Corporate-Higher Education Forum (Newson and Buchbinder, 1988), was created in Canada in 1983. The forum brought together the presidents of most of Canada's universities with the CEOs of Canada's major corporations in order to promote dialogue between the leading entrepreneurial and intellectual resources in the country.

In order to more aggressively pursue the promise of patents, universities and colleges greatly expanded their internal managerial capacity to participate in external markets. The new functions were generally handled by technology transfer offices and included reviewing and evaluating faculty disclosures; technology licensing; supervision of royalty flows; reinvestment of funds in new market opportunities; litigation to defend intellectual property; evaluation of intellectual property for institutional equity investments; monitoring and occasionally administering corporations in which the institution held equity; overseeing initial public offerings (IPOs); and handling bids for downstream research related to patented technology already in the market. As institutions become more involved in academic capitalism, they hired more managerial professional staff. The growth of such managerial capacity is evident in the growth of membership in AUTM over time. Formed by "seven visionaries" as the Society of University Patent Administrators in 1975, AUTM has dramatically grown in membership and has broadened its focus beyond patents (AUTM, 2003). In 1986, its membership was only 381 but had grown to 771 by 1990 and 3,200 by 2003 (AUTM, 2003). These numbers reflect the expansion of patenting and other technology transfer activity among a wider range of universities and the increase in size of technology transfer offices within those institutions.

Copyrighting

Like patenting, changes in copyrighting dramatically illustrate the growth of the academic capitalist knowledge/learning regime. Unlike patenting, which deals primarily with intellectual property discovered by faculty during the research process, copyrighting covers the instructional aspect of faculty work. After the advent of digital technologies, the possibilities of generating external revenues from instructional materials transformed the academic capitalist knowledge regime into an academic capitalist knowledge/learning regime. This shift involved transforming education into yet another new economy service and consumption item to be delivered to consumers.

Traditionally, faculty owned copyrights to their scholarly and creative works or traded royalties for copyrights from third-party organizations, in the form of publishing companies. Other than textbooks, these works had relatively small audiences, made little money, and did not figure in revenue generation strategies of universities and colleges. As digital telecommunications technologies became more sophisticated, universities and colleges began to see instructional materials offered via distance education as a source of external revenue from off-site student tuition. Many institutions developed copyright policies from the mid-1980s through the 1990s. These policies often let faculty retain ownership of scholarly and creative work but made institutional claims to instructional materials, particularly when they were produced with the use of university facilities or resources. These instructional materials were often used in distance education. A startling example of a new circuit of knowledge involving research universities around the world, and including both US and Canadian institutions, is Universitas 21. In 2001, a subsidiary of this group formed a joint venture with Thompson Publishing Corporation to produce and market curriculum distance education packages. These packages are targeted at Asian students and lead to a degree.

Prior to the 1990s, most colleges did not have distance education programs other than correspondence, audiotapes, or closed-circuit television. The Internet technology and telecommunications revolution of the 1990s stimulated enhanced distance education. By 2001, 48 percent of all colleges and universities offered distance education courses, and 22 percent offered graduate-level courses (NCES, 2001). In 2000-1, 2,876,000 college-level credit-granting distance education courses were offered, 82 percent at the undergraduate level. Forty-eight percent of public two-year, 31 percent of public four-year, and 19 percent of private four-year college enrolments were via distance education. Public four-year institutions (48 percent) are most likely to offer virtual degrees, taken entirely through distance education, followed by private four-year (33 percent) and public two-year (20 percent) institutions (NCES, 2001).

Participation in distance education often inducts administrators and faculty into the academic capitalist knowledge/learning regime. Administrators have to purchase or lease and maintain the physical infrastructure that makes distance education possible, construct teams of producers and content providers, and market the product to student consumers. They often work in partnership and consortia with private sector partners. Sixty percent indicated they worked in consortia, most often state wide (NCES, 2001). Unfortunately, national data on how many consortia members are corporations were not available. However, we know from Schiller (1998) that many universities and colleges have corporate partners.

Faculty who develop instructional materials for distance education courses often receive generous royalties for use. However, the nature of their work changes. Rather than being in charge of a classroom where they interact face to face with students, they become content providers on teams of distance education producers in a virtual assembly line. In this process, nonfaculty academic professionals who participate in the teams do not receive royalties even if they contribute to course design because their work is considered work for hire.

Distance education courses offer the promise of new student markets, increased tuition revenues, revenues from educational products, and enhanced efficiencies in the delivery of educational services. As in the dot.com debacle in the private sector economy, the for-profit ventures undertaken by universities and colleges often fail to fulfill the new economy promise. However, other strategies and ventures have been more successful in intersecting with the new economy. Whether it is community colleges marketing courses and programs to international students, or science and engineering departments marketing "professional master's degrees" to employed businesspersons, these efforts have succeeded and mark a substantial change in orientation to education, shifting the focus to the efficient delivery of educational services. Distance education has created new circuits of knowledge that commercialize instruction. For a price, circuits of instruction now encompass campus, state, region, or world, encouraging even "community" colleges to direct attention away from local students and employers in an effort to intersect with the global, new economy.

A number of interstitial organizations have emerged to manage, promote, and regulate distance education. As with patenting, AUTM stresses strategies for institutions to capture and exploit faculty copyrights. Among the many associations that deal with distance education are the United States Distance Learning Association, the Canadian Association for Distance Education, and the International Association of Distance Educators. The Distance Education and Training Council is an accrediting agency for distance education that works with the US Department of Education. Web resources for distance education are too numerous to list.

Many established organizations in higher education have also developed copyright and distance education policies and undertaken conventional interest group activity around these issues. For example, the American Association of University Professors, the American Federation of Teachers, and the National Educational Association have issued statements about copyright and distance education. These organizations generally seek to retain faculty copyright ownership of new, digital forms of intellectual property, including instructional materials used in distance education. Although they articulate some traditional stances concerning professional control of work and professional standards of quality, by endorsing faculty claims to new forms of intellectual property these organizations also promote faculty complicity with and commitment to the academic capitalist knowledge/learning regime.

The emergent and rapidly expanding for-profit postsecondary sector is one of the most important new organizational forms with regard to academic capitalism in the delivery of educational services. The lobbying by these entities of state boards of education and regional accrediting associations has served to legitimate and advance an academic capitalist knowledge/learning regime, relaxing restrictions and creating exceptions to professional quality standards regarding the percentage of classes that are taught on campus, the percentage of staff who are part time, and the involvement of faculty in curricular matters. Their efforts have encouraged a shift away from treating distance education as another form of education, with a focus on key inputs and standards, and toward regarding it more as a new economy delivery of information and services.

Many organizations intermediate among public, non-profit, and private entities concerned with copyrighted intellectual property. Members from the educational and corporate sectors in these intermediating organizations are committed to improving education through information technology. Their education goals operate in tandem with commercial objectives. EDUCAUSE and the League for Innovation in the Community College are among the most well known. Such organizations link universities and colleges to corporations that market information technology hardware and software, often in packages that can be sold to campuses as discounted systems.

These intermediating organizations span the boundaries of public, nonprofit, and private entities and expand higher education institutions' commitment to information technology. They pursue legislative strategies that increase public monies for information technology, subsidizing tighter connections between universities and colleges and corporations. They support distance and on-campus education delivered through more advanced information technologies, which encourages new economy corporate production and sales. It also encourages universities and colleges to market distance education and educational materials to new student markets as a new information and educational service intended to generate new revenue streams. Intermediating organizations, then, support the commitment of universities and colleges to an academic capitalist knowledge/learning regime.

Like patents, copyrighted instructional materials must be managed to enhance revenues. Although technology transfer offices often manage copyrighted intellectual property along with patents, college and university commitment to distance education and to copyrighting of instructional materials has also resulted in the creation of offices to manage these initiatives. For example, many institutions have distance or continuing education offices that manage virtual education, including its many physical manifestations, like networking infrastructure, computer labs, one- and two-way video equipment, and marketing. In addition, most institutions now have offices that encourage the use of technology in on-campus education, from teaching centres to professional development centres that develop or help faculty to develop and incorporate information and multimedia technologies into their instruction.

Enhanced managerial capacity also means expanded managerial capacity. The use of information technology generally calls for more support professionals to operate, repair, handle, and conceptualize educational materials and curricula. Part of what is driving the increase in support professionals is the establishment of a new production process for the delivery of information and educational services, which involves a matrix of professionals rather than a single professor in constructing and delivering a course. Faculty are being decentred not only in absolute numbers, and in the increased numbers and percentages of part-time faculty, but also in the educational process itself. Because managerial professionals report to administrators rather than to the faculty as a collectivity, whether in departments or senates, there is a shift toward expanded administrative authority.

In a related development, many universities and colleges established the position of CIO (chief information officer) in the past decade. The CIO manages infrastructure for information technology, ranging from technology-infused classrooms to high-speed computer wiring systems for dormitories. These officials also develop forward planning for the institutional information technology system. Furthermore, they represent a new force promoting the increased use of and investment in information technology.

Departments

We found departments very involved in academic capitalism but in unanticipated ways that speak to the complex and sometimes conflicted nature of academic commitment to entrepreneurial activity. Although most departments we interviewed generated external revenues by competing for grant and contract funding, we were somewhat surprised at the relatively limited collective initiatives to pursue entrepreneurial research markets as a unit. More common were educational initiatives designed to generate external and internal revenues through new programs. These programs articulate with the new economy.

Several examples of new circuits of knowledge were evident in the activities of academic departments. New master's programs targeting prospective students in business were established. These "professional master's degrees" were terminal and did not require a thesis. The idea was to make them more attractive to employed persons who would not have time to do thesis work and who would be neither interested in nor able to pursue a doctorate in the field. In addition, such programs were cheaper to run since there was no provision for tuition waivers or assistantships for students and since there was little need to hire additional faculty because the courses could be taught by doctoral students. The new programs represent a substantial shift away from past practices, which treated masters degrees as a step on the way to a doctorate, which was largely a step on the way to academic employment. The professional master's degrees can be seen as a new economy form of continuing education, with traditional academic departments reconfiguring their programs to integrate them with new economy employees.

A variety of new organizational forms and arrangements have emerged around academic departments, and these new forms clearly are supporting and facilitating the academic capitalist knowledge/learning regime. Essentially all of the academic colleges in our sample have development officers, and some departments undertook fundraising activities. One of the organizational mechanisms for pursuing such efforts was advisory boards, which included members who represented or were connected to large corporations and potential donors. These boards mediated between the worlds of academe and industry. Although they were largely focused on fundraising, their existence also made possible a more direct flow of feedback from the external world to the department in regard to employment needs. Since the mid-1980s in the United States and the early 1990s in Canada, most public universities have aggressively pursued large capital campaigns. Some years later, colleges and faculties within these universities began to hire their own development officers and to appoint advisory boards. Such initiatives were initially most common in business and engineering colleges but have since expanded. Now we are finding evidence of academic departments within the colleges developing these sorts of links to the private sector market.

A more long-standing organizational form in universities is centres and institutes. In the past two decades, new types have emerged, with more direct partnerships and connections with private enterprises. Indeed, at the initiative of federal funding agencies such as the National Science Foundation and the Canadian Foundation for Innovation, many such centres and institutes require and promote university-industry partnerships. These entities facilitate the movement of faculty and students between academic and business worlds. Like advisory boards and development offices, they normalize and expand managerial capacity in areas in which faculty have long had networks of relations, as individuals, with the private sector and government and non-profit agencies. We are seeing greater co-ordination and management of such networks with the emergence of various interstitial and intermediate organizations.

Yet for all these developments of the academic capitalist knowledge/learning regime, elements of and some commitment to old (public good) regimes and prestige systems persist. Even those department heads who sought more aggressively to intersect their units collectively with the business world were clear that they had to maintain and, in fact, expand federal grant and contract revenues. Such peer-reviewed grants were considered by almost all heads and faculty as more prestigious than private sector support and as key to the tenure and promotion process of individuals as well as to the collective prestige of the department. Some resistance to the academic capitalist knowledge/learning regime was grounded in a continued commitment to alternative conceptions of the functions of a university.

In this sense, there is clearly a co-existence of academic capitalist and other knowledge regimes. At the same time, it would appear that the prestige system is increasingly being defined in academic capitalist terms. That is, grant revenue rankings are increasingly important relative to National Research Council prestige rankings, and the prestige of the institution as well as the academic unit is increasingly being defined by how much money it can command from external markets. Such developments, in our view, speak to the ascendance of the academic capitalist knowledge/learning regime.

Administrators and Trustees

The networks of administrators and trustees distinct from faculties are senior academic administrators, such as presidents, and trustees of universities and colleges who advance the academic capitalist knowledge/learning regime and intersect the new economy directly – through intermediating and interstitial organizations that foster the development of new circuits of knowledge and involve expanded managerial capacity. We analyzed Internet2 as an intermediating organization that networks public organizations and private corporations. Internet2 was initiated by presidents of research universities but now encompasses postsecondary institutions from across the spectrum. The purpose of Internet2 was to create new Internet infrastructure that was not overly burdened by commercial traffic and that tested and deployed hardware and software for new economy telecommunications corporations.

The network unites its participants around the electronic infrastructure and commercial purpose that play a part in building the new economy. Internet2 enables corporations and public and non-profit entities to adopt the others' practices, enhancing potential profit/revenue streams and expanding markets. Corporations benefit from the network in that new infrastructure is constructed that may be privatized, allowing corporations to benefit from public and non-profit sector resources. Universities and colleges benefit in that they build infrastructure that expands their telecommunications capacity, furthering research and educational service delivery goals that depend on that capacity. Universities and colleges are able to reduce the costs of Internet2 through corporate contributions. Corporations are able to deduct their contributions as either research tax credits or charitable donations yet are often given contracts to construct components of Internet2. As colleges, universities, and corporations build Internet2, they create intellectual property in which they hold shares according to their agreements, and they profit from the marketing of knowledge economy products that are by-products of Internet2 construction. Universities and colleges serve as test beds for corporate information technology products, often receiving deep discounts. Corporations benefit from the knowledge generated by student use and faculty expertise.

The networks created by intermediating organizations such as Internet2 normalize corporate-university relations around commercial activity. They create new organizational fields across very different sectors (DiMaggio and Powell, 1983), operating through fluid networks rather than stable fields. These new networks create common ground for actors to develop shared values and norms, and the organizations within the network become more similar.

Many of the organizations affiliated with Internet2 have emerged from the interstices of public entities to connect them to for-profit entities, often through intermediating boundary-spanning organizations such as Internet2. For example, Media Center North Carolina (MCNC) was founded by the North Carolina General Assembly in 1980, the Indiana Higher Education Telecommunication System (IHETS, 2003), the LaNet (Louisiana), the NYSERnet (New York State), and the University of Florida System. In other words, Internet2 replicates itself through its affiliates, expanding the networks that experience commercialization as normative in higher education.

As faculty academic capitalist networks are distinct from but related to presidential networks, so presidential networks are related to but distinct from trustee networks. The trustee networks are another form of intermediating organization. Historically, trustees may not have been tightly networked. Currently, private sector trustees at elite research universities directly connect private universities to the new economy. Public university trustees, aware of private trustees' network and resource advantages, may engage more aggressively in commercial endeavours in an effort to compete successfully. Despite not participating directly in the private trustee network, public university trustees may embrace more closely academic capitalism in the new economy in the hope of generating external revenues to keep the resource gap between private and public universities in the United States from further widening. Although we found that elite public research universities are not directly linked to new economy corporations through their boards, they are indirectly connected through other networks they share with private universities. Moreover, direct connections are very likely evident in various interstitial fundraising entities that have emerged and expanded within public universities since the mid-1980s. Public universities have aggressively taken on development activities that not only are co-ordinated by central offices and foundations separate on paper from the university but directly connected to it, but also are effected through advisory boards of the academic colleges. These boards link colleges directly with the external world, particularly with large companies and potential donors. Although the records of the central offices and the college boards are difficult to access, there is good reason to believe that numerous connections with new economy corporations may be found there, particularly in the boards of professional schools such as agriculture, architecture, business, engineering, and medicine.

Presidents networked in intermediating organizations such as Internet2 create new circuits of knowledge, different from but aligned with those created by faculty, technology transfer officers, and corporate licensees or partners, or faculty, distance education officers, and corporate licensees or partners. The presidents, in organizations like the Business-Higher Education Forum, EDUCAUSE, Internet2, and biotech consortia, create new circuits of knowledge when they engage in forward planning for research, deployment, and testing of infrastructure and developing products, processes, and services for the knowledge economy. In effect, these new circuits of knowledge lay the groundwork for orienting faculty research and teaching in commercial directions. They augment, expand, and enhance opportunities for faculty and staff to become academic capitalists.

New circuits are evident as well in the activities of trustees and development officers in their interstitial and intermediating organizations. At the central level, as well as at the level of colleges and departments, boards and donors open up new economy opportunities that encourage and channel faculty research and educational activity in directions seen as potentially generating new revenues. These new and expanding organizations create new opportunity structures, realized through closer interaction with and direct engagement in the market.

In the case of fundraising and development, we see an expanded managerial capacity that is comparable to the growth of personnel managing patents and copyrights. In the past twenty years, development offices have increased substantially in size and activity and have emerged at the level of academic colleges, expanding the number of personnel there as well. Increasingly, these managerial professionals, focused on generating entrepreneurial revenues from closer connections to the private sector, have a role in and impact on the strategic directions and initiatives of private and public universities.

Markets in Students and Marketing to Students

The theory of academic capitalism explores new levels of marketing and consumption within the institution by focusing on school logos as brands. It also moves beyond students as consumers to institutions as ever more sophisticated marketers, increasingly able to capture the student markets they target. Student markets are heavily state subsidized, whether through state block grants or state and federal student financial aid funds. Nonetheless, the greater the degree to which tuition dollars constitute a share of universities' and colleges' annual operating budgets, the more aggressive institutions' marketing behaviours. Moreover, as the academic capitalist knowledge/learning regime intensifies, students, once recruited, are transformed into captive markets to which institutions market branded products as well as an array of other revenue-generating products and services.

Branding is a new economy marketing strategy that universities and colleges use to sell goods and services to matriculated students, who are captive audiences. Universities and colleges brand products and services with trademarked college and university logos, which they sell to students and alumni to increase external revenues. Like for-profit and non-profit marketing activities, the stores and websites that sell logoed paraphernalia are virtually indistinguishable from their commercial counterparts.

However, colleges and universities have gone beyond marketing to students; they also market their students. Many regard their student bodies as negotiable, to be traded with corporations for external resources through all-sports, test-bed, single-product, and information (names, addresses, telephone numbers) contracts. When students graduate, universities and colleges present them to employers as output/product, a contribution to the new economy, and simultaneously define students as alumni and potential donors. Student identities are flexible, defined, and redefined by institutional market behaviours.

Trademarking groups have their own interstitial organization that emerged in the 1980s, the Association of Collegiate Licensing Administrators, which is more comprehensive than the older, less commercially oriented licensing groups. Their work is augmented by Royalty Management Associates, an organization led by a former Disney auditor, which provides compliance review services to licensors, including colleges and the Collegiate Licensing Group. Sometimes interstitial organizations and intermediating organizations overlap. In 1992, the Collegiate Licensing Company, which licenses logos for a number of universities, joined with professional sports leagues (MLB Properties, NBA Properties, NFL Properties, and NHL Properties) to form the Coalition to Advance the Protection of Sports Logos (CAPS). Since its establishment, CAPS has developed a network of private investigators and law enforcement officials that brings civil or criminal actions against trademark violators, protecting college and university commercial assets.

In addition, for-profit, non-profit, and public organizations have emerged around postsecondary marketing opportunities. For example, the Independent Educational Consultants Association (IECA) is a national private, fee-for-service organization of counsellors who aid high school students applying to universities and colleges. In 1994, the National Academic Advising Association, the non-profit counterpart of the IECA, emerged to share information about how to help prospective students choose universities and colleges. The University Marketing Professionals Association was established in 1999 and performs functions similar to associations organized by for-profit marketers.

The new circuits of knowledge, interstitial organizations, and intermediating organizations call for enhanced managerial capacity in universities and colleges. If institutions increase their enrolment management capacity, they hire staff, as they do if they develop stores to sell products branded with trademarked logos. When universities and colleges develop facilities and services to recruit students and sell products to them after they arrive, they hire new support professionals. Recreation centres and mini-malls require personnel. Even when business opportunities are outsourced – to Starbucks, McDonald's, or Barnes and Noble – universities and colleges have to manage the licences and external revenues. Enhanced managerial capacity creates a stratum of on-campus professionals who are committed to expanded commercial opportunities.

Inherent Fault Lines in the New Knowledge/Learning Regime

Several fault lines are evident in the academic capitalist knowledge/learning regime. They undercut the market logic and claims of increased efficiency that are embedded in academic capitalism in the new economy. Several themes emerge from our analysis. Academic capitalism blurs the boundaries between public and private sectors, but it sustains a substantial level of public subsidy of higher education. Simultaneously, the public space in the academy is redefined as public monies shift to subsidize different activities, fields of work, and professionals. In many cases, capitalism – academic style – is not very successful in generating net revenues, and it leads to unanticipated, undesirable practices and outcomes. In the context of a conception of institutional purpose that is reduced to revenue enhancement, the academic knowledge/learning regime leads to an expanded range of educational services to a reduced range of traditional-aged students. In perhaps a final irony, we see an increasingly similar pattern of effort to intersect global information, new economy opportunities in ways that reduce distinctive involvement in local communities by various types of universities and colleges.

The redefinition of the public space as part of the academic capitalist knowledge/learning regime is particularly noticeable in Canada. Since 1997, the federal government has used a number of new policy instruments, as well as the three established funding councils, to dramatically increase research funding going to universities. Between 1997-98 and 2004-5, the federal government added a total of approximately $11 billion in university research spending. Approximately 70 percent of the funding was received in the past four years (see AUCC, 2005, p. 22). The natural, applied, and health sciences were favoured to the extent that, between 1997-98 and 2004-5, only $1.4 billion or 12 percent of this funding went to the humanities and social sciences. A key development in the academic research enterprise over the past fifteen years has been the emergence of a clear and separable strata of research-intensive universities. The increase in research funding has been concentrated into this relatively small group of universities, between ten and fifteen out of a total of seventy-six to eighty-three.[2] In 2004, fifteen[3] of the eighty-three universities listed by Canadian Association of University Business Officers (CAUBO) accounted for 80.69 percent of the total university research income.[4] All Canadian university departments in the natural, applied, and health sciences have been favoured, thereby exacerbating the level of internal stratification.

The redefinition of the public space in Canada is illustrated by the increases in federal funding going to support university research and development (R&D). In 2005-6 at $2.5 billion, for the first time the amount exceeded its own internal R&D expenditures (Council of Canadian Academies, 2006, Figures 4.2 and 4.3, pp. 39-40). In 2004, the federal government intramural spending on R&D was almost $2.3 billion, a figure that remained fairly constant in the previous six years (Box 6.4, p. 109, and Figure 4.3, pp. 39-40). At the same time, and in spite of the very generous tax credits offered as an incentive to make these investments (p. 104), Canada records a relatively low business expenditure on research compared to other OECD countries (Figure 4.4, p. 41).

The federal policy changes in the United States created new opportunities for public and non-profit entities to engage in commercial activities. In redefining public space in ways that foreground and feature market activity and logic, these federal policies continue a pattern of substantial public subsidy in various forms. When the neoliberal state withdraws broad support for social services and promotes entrepreneurial activity, ironically, non-profits proliferate. US non-profits tripled in the past three decades, growing from about 300,000 in 1970 to approximately one million in 1998. In 1975, their total revenues were less than 6 percent of the gross national product (GNP), while in 1990 they exceeded 10 percent. Between 1980 and 1990, paid employment in non-profits increased by 41 percent, more than double the growth of employment in other sectors.

Perhaps even more ironically, non-profits are turning to commercial activity to expand their operations. The legislation enacted by the competitiveness coalition created commercial opportunities not just for universities and colleges but also for the majority of non-profit organizations (Weisbrod, 1998). Commercial activity increased across non-profits, from gift shops in museums to health clubs in hospitals. Many non-profits are forming for-profit subsidiaries. Public and private universities and colleges have led the non-profits that have engaged creatively in commercial activity.

As commercial activity expands in the not-for-profit sector, it may become an end in its own right. James (1998) suggests that there may come a point when non-profits become "false nonprofits" or, as Weisbrod (1988) calls them, "for-profits in disguise." That certainly is a possibility in private, not-for-profit higher education as well as in some sectors of public higher education. Public universities and colleges have no interest in becoming for-profits, but many public research universities make the case that they should become "private" entities because state appropriations in some cases provide as little as 15 to 30 percent of institutional revenues. However, they do not want to pay taxes, whether on property, the proceeds of their intellectual property, or their commercial revenue from an array of marketing activities, all of which are currently not taxed so long as they are used for institutional rather than individual purposes. Nor do not-for-profit universities and colleges want to forgo public subvention in the form of state and federal student financial aid and loan programs. In short, they want the best of both worlds – the protections and continued subsidies of the public sector and the flexibility, opportunities, and potential revenue streams of the private sector.

Although universities and colleges usually present their commercial activity as win-win, building the economy, generating external revenues, and expanding educational capacity, the commercial activities of institutions can be problematic in several ways. First, higher education institutions are often not very successful capitalists, and students and the public have to pick up the tab for their failures. For example, while technology transfer brings external revenue to universities and colleges, it also takes funds from them. Universities and colleges or state systems have to pay for legal fees and for technology transfer offices. Nationally, legal fees are in the hundreds of millions of dollars. The magnitude of non-reimbursed legal fees has increased about 250 percent over the eleven years that AUTM has surveyed technology transfer activities. These costs could be substantially higher, since AUTM modified its definition of legal fees in 1999, omitting major litigation to better focus on benchmarking patent prosecution costs. A relatively small number of universities are responsible for the lion's share of patenting activity and are likely to actually run in the black in their technology transfer efforts. In the 1990s, the 100 largest universities received more than 90 percent of all patents awarded. Income from patents was also concentrated in the top 100 institutions; the most recent survey indicates that two-thirds of the monies were generated by thirteen institutions. However, most doctoral-granting institutions maintained technology transfer offices, as did a few comprehensive universities. In other words, a number of universities bore the expense of technology transfer offices but reaped relatively few benefits. Similarly, many for-profit ventures in the realm of on-line and distance education have gone bankrupt.

In addition, there are some undesirable, even dysfunctional, outcomes that can attach to the entrepreneurial activities of universities and colleges. For example, those who support patenting argue that it will contribute to economic growth beneficial to the citizenry as a whole. However, the overall pattern of the knowledge/information economy, at least as configured in the United States, has resulted in greater income and wealth stratification within and outside the academy than was the case under the public good knowledge regime. Moreover, actors in patent networks often present commercialization as an activity that benefits taxpayers through new discoveries made through university-industry partnerships, a presentation that obscures the continued contributions made by federal tax revenues to pay for R&D. And patent income does not get used to offset other costs in educational institutions; most institutions dedicate patent income to generating more intellectual property. Despite an elaborated market discourse, the public sector continues to bear the lion's share of the costs of technology transfer.

Patent policies and practices also contribute to some undesirable outcomes in regard to the activities of professors. They increasingly straddle two worlds, retaining a place in the higher education community but also assuming the role of (state-subsidized) entrepreneurs, with several attendant problems. Professors who delay publication or do not publish all of their results make it impossible for other scientists to replicate their work, which makes judgment of science difficult. Professors involved with the market are likely to be "interested," not "disinterested" in the Mertonian sense, in certain results and perhaps less likely to see problems that are unlikely to bring commercial returns. Such professors are less likely to be engaged in undergraduate instruction and frequently involve their graduate students in commercial activities in ways that disrupt the students' graduate work and their freedom to complete and publish their dissertations.

As more students and professors engage in entrepreneurial research markets, more knowledge becomes "commodified" or owned. When information and knowledge are owned, they circulate less freely. Sometimes information is strategically incorporated into companies' growth strategies and removed from markets. In other words, in a perverse inversion of purpose, patents are used to keep information from the market. Granstrand (2000) makes the case that, "if the rate of knowledge growth is consistently larger in the private domain than in the public domain, then at some point in time privately held knowledge will start to dominate" (p. 24). If private knowledge control dominates, then public science and technology as well as education become more difficult to maintain. The academic capitalist knowledge/learning regime may contribute to this process.

Finally, in regard to patents, it's not that academic capitalism and the commercialization of knowledge is all bad, it's a question of where the line is drawn, who draws the line, and what sorts of products are promoted. What are educational institutions' terms of engagement with the corporate world and the world of commerce? Currently, universities and colleges have no policy about how they select discoveries to patent or exploit commercially. Some are more likely to patent when a corporation will pay the cost. Others are likely to patent when the market for the product looks promising. Academic patent and intellectual property policies and practices do not attend to the issue of selecting patents or copyrights that might have social utility. In other words, universities and colleges are as likely to patent cosmetic properties, for example RetinA, as they are discoveries that might contribute broadly to the social welfare of the citizenry, for example AIDS vaccines. When they license their patents to corporations, higher education institutions tend not to add clauses that contain costs so as to benefit the citizenry, for example prescription drugs (an important point since such a large portion of patent royalties relates to biomedical, pharmaceutical products). Universities and colleges follow a market rather than a social welfare logic. As non-profit and public institutions, they might well increase their public support and legitimacy by commercializing in areas of great public utility and seeking less than the maximum profit the market will bear when selling products.

Copyrights raise many of the same problems as do patents. Commercializing copyrightable materials increases educational costs in terms not only of tuition but also of the costs of educational materials themselves. Whether in the form of courseware packets, CDs, or other technology-enhanced educational materials, academic capitalism has increased the costs of education. As with patents, the more costly educational materials are, the more the free flow of knowledge is constrained. Ironically, the public space of academic publication becomes less a place of the free flow of ideas and information in an information-based new economy.

Academic capitalism in the new economy also restructures work in the academy, with some undesirable and unintended consequences. As in industry, universities and colleges have downsized and essentially outsourced their instructional production workers, replacing full-time faculty with part-time and contingent faculty. The increased use of contingent faculty is related to the underfunding of universities' and colleges' instructional mission relative to the tuition monies and state dollars that come to them as a result of enrolments. Moreover, the percentage of faculty who are part time has doubled in the past twenty years despite research pointing to the significance of contact with faculty for student learning, satisfaction, and success. Part-time faculty are by definition and by working conditions (e.g., no office space) less available to their students than are full-time faculty.

In contrast to the pattern in industry, where the numbers of middle managers have declined, universities and colleges have greatly expanded middle management, whether to supervise commercial endeavours and engagements with various external communities or to support students and information technology. Thus, in regard to student customers, academic capitalism in the new economy has involved universities and colleges reducing instructional and faculty labour costs and expanding costs in various support, entrepreneurial, marketing, and consumption realms of and professions in the academy. The managerial, non-faculty professionals who manage infrastructure, economic development, endowment, and entrepreneurial activity are less directly focused than are faculty on teaching and research, and they are more closely linked to intermediating networks of senior administrators involved in promoting university-business co-operation and partnership and new economy academic capitalism.

In addition to restructuring professional work, academic capitalism in the new economy brings restratification of and competition among academic fields. This can be a very healthy development, but it can also entail some dysfunctionalities. Among them are a restricted conception of what a college or university education is, a heightened and counterproductive sense of struggle between and within academic units, an orientation to short-term educational markets that prioritizes market share and revenue enhancement over educational quality, and an internal resistance to some of the directions embedded in academic capitalism.

As institutions move more aggressively to intersect with new economy corporate and employment markets, conceptions of a college and university education become more and more constrained by a sense of opportunities in the marketplace. The idea of a college or university as a space for public discussion, debate, commentary, and critique is pushed to the background. Ascendant is the idea that college education is about preparation for employment in the new economy. Thus, for example, at the graduate level, there is an increasing emphasis not on generating knowledge but on what is essentially continuing education that advances employees up career ladders. A dramatic expansion of "professional master's degrees" is a product of academic capitalism in the new economy, as are contract education and certificate programs in community colleges. The focus of these educational innovations is in considerable part on efficiency and revenue generation, in narrow ways that have little to do with a range of educational functions that universities and colleges might be expected to play with regard to employers and employment (e.g., participating in defining the contours and conditions of work in the new economy, as social scientists did at the turn of the past century with regard to industrial and professional employment).

From the standpoint of academic departments seeking to survive and thrive in academic capitalist universities and colleges, there is similarly an increasingly short-term perspective that focuses on productivity measures in research, grants, and student credit hour production. Increasingly, academic units are conceptualized as cost centres, as production units, seeking to maximize their productivity. That can lead them to compete with each other for students in some counterproductive ways (Rhoades, 2000). It can mean reducing standards for general education students or majors or expanding student numbers beyond those that make sense for local labour markets. It can also inhibit patterns of collaboration and interdisciplinary activity, pitting departments within the same institutions against each other in a cutthroat and cannibalistic competition for internal university resources.

At the departmental level, the ascendance of academic capitalism in the new economy is sometimes met with confusion or resistance. That was clear in our analysis of department heads and faculty in science and engineering. Heads responded unevenly to the possibilities of entrepreneurial activity. In some cases, heads seemed unsure what to do strategically or how their department could possibly fit within the current agenda of their institution. In other cases, heads were resistant to the push from central academic managers for more entrepreneurial activity and engagement with business in the area of research. One of the fault lines within academic capitalism is that there are often disjunctures between where presidents, provosts, and other senior academic administrators want to take an institution and the commitments and interests of significant numbers of faculty within the institution.

Nevertheless, presidents and senior administrators operating in intermediating institutions have greatly enhanced managerial capacity. They direct the forward planning of their institutions by committing resources to projects such as Internet2, shaping future directions for decades to come. However, members of the intermediating organizations often do not consult extensively with their internal institutional constituencies, which may undercut local support and willingness to participate in the projects. Members of intermediating organizations often redraw the boundaries of public, non-profit, and for-profit entities. In cases such as Internet infrastructure (Internet2), distance education (EDUCAUSE), the League for Innovation, and start-up corporations (boards of trustees), the functions of public, non-profit, and for-profit entities are indistinguishable. Public institutions do not serve the citizenry as a whole but provide service to the same students targeted by for-profit and private institutions, as is especially clear in the case of distance education. Non-profit institutions, whether public or private, seek to maximize profits on the market activity, ranging from taking their start-up companies public through initial public offerings (IPOs) to intellectual property to marketing computers to students in bookstores. For-profit corporations become deeply involved in the business of education, using universities and colleges as test beds for developing and marketing educational products. Only their designation, and the costs and benefits that stem from it, are different. When public, non-profit, and for-profit entities combine in intermediating networks, each seeks to attain as many of the benefits, and as few of the costs, as possible attached to the others. The greatest problem stemming from such intermediation is that public resources are transferred to private networks that underwrite the new economy. This transfer, which is not subject to broad public debate or voted on, may undermine public trust in universities and colleges, manifesting itself in less public support for state and federal resource allocations to postsecondary education.

Densely networked boards of trustees who share information but whose institutions compete with each other may move universities and colleges from non-profits to "disguised for-profits" (Weisbrod, 1988). Presidents of research universities take on the appearance of chief executive officers. Four presidents of private universities earned more than $800,000 in the 2002 fiscal year, and, if pay for serving on corporate boards is included, the compensation for three went over the million-dollar mark (Basinger, 2003). James (1998) sees this as an indication of non-profits becoming disguised for-profits when "nonprofits maximize profits and distribute them in disguised form (as higher wages and perks), or they may maximize revenues that lead to power and prestige for their managers" (p. 273). The trustees, who intermediate between universities and the corporate sector, normalize presidential salaries that far outstrip the salaries of most other US professionals, making some university presidents' salaries more like those in the for-profit sector than the non-profit sector. Marketization of student recruitment raises questions of access. When elite public and non-profit universities and colleges compete for students who score well on standardized tests and are able to pay high tuition, low-income and minority students are less likely to attend. The heavy attendance of low-income and minority students at community colleges is in part a reflection of the marketing strategies of elite universities and colleges. Marketing of distance education to non-traditional students, even when such projects are arms of elite schools, contributes to bifurcated access patterns in which increasing numbers of students are educated off-site. Competition for student markets does not reduce tuition; on the contrary, it may have increased tuition as institutions vie with each other to offer students more non-instructional activities.

Marketing to students once they matriculate raises questions about the part universities and colleges play in student identity development. When universities and colleges seek to market non-instructional, commercialized goods on campus, they develop students' identities as consumers rather than learners. Students, their families, and alumni respond to the brand through purchasing and giving. However, universities and colleges lose their claim to full development of students in the students' best interests.

Alternatives within and beyond Academic Capitalism in the New Economy

The academic capitalist knowledge/learning regime is ascendant and, as we have argued, embedded in a complex array and network of policies, intermediating and emergent interstitial organizations, and actors and practices. Yet this regime is not inevitable, in its current configuration, and it does not stand alone. This chapter maps a general pattern that is in place. However, what academic capitalism in the new economy means concretely for the future direction and work of individual universities and colleges in the United States and by extension Canada is yet to be fully defined.

Just as there are many forms of capitalism, so too there can be many forms of academic capitalism. It does not have to take laissez-faire form. Rather than simply seeking to maximize external revenue generation, academic capitalism could seek to enhance the social benefits of intellectual property and educational services. Universities' and colleges' commitment to revenue generation could also encompass commitments to increased access for underserved populations and expansion of opportunities for women and minorities.

For many universities, a current principal target of investment is biotechnology. However, all universities are unlikely to succeed in the biotech arena; competition is too intense. Instead, universities and colleges could try to discover distinctive niches that build on their research strengths or their geographic locations. These niches might well be targeted because they provide opportunities for social benefits. For example, there is enormous potential in the realm of environmental engineering, a sustainable environment, and clean energy alternatives, which are all significant sectors of the new economy. In the case of our own university, there would be great promise in an initiative that focused on environmental issues and enhancing the quality of life in the borderlands. Such an initiative would involve investing not only in the sciences but also in various social sciences, humanities, and fields of education, integrating in interdisciplinary ways that creatively cut across the divide between science fields and the rest of the university. The promise of such an initiative would be to intersect successfully with growth areas in the new economy and to impact positively the region within which the university exists. Such a strategy would play not only to the geographic location of our university in the southern Arizona borderlands but also to our academic strengths in environmental sciences, arid land studies, borderland studies, anthropology, sociology, American Indian studies, bilingual education, and linguistics (and higher education!), among others.

In addition to biotechnology, many higher education institutions are seeking to intersect with the information technology sector of the new economy. Community colleges and comprehensive and urban universities see this general realm as a target for substantial investment. In pursuing such a strategy, universities and colleges are intersecting with a global economy in ways that do not always pay dividends for local economies and regions. They prepare relatively privileged students for computer-related careers or generate revenues through distance education that serves audiences far from their geographic locations.

We see an alternative for such institutions. They could focus on local needs, attending to issues of immigration and integrating immigrant and low-income populations into the middle layers of the new economy. What does that mean concretely? It could mean a community college combining a computer-tech program with an ESL program targeting immigrant populations. It could mean a comprehensive university combining an information technology program with a teacher preparation program, training educators who would contribute to enhancing urban populations' ability to intersect with and work within the new economy. The point is to leaven the new economy focus on technology with the ongoing and emergent human challenges and opportunities that we confront in a globalizing world. We believe that such an approach would yield substantial dividends for the higher education institutions as well as for the communities in which they are located.

Of course, these are not either/or choices. The issue in most universities and colleges is how to balance various alternatives. We are simply suggesting the foregrounding of possibilities that currently are very much in the background and that involve human sciences and services fields that are currently the target of deinvestment in many higher education institutions.

The educational mission of higher education could be reinvested in by judicious use of the proceeds from intellectual property. Alternatives to current patterns of faculty and institutional ownership of and claims to royalties from intellectual property could be explored. A share of revenues generated by the intellectual property could be placed in a public trust that could have as its purpose directly aiding students and communities in a variety of ways, whether through scholarships, research internships, or direct grants toward community development.

Rather than focusing only on the revenue potential of intellectual property, universities and colleges could provide some discount for the sale of products developed by faculty, which, after all, were publicly subsidized in their production. Faculty and university involvement in the production of goods and services could ensure that these goods be treated as generics, with less focus on maximizing revenues than on the wide distribution and availability of the products. The implications in the field of biomedical products would be enormous.

Each of the above alternatives requires a network of policies, organizations, and actors to become viable, as was the case with the academic capitalist knowledge/learning regime. We must imagine a new university with organizational structures, incentives, and rewards for the kind of society we want and then create the new circuits of knowledge, interstitial organizations, and intermediating networks to achieve it. This is a task that will take time, patience, and commitment and will have to be linked to appropriate organizations and social movements outside the university. Perhaps we could begin by developing networks of citizens, faculty, academic managers, and students to formulate policies that frame the terms of engagement of universities and colleges with corporate partners, that create incentives for developing products that have socially productive purposes, and that work out ways for shares of revenues from intellectual property to be directed to undergraduate instruction. We must imagine a university that emphasizes the "use" value of the knowledge it creates. The "exchange" university (see the Introduction to this volume) will become an institution whose raison d'être is to serve the public good.

Notes

1 A similar trend developed in Canada. While the responses from Canadian institutions to the AUTM surveys (AUTM, 2003, pp. 66-67) have not been as inclusive as their US counterparts, we do see an increase in the number of US patents issued to Canadian universities, from 52 in 1994 (N=12) to 172 in 2002 (N=22).

2 The variance depends on who is counting.

3 The fifteen universities in order of the amount of research funds received are Toronto, McGill, Montreal, British Columbia, Alberta, Laval, Calgary, McMaster, Western Ontario, Ottawa, Queen's, Manitoba, Guelph, Waterloo, and Saskatchewan.

4 Calculated from *CAUT Almanac* (2006, Table 5.6, p. 46).

References

Association of Universities and Colleges of Canada (AUCC). (2005). *Momentum.* Ottawa: AUCC.

Association of University Technology Managers (AUTM). (2003). *2002 licensing survey.* Northbrook, IL: AUTM.

Basinger, J. (2003). Closing in on $1-million. *Chronicle of Higher Education, 50*(12), S1.

Bok, D. (2003). *Universities in the marketplace: The commercialization of higher education.* Princeton: Princeton University Press.

Canadian Association of University Teachers (CAUT). (2006). *Almanac.* Ottawa: CAUT.

Clark, B.(1998). *Creating entrepreneurial universities: Organizational pathways of transformation.* Oxford: IAU Press and Pergamon.

Council of Canadian Academies, Committee on the State of Science and Technology in Canada. (2006). *The state of science and technology in Canada.* Ottawa: Council of Canadian Academies.

DiMaggio, P.J., and Powell, W.W. (1983). The iron cage revisited: Institutional isomorphism and collective rationality in organizational fields. *American Sociological Review, 48,* 147-60.

Etzkowitz, H., Webster, A., and Healey, P. (1998). *Capitalizing knowledge: New interactions of industry and academe.* Albany: SUNY Press.
Evans, K. (2005). *Going global with the locals: An examination of international activity at the university colleges in British Columbia.* Unpublished doctoral dissertation, University of British Columbia, Vancouver.
Finkelstein, M.J., Seal, R.K., and Schuster, J.H. (1998). *The new academic generation: A profession in transformation.* Baltimore: Johns Hopkins University Press.
Fisher, D., and Atkinson-Grosjean, J. (2002). Brokers on the boundary: Academy-industry liaison in Canadian universities. *Higher Education, 44,* 449-67.
Fisher, D., Atkinson-Grosjean, J., and House, D. (2001). Changes in academy/industry/state relations in Canada: The creation and development of the Networks of Centres of Excellence. *Minerva: A Review of Science and Policy, 39,* 299-325.
Granstrand, O. (2000). The shift towards intellectual capitalism: The role of infocom technologies. *Research Policy, 29*(9), 1061-80.
Indiana Higher Education Telecommunications System (IHETS). (2003). *About us.* www.ihets.org.
James, E. (1998). Commercialism among nonprofits: Objectives, opportunities, and constraints. In B.A. Weisbrod (Ed.), *To profit or not to profit: The commercial transformation of the nonprofit sector* (pp. 271-86). Cambridge, UK: Cambridge University Press.
Metcalfe, A.S. (2004). *Intermediating associations and the university-industry relationship.* Unpublished doctoral dissertation, University of Arizona.
National Center for Education Statistics (NCES). (2001). *Digest of educational statistics.* Washington, DC: US Department of Education.
National Science Board (NSB). (2002). *Science and engineering indicators: 2002.* Arlington, VA: National Science Foundation.
Newson, J., and Buchbinder, H. (1988). *The university means business.* Toronto: Garamond Press.
Noble, D.F. (2001). *Digital diploma mills: The automation of higher education.* New York: Monthly Review Press.
Rhoades, G. (2000). Who's doing it right? Strategic activity in public research universities. *Review of Higher Education, 24*(1), 41-66.
Schiller, D. (1998). *Digital capitalism.* Cambridge, MA: MIT Press.
Slaughter, S. (1990). *The higher learning and high technology: Dynamics of higher education policy formation.* Albany: SUNY Press.
Soley, L. (1995). *Leasing the ivory tower: The corporate takeover of academia.* Boston: South End Press.
Weisbrod, B.A. (1988). *The nonprofit economy.* Cambridge, MA: Harvard University Press.
–. (1998). The nonprofit mission and its financing: Growing links between nonprofits and the rest of the economy. In B.A. Weisbrod (Ed.), *To profit or not to profit: The commercial transformation of the nonprofit sector* (pp. 1-24). Cambridge, UK: Cambridge University Press.

2
Academic Culture and the Research-Intensive University: The Impact of Commercialism and Scientism

Adrienne S. Chan and Donald Fisher

Academic culture is defined by Ringer as "the network of interrelated and explicit beliefs about academic practices of teaching, learning, and research, and about the social significance of these practices" (1992, p. 13). Academic culture has also been discussed in relation to different cultures and identities, academic tribes and ethics, external influences, internal directives, and social, political, and educational agendas (Becher and Trowler, 2001; Clark, 1987; Elzinga, 1985; Neave and van Vught, 1991; Shils, 1997; Tierney, 1991). In this chapter, academic culture includes conceptions of knowledge production and institutional practices and is therefore understood through the discourses of the social actors in the university, and their understandings of knowledge, and "life" within the academy. Internal and external forces impose direction on the academy and are evident in the debates and priorities that are articulated by faculty and administrators. The state is a significant external force that, through funding and policy, exerts influence over the direction of research in universities. They develop strategic priorities and policies that also determine the direction of research and knowledge production. This chapter examines a number of internal and external factors that have shaped changes in academic culture in Canada over the past fifteen years. In particular, we focus on the case study of the University of Ottawa.

Becher (1989) studied the interconnections between academic cultures and the cultural worlds of disciplines or tribes and suggested a range of cultures across a disciplinary continuum of hard pure sciences through to applied professional sciences, the social sciences, and the arts. This work is considered seminal among studies of academic culture. Although the interviewees were mainly from senior male faculty and thus representative of a particular subculture of the academy, the research does suggest an important thesis concerning the development and evolution of academic cultures, territories, and tribalism. The continuum of disciplines is significant, particularly when considering the current emphasis on the natural and applied sciences and the corrosion of the boundary separating the academy from industry.

Canadian universities are almost exclusively public institutions. They are also the location of the majority of the research conducted in the country. In 1986, the Canadian government introduced a matching funds policy requiring its granting councils to earmark funding for university-industry collaborations. Since that time, universities in Canada have been forced to examine their role in the "knowledge economy" and the weighting they give to science, technology, and innovation as part of their response to state policy (de la Mothe and Pacquet, 1999; Fisher, Atkinson-Grosjean, and House, 2001). Higher education in Canada has become strongly implicated in the market language of production, distribution, and utilization of knowledge. The debates concerning the selection of priorities for knowledge production are ongoing and have been at times acrimonious.

Three studies preceded this research: a case study of Canadian university industrial liaison offices (Fisher and Atkinson-Grosjean, 2002), a case study tracing the development of the federal government's Networks of Centres of Excellence program (Fisher, Atkinson-Grosjean, and House, 2001), and a history of Canadian science policy that traces the development of public-private partnerships from the turn of the twentieth century (Atkinson-Grosjean, House, and Fisher, 2001). These studies implied that "campus culture" and the "culture of academic science" have changed through the evolution of public policy and that new types of research and researchers are becoming more prominent in the academy.

The purpose of our research[1] was to increase our understanding of how academic culture in English-speaking Canadian research universities has changed over the past fifteen years. We were particularly interested in the linkages between the state, the academy, and the private sector. These links have been facilitated by a series of federal and provincial policies that require or encourage matching funding for research. The specific funding envelopes made available to universities were framed within this ethos of collaboration. Funding from private sources (e.g., industry, venture capitalists) has also increased and influenced the research agenda.

This chapter reports the results from one case study: the University of Ottawa. Through this example, we draw some conclusions about the changes that have occurred with regard to academic culture.

Methodology and Research Design

Canadian universities are usually divided into three categories: mainly undergraduate, comprehensive, and medical/doctoral. Before deciding which universities would be the subject of our case studies, we examined the funding patterns of twelve of the most research intensive,[2] medical/doctoral, English-speaking universities in Canada.[3] From there, the University of

Ottawa became one of our four case studies. Three weeks were spent conducting fieldwork in Ottawa. Interviews were conducted with tenured faculty or members of the senior administration who had held their appointments with the institution for at least ten years. Faculty interviewees represented a cross-section of disciplines from among the "hard" sciences, engineering, arts, social sciences, and humanities. The interviewees were a mix of gender and racial/ethnic groups as well as language groups at the University of Ottawa. Some of the faculty were serving or had served on the senate or an equivalent body. Interviews included deans, department heads, vice rectors, and esteemed researchers (Canada Research Chair holders and/or members of an NCE). We also interviewed faculty whom we identified as critics of the cultural changes in their institutions. In these cases, the faculty members were well known to us through their opinions voiced in the media or had been recommended to us by the faculty association or one of the interview participants. From a research and institutional perspective, we interviewed some administrators in the industry liaison or technology transfer office. A total of twenty-six interviews were conducted at the University of Ottawa (twenty-three were taped and transcribed).

This chapter identifies some of the themes that characterize the changing academic culture at the University of Ottawa.We provide some background information about the university that was developed through the examination of documents from the university (e.g., Draft Business Plan, 1998c; Performance Report, 1998d). Our analysis highlights the concept of changing culture through six key themes: research, science, commercialization, changing roles, collegiality, and generational differences.

The University of Ottawa

The University of Ottawa was founded in 1848 in the national capital of Canada and has a history housed in its pontifical charter of 1889. Faculties and schools with ecclesiastical status were transferred to St. Paul's University in 1965, when the university was granted a provincial charter and joined other publicly funded institutions in Ontario. The University of Ottawa is a bilingual university in the Province of Ontario, which is largely anglophone. The history of the university emerges from both a traditional European model and francophone culture.

The University of Ottawa is consistently ranked among the top ten research universities in Canada. In 1999 and 2003, it was ranked eighth in research intensity[4] in Canada. The university has an industrial liaison office that is part of the administrative structure. As the owner of intellectual property, the university is either the outright owner or requires a compulsory agreement with faculty. In 1999, the University of Ottawa received gross royalties and licence income of $330,300 (US funds, thousands of constant dollars). Sponsored research income in 2000 was $114,612 (US funds, thousands of

Table 2.1

University of Ottawa sponsored research income

Income source	1986	1991	1997	1998	2002	2003
Total government	16,807	34,365	28,589	32,612	102,466	126,395
	69.6%	*64.4%*	*48.1%*	*37.7%*	*67.3%*	*67.9%*
Non-government	6,524	17,237	30,574	53,694	43,830	51,993
	27.0%	*32.3%*	*51.4%*	*62.0%*	*28.8%*	*28.0%*
Other income	800	1,755	332	235	5,902	7,666
	3.3%	*3.3%*	*0.5%*	*0.3%*	*3.9%*	*4.1%*
Total	24,131	53,357	59,495	86,541	152,198	186,054
	100.0%	*100.0%*	*100.0%*	*100.0%*	*100.0%*	*100.0%*

Note: Figures are in thousands of constant US dollars.
Source: Canadian Association of University Business Officers (CAUBO).

constant dollars), an increase of 28.2 percent over the previous year; in 2004, sponsored research income was $190,343 (US funds, thousands of constant dollars).

Table 2.1 examines the trends in sponsored research income[5] at the University of Ottawa. In a fifteen-year period (1986 to 2003), we see that total government (federal, provincial, and municipal) contributions decreased from 69.6 percent (1986) of the total sponsored research income to 37.7 percent (1998) and increased again to 67.9 percent (2003). Non-government sources increased from 27.0 percent (1986) to 62.0 percent (1998) and decreased to 28.0 percent in 2003. Other income sources (revenues, bequests, donations, and interest income) ranged from 3.3 percent (1986) to 0.3 percent (1998) and then to 4.1 percent in 2003. A peak in non-government income occurred in the years 1997 and 1998. The most dramatic change occurred between 1998 and 2003 in the research income coming from government. The increase from approximately $32 to $126 million was a result of the drive by the administration to change the research culture of the university.

The distribution of federal funding from research councils and other federal sources is outlined in Table 2.2. The CFI and CRC programs account for a significant increase of federal funding in 2002 and 2003. The natural, applied, and health sciences continue to represent a higher proportion of funding over the humanities and social sciences. In 2003, SSHRCC accounted for 1.9 percent of the total sponsored research income, while NSERC, CIHR, and CFI accounted for 29.6 percent.

In the Province of Ontario, the focus on "economic leadership and technological innovation" was the mandate given to the Premier's Council of On-

Table 2.2

University of Ottawa sponsored research income: Distribution across federal sources and as a proportion of total sponsored research income

Income source	1986	1991	1997	1998	2002	2003
SSHRCC	1,117	1,953	1,803	1,796	3,769	3,530
	4.6%	*3.7%*	*3.0%*	*2.1%*	*2.5%*	*1.9%*
Health Canada	567	1,604	852	1,112	1,783	1,454
	2.3%	*3.0%*	*1.4%*	*1.3%*	*1.2%*	*0.8%*
NSERC	6,197	9,197	7,428	7,739	10,608	11,793
	25.7%	*17.2%*	*12.5%*	*8.9%*	*7.0%*	*6.2%*
MRC/CIHR	4,488	4,960	7,414	7,746	9,371	21,499
	18.6%	*9.3%*	*12.5%*	*9.0%*	*6.1%*	*11.6%*
CFI					12,653	21,981
					8.3%	*11.8%*
CRC					2,299	5,330
					1.5%	*2.9%*
Other federal	2,769	10,229	6,265	9,730	29,420	20,782
	11.5%	*19.2%*	*10.5%*	*11.2%*	*19.3%*	*11.2%*
Total federal	15,138	27,943	23,762	28,123	69,903	86,369
	62.7%	*52.4%*	*39.9%*	*32.5%*	*45.9%*	*46.4%*

Note: Figures are in thousands of constant US dollars.
Source: Canadian Association of University Business Officers (CAUBO).

tario (1988) in order to develop the competitiveness of the province. The council produced a report entitled "Competing in the New Global Economy" (1988). Among the recommendations of the report was that greater resources were to be placed in industries that would benefit from investment in R&D and marketing. These early innovations set the stage for universities in Ontario to increase academic "investment" in research.

Throughout this period, we see an emerging discourse that highlights the objective of further development of research activity in universities, to develop and maintain a competitive position in the world economy. Technology was also emerging as an important element in global competitiveness. Linked to these notions of technology, the University of Ottawa requires that all inventions, industrial designs, new circuited topographies, and new plant varieties be reported through its intellectual property policy (2001). We see the emphasis of pushing research to the market (Slaughter and Rhoades, 2004), although there are also internal contradictions where public funding has been increased.

In Ontario, the Ontario Centres of Excellence (OCE), the University Research Incentive Fund (URIF), the Premier's Council Technology Fund, and the Industry Research Program were all established in 1987. Ten years later, the Ministry of Energy, Science, and Technology was created, and the Research and Development Challenge Fund was established (1997). The fund emphasized university-industry liaisons to support job creation and economic growth and to attract and keep skilled researchers in Ontario.

Supporting the Ontario R&D Challenge Fund, a 20 percent refundable research and development tax credit was established for corporate-sponsored R&D in Ontario universities and other postsecondary institutions. A co-operative education tax credit in information technology was expanded, and an intellectual property tax credit was established. Other provinces have also introduced a tax policy (e.g., Quebec in 2001) to provide particular incentives for research and development and technology.

In 2002, the Ontario Research Performance Fund was announced. The fund provides an additional $30 million annually to colleges, universities, and research institutes to cover the overhead costs associated with Ontario-funded research. The R&D Challenge Fund was also increased to $100 million. One example of how these funds have assisted the University of Ottawa is the commitment of $5.4 million from the province to help create the Ottawa Biotechnology Incubation Centre, with the objective of boosting competitiveness and creating jobs in the biotechnology industry.

Changing the Culture

The dramatic change in the policy environment at both the provincial and the federal levels of government had an impact on the internal life of the University of Ottawa. The overwhelming emphasis over the past decade has been upon attracting an increasing amount of research funding as a means to transform the institution into a leading research intensive university. Inevitably, given the focus on the "sciences" at both the federal and the provincial levels of government, the "sciences" as an ideology and a set of practices have been a central component of the redefinition of academic culture.

Research

A major theme at the University of Ottawa was its strategic goal to become a research intensive university. The decision arose out of discussions and planning sessions within the senate. Discussions that began in 1992 produced several documents in 1993 and 1994 and a "yellow paper" in 1995 that articulated the emphasis the university would place on graduate studies and research that would be in keeping with the role of a full-service, research intensive university. The yellow paper identified a commitment made by the administration to "actually assist researchers in their efforts to obtain external funding for their work" (University of Ottawa, 1995).

The development of a research intensive university has accelerated with the creation of the position of vice rector research and the subsequent creation of the position of associate vice rector research. In this time period, a number of cross-disciplinary research centres were developed, and there has been an aggressive campaign for SSHRCC funding, Canada Research Chairs, CFI grants, and innovation funding at the provincial level. The emphasis on research has been articulated in a number of planning documents: "Fostering excellence is pivotal to our success in research, whether the research is basic or applied, of intrinsic value or commercial importance. By launching new initiatives in strategic areas, by promoting collaboration within and across faculties and affiliated institutes (e.g. an Interfaculty Collaborative Research Grants program has been established), and by increasing our partnerships with the private sector, we intend to provide the milieu in which creativity can flourish and to secure a leadership position among the research intensive universities in Canada" (Canada Research Chairs, 2001, p. 4). Thus, the university has worked to establish a national presence in research and by 2003 had achieved success.

Academic culture includes notions about everyday life as well as beliefs about teaching and research. Change in the culture of research was identified as a result of a number of factors, including the pressure placed on faculty to obtain research grants and to contribute to knowledge production within a highly competitive environment. Academic life has become much more complicated in the past fifteen years. Research intensive universities have a larger role as they are expected to contribute to the knowledge economy.

Funding envelopes such as the SSHRCC Initiatives for the New Economy (INE) and the CFI infrastructure grants clearly set limits on what will count as legitimate research and knowledge. Emphasis on teams and networking in research programs brought about another shift in the culture. The NCEs were cited as a motivating factor at the University of Ottawa. The university is seen to have "made an effort to break down the walls between faculties" (P15 OT, research chair, applied sciences[6]), to involve graduate students, and to increase multidisciplinary programs. "I think things have become more collaborative, obviously. You know, the research councils want us to collaborate, but science in general is becoming more complicated. You know, for example, I think for the first maybe twenty-five years that I was here we didn't really have, or I didn't really have, graduate students that were associated with other professors" (P13 OT, faculty researcher, sciences). The NCEs are regarded as a factor in the shift to interdisciplinarity and a weakening of the boundary separating industry and the university. Historically, teams and networks operated at the informal level, particularly in the arts and social sciences, but the NCEs have made it a necessary condition. The NCEs have created a system of connections across disciplines and universities, particularly across the sciences, where such networks might not have occurred otherwise. The arrival of the NCEs meant that networking became an important part of knowledge. This is mode 2 knowledge production and diffusion (Gibbons et al., 1994).

In 2000, the University of Ottawa was ranked second in the Province of Ontario in grants from the CFI, the Ontario R&D Challenge Fund, the Premier's Research Excellence Awards, and the Ontario Innovation Trust. The university ranked eighth in Canada in sponsored research and sixth in research intensity (Re$earch Infosource, 2001). In 2002, the University of Ottawa received $17.5 million from the Canada Foundation for Innovation for seven projects, ranking ninth in Canada. In the same year, the university received private sector support for research that ranked second in Canada. This support continued in 2003.[7]

A decision was made by the university to focus on four main areas of research. This discussion and the associated strategic planning began in 1998, and the four areas were confirmed and articulated in the strategic research plan for the Canada Research Chairs (2001). The four areas are Canada, health, information technology, and molecular sciences. While other areas of research (not falling within this range of themes) may be pursued, they are not emphasized in this context. This focused strategy has given the university strength in pursuing sponsored research income and research direction: "The CRC and CFI programs are a cohesive, quintessential prescription for competitiveness on a global basis" (Canada Research Chairs, 2001, p. 4). As one administrator put it, "the key in why we are so research intensive now was the decision to focus, to not try to do everything. And so there was a pretty overt decision to pursue what are called strategic areas of development. And I think that was the key to it" (P6 OT, humanities). The effects of becoming a research intensive university have been significant. The transition has required an engagement by faculties in a research model that is seen as competitive and relevant: "Obtaining grants and funds is a major factor in being competitive" (University of Ottawa, 1998a). This was not a significant shift for medical and science faculties; however, it was a cultural shift for faculties that had not been research oriented or research competitive (e.g., management, education): "There has been a major shift towards the scientific model or the medical model that is even in the other disciplines, humanities and social sciences. Much more importance given to outside research funding. Basically, when I came in here the humanities professors paid out of their own pocket for their research activities. And didn't or weren't encouraged actively to pursue outside funding. That is not the case now" (P1 OT, senior administrator). The shift in research has also meant thinking about research differently: partnerships with the private sector, competing for grants, and the use of a science model. This is "not an easy revolution because people in humanities and social sciences have a tendency to resist this scientific model" (P1 OT, senior administrator):

> We're the sixth best university in terms of research in Canada now. And there's a lot of money for research, but there are problems entailed. I think the emphasis on research is great. And the majority of people we're hiring now have a great emphasis on research and writing. Some of the older people in the faculty aren't interested in research, and so we're going to clear away those [people]. (P12 OT, administrator, humanities)

> The U of O has become much more research intensive. And there is a significant stress on that. I think the importance of that to the university is reflected in its change in status among those institutions that are competitive for the big research grants in Canada. We have moved up actually in the last six or seven years from position number thirteen to position number five or six in terms of total research funding, which is significant. Therefore, the recruitment has largely been placed on people who are researchers, with teaching skills moving very much to the background. And in fact their time is significantly protected so that they can be competitive for research grants. (P7 OT, research chair, sciences)

The priorities of research are the first "screen" for recruitment. Faculty are recruited because of their portfolio of research. As one respondent noted, "your research dossier gets you the interview for the job, and your ability to communicate gets you the actual job" (P6 OT, administrator, humanities).

The selection of faculty is key to funding and research goals:

> Teaching is definitely not a major consideration for the Faculty of Medicine in terms of those undergraduate programs that are not medicine [e.g., biology]. Whereas in the Faculty of Science, of course, it's front and centre, along with research ... Most of the research ranking of the university is due to the activities within the Faculty of Medicine. (P7 OT, research chair, sciences)

> People want to do research, ... and it is certainly true that there is increasing pressure to figure out ways to give people reductions in teaching loads. Which for a university, at least its faculty, which started out from a totally egalitarian, very strong egalitarian tradition, is proving very complicated in terms of people getting their heads around and discussing this question – should people do less teaching if they do more research, and in what ways do you do it? So there are huge pressures in that. (P11 OT, administrator, social sciences)

The emphasis on research, the competition for research funding, and the effect on teaching comprise a troubling discourse. Inevitably, there are greater pressures to perform and more competitiveness in the environment. Faculty are concerned about what counts as research funding, but as one respondent noted there is "little debate" (P12 OT, administrator, humanities). Some faculty had reflected on the complexity of the issue, particularly in relation to funding from industry. A related issue is the worry that external influences will determine the research agenda.

The role of teaching in a research intensive university was an emerging theme in the interviews. This involved re-examining the commitment to teaching and its relationship to research. The importance of pedagogy at the University of Ottawa was articulated by faculty and administrators.

> So now you must have a strong research dossier to be a prof here, but you will not be hired if people don't think that you are going to be a good educator as well. And the emphasis now on teaching dossiers and so on is just exponentially increased, and I think we pride ourselves a lot on being good educators. (P6 OT, administrator, humanities)

> The essence of the academic life, I tend to think, is a balance between teaching and research. And as a dean, I still teach. I've taught three different courses on the graduate level. (P12 OT, administrator, humanities)

How the mutual reinforcement of teaching and research is manifested varies. Some new faculty members, particularly in the sciences, have come to the university with an expectation that they will not have to teach.

Science

The emphasis on science at the University of Ottawa is marked by activity in life sciences, photonics, and technology. A number of initiatives emphasize work across disciplines. An example was a proposal for a Chair in Science and Technology Policy and Corporate Strategy. This was approved in principle in a Draft Business Plan at the senate (University of Ottawa, 1998b). This interdisciplinary initiative entailed discussion among the deans from the relevant disciplines. The intention was to develop a chair with joint funding from two councils, NSERC and SSHRCC, as well as corporate sponsors. This position was eventually funded as a Canada Research Chair in Innovation Strategy (Canada Research Chairs, 2003).

Thirteen of twenty-two Canada Research Chairs are in the sciences (the natural, applied health, and life sciences), technology, and health and medicine (2003). Of the remaining nine chairs, two are in a general category of population health, and the remaining seven are in the humanities and social sciences. Furthermore, eighteen of twenty-four research centres focus on science and technology, with six of these centres based in hospital research. The majority of Canada Research Chairs are men.

Faculty and administrators expressed their concern about a perceived imbalance in support for the "hard" sciences versus the humanities and social sciences:

> I thought, in terms of the Canada Research Chairs, that the percentage of new hires ... on the life sciences side, a significant proportion of them could be chairs. Whereas in the social sciences, considering the very small number of chairs and the huge numbers in the social sciences, [the proportion] was zero. I mean it was about 0.1 of the new hires would be chairs. (P11 OT, administrator, social sciences)

> Well, I think there isn't enough money going to the humanities; on the other hand, what humanities needs is time to research and write, and they don't have these big, huge proposals. (P12 OT, administrator, humanities)

> The humanities have been sidestepped in the past twenty years or so, and there's an emphasis on technology, on information technology, on engineering, but I don't think the humanities have anything to apologize for. We just have to do what we do as best we can. (P12 OT, administrator, humanities)

There continues to be tension regarding what funding is available and for which areas and disciplines. This is a competitive environment, and concern is expressed in terms of what is available and what is protected.

> A lot of people were very upset on the biomedical side by the fact that CIHR expanded its mandate to include humanities input. The humanities were very upset because that was seen as a diminishment of the impact of biomed. The social sciences were very upset because the door wasn't sort of kicked wide open, it was only just sort of partially opened. But that partial opening was probably bigger than certainly any of the biomed folks would have been happy with. I think it's a foot in the door. Similarly, the decision to allocate the CRCs was another way of saying can we redress some of the perceived imbalance, and that wasn't happily received by a large number of the science-based folk. So I guess partly it's in the eye of the beholder. (P14 OT, administrator, sciences)

> Science and medicine are getting all the money, and therefore they are getting all the money. At Toronto, I saw the list of the Canada Research Chairs, and almost every one was non-humanities for the new list. And so, if you're going to put people into where it's already getting the money, I can see the reasoning, but what's happened to the arts faculty or the social sciences? That's what has to be protected. (P12 OT, administrator, humanities)

Sciences, social sciences, humanities, and the arts disciplines are part of the necessary range of university teaching and research. However, there is a tension surrounding funding and research that is market driven. This is an issue for the University of Ottawa as well as for other universities in Canada.

Commercialization

Supported by the report of the Advisory Council on Science and Technology (1999) regarding the commercialization of university research, offices of technology transfer are ideologically equipped to emphasize commercialization in a broad sense: creation and disbursement of intellectual property, patents, spin-off companies, and linkages to industry. This ideology is key to strategies for globalizing education (Morrow and Torres, 2000). Nevertheless, the visibility of the commercialization process makes it more vulnerable to criticism among faculty.

Linkages to industry are part of research relationships based on relevance to particular communities, and there are benefits to these relationships. Industry research funding has also given faculty some flexibility to conduct additional research "on the side" – an opportunity that they would not have otherwise. While commercialization is another debated subject that a minority of faculty resist, it is acknowledged as part of the university reality.

The emphasis on relationships with private sector research and on industry relevance was articulated by the university:

> Due to the unique location of the University of Ottawa and its affiliated institutes, researchers are well positioned to take advantage of the opportunities for collaboration with individuals at leading private sector research laboratories and government laboratories. Maintenance of close interactions with non-university research of economic or industrial importance is an important part of our strategy. It also forges closer links that ensure the continued excellence of research programs that provide industry relevant training to students. (Canada Research Chairs, 2001, p. 4)

In the past fifteen years, links to business and industry have become stronger, and the private sector is recognized as a legitimate partner with the university. Demand has increased for "economically relevant output" (PX3 OT, faculty, sciences). To achieve this objective, "the university gives strong encouragement to seek external funding" (P21 OT), and the university is "more market driven" (P23 OT, endowed chair, social sciences).

However, others are circumspect about how these relationships are working and how they serve industry and not the university.

> We've been pushed out to develop these relationships with [the] private sector. The moment that it is not in the private sector's interest to do that,

> because their profit margins are shrinking, guess who walks away from the table? It's not that they're going to sustain it through thick and thin. They're backing away from the table. So, when it suits their interest, everyone has to jump. And when it doesn't, well, we're left in the lurch. (P14 OT, administrator, sciences)

> And when you talk about your links with industry and matching funds, that is the whole area where this is very predominant. And certainly now even within your grants, within the way that you present your material and what happens once the findings are there, there used to be and I can still recall many debates that were so anti-commercialization, so anti-moving forward with a product, a research product. Now it's why haven't you done it? What's stopping you here? This is another spin-off of your research that you should take full benefit from. So we have an attitudinal change that has taken place. And we have also sought out relationships. Universities didn't seek out those relationships before. (P4 OT, administrator, health sciences)

These linkages to industry and the private sector help to define knowledge and how it is produced. The increasing emphasis on the commercialization of knowledge and the creation of intellectual property raises concerns and some cynicism.

> But certainly it's [i.e., commercialization] changed the way the university has looked at me and looked at the kinds of things that they would like to see me do, because we now have these officers that go around, that are commercial experts and IP experts. And they constantly talk to us, and they say, you know, go out and get contracts and all these kinds of things. I'm not interested, so I don't do it. Some people in our department probably do do it, but I'm not interested. (P13 OT, faculty researcher, sciences)

> I think that universities are trying to be businesses, and they're not. So I think what the university should be doing is to facilitate this transfer of technology to the outside business world, but beyond that they shouldn't get involved. And I think when that happens you have real conflicts. And there are examples where this has happened. They are trying to get involved, for example in getting venture capital in and getting companies starting up, and I don't think universities should do that. (P18 OT, former administrator, sciences)

> The great incident here is when the high-tech sector went ... through the roof, the universities weren't doing enough to prepare students for the high-tech sector. So they [the industry] got on the university's case, they got on the government's case. Government responds, of course, by insisting that the universities pump through a bunch of students. So we wind up doubling and tripling the enrolment in the computer engineering side. This happened

> across the country. Then there's the implosion, and these kids have been trained to work where? You don't hear the high-tech industry standing out there saying "mea culpa." (P14 OT, administrator, sciences)

A utilitarian imperative has become important in the university, and this can be problematic if it is the only consideration: "If industry is interested in your research, therefore it must be useful – and if they're interested and it's useful, therefore it will be picked up and applied" (P2 OT, research chair, applied social sciences).

Changing Roles and Complexity

The concept of multiple and changing roles among faculty and administrators was expressed in the context of the changing nature of collegiality, the pressures of time, space, and intellectual productivity, and the emergence of a managerial culture.

At the University of Ottawa, the roles of both faculty and administrators have become more complex. Deans do not simply administer the activities of their faculties. They are now engaged in fundraising, community liaison, and development. For one dean, the changes with respect to fundraising brought the University of Ottawa closer to an American model.

> I would say the major difference is that there's an expectation now of considerable engagement in fundraising activities. And that's more what the dean of a US school does than historically a dean of a Canadian school. And I was sort of in that transition period. We raised money for this chair. (P23 OT, endowed chair, social sciences)

> I think what's increasingly happening now is that the dean is going to be almost exclusively externally focused: fundraising, which has its positives and its negatives. You know, that's a very American model. I kind of like the mix. I don't mind doing some of that, but I love the conceptualization of the building, but you can't do that alone, nor should you. (P14 OT, administrator, sciences)

Deans are required to deal with a more complex administrative structure: "I would suggest that it is [being a dean] more demanding, because you have to deal with all internal matters. And even within the faculty, there was a time where, for example, there was no collective agreement. Now we have three. So just dealing with different collective agreements. Then also in terms of contact with the external community" (P21 OT, administrator, arts and education). External as well as internal pressures have an impact on faculty and administrators. Individuals who represent the university in some way are reaching out from the institution, engaging on a number of levels with the public and the community.

> [We] have to deal with the community at large. In the case of this faculty, ... because we are a bilingual university, it means we have to deal with the francophone community, with the anglophone community. And with the francophone community, it is not only in the Ottawa area of eastern Ontario region, it's across the province. (P21 OT, administrator, arts and education)

> Fifteen years ago you had your teaching load, you had your one grant, and you had your project. And now you are expected to be on CBC, you are expected to be on tap as a media personality for the university, you are expected to be at committee meetings of all kinds, both inside and outside the university, you are expected to be quoted in the newspapers. You are expected to be writing articles. (P2 OT, faculty-administrator, arts and education)

The emphasis on accountability to external audiences indicates a change in university culture. This trend is similar to the one described by the OECD as universities move from a collegial mode of organization toward more bureaucratic and managerial modes (Fisher, Rubenson, and Schuetze, 1994; OECD, 1990). Almost everything has to have a strategic justification that is time consuming, part of a more complex administrative structure, part of an accountable, outcome-oriented, and performance-based culture. "Academic work" has been changing rapidly and dramatically over the past decade, and the structure and mission of universities are in question (Currie et al., 2003; Currie and Newson, 1998; Fisher and Rubenson, 1998).

Collegiality

The change in collegiality was framed discursively. Collegiality has changed given the multiple roles that faculty perform. A majority of faculty and administrators note the move toward the commodification of time and space, the sense of time related to their experience of "a lot more competitiveness" (P5 OT, administrator, sciences), and overloaded schedules. Faculty in the same discipline are often dispersed across the campus. Daily life has become even more solitary than in the past: "It was a funny comment that ____ made the other day, talking about getting crumbs – you know – maybe coming to a joint coffee room rather than getting crumbs in your computer during lunch. And that's what we do. We sit down, and because we don't have the time that we used to have, we get crumbs in our computers. Instead of sitting down with a bunch of people and having lunch together" (P13 OT, faculty-researcher, sciences). Crumbs on your computer is a poignant metaphor for the time pressures and lack of connection being experienced by faculty, who spend their lunchtime at their desks, working on their computers. The nature and demands of the work have changed, and these are pressure points on faculty as well as administrators.

The ability to close the door and protect the space for thinking was highlighted as an important requirement, but closing the door is very difficult to maintain.

> Where your job is partly to read books and come up with new ideas and be on top of your field, that takes time, and it's very hard to close the door so you can actually do that. (P2 OT, faculty-administrator, arts and education)

> I need space, ... the door shut, alone, and then I can think it through. It is very difficult to do that in a full day at the university right now as a dean. I mean ... deans just can't go off into a corner anywhere anymore. And I think that is a negative. I really do. I think you are going to be far more productive and innovative, and you will advance the entire faculty if you could just take a day. But I took a day for my research, and people knew what day it was, and so they thought, you know, s/he doesn't have any appointments that day. (P4 OT, administrator, health sciences)

The reflective spaces are diminished by the culture of the university – a culture that is distinguished by time within a scarcity model, a culture that demands intellectual thought and creativity but has fewer safeguards to protect the space required for that thought and creativity. Engaging in a highly competitive environment takes a toll. Different kinds of time are considered to be lost, including time for scholarly writing and preparation and teaching time (Slaughter and Leslie, 1997).

Generational Differences

Faculty have a strong sense that the generation of new scholars is different from the previous generation. Among newer faculty, particularly in the science disciplines, there is less resistance to rethinking research in terms of funding and competitiveness. This is accepted as a "given" among these new academics; this is part of their reality.

However, these new scholars are working in a more "tense, stressful environment with a need to produce" (P11 OT, administrator, social sciences). Funding councils have supported this new generation by giving "the younger researchers a lot more opportunities to get funding" (P4 OT, administrator, health sciences). The support provides the base for "getting new scientists off the ground," and it has made "a huge difference" (P8 OT, research chair, sciences) to the university. "So it's a different generation that's taking over. And like any new generation, it's very, very good and very bad too. Because they'll talk about – well, one person came to see me whom we didn't hire who wanted a position, and she thought that we were a good university, and we were very good, and therefore she didn't really want to teach for the first couple of years. Well, I said, 'I'm sorry, you'll have a full teaching load'" (P12 OT, administrator, humanities).

Newer academics who have been in the university for less than seven years can see the generational and funding divisions among themselves and among the faculty at large. The cultural distinction between generations, and the pressure for faculty to change their perspective, are intensified by a university governance imperative to become more responsive to external objectives and criteria for performance, particularly through research. While responsiveness is seen as appropriate and important, there are unanswered questions of balance (e.g., responsiveness, accountability) and a considered strategic decision-making process. "I have funding from NSERC, and I have funding from industry, and that's sort of a natural progression because I'm more experienced now, I have more contacts ... And I think the whole Faculty of Science is starting to segregate into two categories which weren't there before, which is the people who have only NSERC funding, or one grant from NSERC, the basis grant, and the people who can leverage all kinds of other money, because they're doing other stuff that's relevant to the needs of outside sources" (P17 OT, research chair, sciences). Some newer professors are not as involved in teaching and its administration. They contribute less time to the department, and they teach less. Others are seen as bringing large grants into the discipline, and even this can be a source of tension.

> I think the relationship between, shall we say, the old farts and the young guys, or the young professors, has changed a lot. There's a lot of, this will probably sound inappropriate, but there's a little bit of jealousy, OK, but that jealousy isn't, doesn't, come out as ... what am I thinking of here? We're jealous of the fact that the young guys are coming in, and they're receiving huge amounts of money. Some of which is of great use to us, because we can piggyback on some of it, but we always say, well, back in the old days things were a heck of a lot harder. And in fact they were. When I came here, I can recall getting very little money to set up a lab. (P13 OT, faculty-researcher, sciences)

Increased involvement of contingent faculty has become the "norm" at the University of Ottawa: "You also have people who work on contract, who teach part time and do consulting work. So there is a real collection of people teaching at the university. You have people who don't have office hours. People who don't live in the same city" (P2 OT, research chair, applied social sciences).

At the same time, new doctorates may not pursue careers in the academy. This raises a concern about who will fill the enormous gap created through the retirement of the "older generation."

> A lot of new people don't want to take academic jobs. They say the lifestyle isn't very good, the work is too hard, the rewards are too few. And they will go to research institutes where they can do pure research, or they will go to industry. And I would say that a very, very small percentage of our grad students have an express wish to be a professor ... Most of our students will not end up in academia. We don't actually train them for academia anymore. Whereas when I was a student, it was assumed you were just going to be a professor, whether it was true or not. It was hard on people who wanted to go into industry. Research institutes were almost unheard of, except for Toronto and a few other places. Now it is exactly the reverse. (P7 OT, research chair, sciences)

The face of the faculty is changing. If new doctorates are not necessarily interested in pursuing academic careers, this trend raises questions. Who will comprise the new faculty? Who will comprise the next generation? Currently, faculty are divided by generation, with the newer faculty engaging more readily in the competitiveness for funding and faculty who are divided among themselves by virtue of the size and type of research grants.

Conclusion

The nature of academic culture is part of an ongoing, dynamic, and transformative process within the university. New territories and competitive modes have emerged among disciplines. The purpose of the academy has been called into question by both modernist notions, in which knowledge production results from objective and scientific approaches, and postmodernist notions, in which knowledge is divergent, produced, and disseminated under political and economic conditions (Tierney, 2001). Bauman (1997) suggests that universities have become obliged to embrace business as a normative practice. The story of the University of Ottawa is dominated by the motivation and determination to become a research intensive university and the need to change the relationship with industry and the private sector. Other universities, at least the top five research intensive universities, follow a similar determination – which is evidenced by the increased sponsored research income. While the University of Ottawa has achieved the goal of research intensity, the cost has not been fully realized.

Academic culture is far more "market oriented" than in the late 1980s. The university in many ways exemplifies the norms of "academic capitalism" (Slaughter and Leslie, 1997; Slaughter and Rhoades, 2004). Commercialization through the production of "intellectual property" has become the watchword of internal research policy. Research intensity has become linked to both private sector activity and industry relevance. The continuing and increased emphasis on the natural and applied sciences defines the university's mission. Academic science in universities increasingly fits into a mix of what Stokes (1997) has described as the "Pasteur" and "Edison" quadrants. Research in the "Pasteur Quadrant" is dedicated to understanding and use, while research in the "Edison Quadrant" searches only for utility.

In Becher's terms (Becher, 1989; Becher and Trowler, 2001), those disciplines in the pure and applied "hard" sciences are dominant. The lines of tension that strengthen the boundaries between groups of disciplines correlate with age as "new" scholars are much more likely to accept and at times celebrate the commercialization trend. This trend has been encouraged and facilitated by both the federal and the provincial governments. As academic culture has changed, so has academic work. Faculty are pressed into competing for research funding at the expense of their other functions. Collegiality in some disciplines has diminished as a result.

Although proponents of globalization and academic capitalism might suggest that the university must come into line with government and industry priorities, there is also a lament that such an ideology is causing the demise of the university as it once was – a thriving institution of intellect, creativity, and exploration (Readings, 1996). These notions are part of a dialectic, a contested discourse, that has emerged at the University of Ottawa and at other universities in Canada.

Notes

1 This research was funded by the Social Sciences and Humanities Research Council of Canada, grant number 410-98-1577.

2 We began with the top twelve ranked in 1999 and followed them through to 2004. Each university was examined across five dimensions indicating levels of research intensity and research excellence: (1) sponsored research income by source; (2) royalties and licensed income; (3) presence of an industry liaison office (ILO) to address inventions, patents, and intellectual property; (4) level of participation in the Canada Research Chairs program; and (5) level of participation in the Networks of Centres of Excellence program. Comparative tables were developed for each university, taking into account sponsored research funding received from the federal granting councils.

3 The University of Ottawa was included in our list of twelve universities even though it is a bilingual institution. In part, this decision was made because of the location of the university in the federal capital but also because of the phenomenal shift in research funding that took place during the 1990s.

4 Research intensity refers to sponsored research income per full-time faculty position (Re$earch Infosource, 2001).

5 Sponsored research income includes grants from federal sources (e.g., funding councils, specific funding envelopes), provincial sources, municipal sources, industry, and private contributions.

6 P15 OT denotes the code given to the fifteenth person interviewed at the University of Ottawa.

7 Table 2.1 indicates "other income," which largely represents private sector support as well as donations.

References

Advisory Council on Science and Technology. (1999). *Public investments in university research: Reaping the benefits. Report of the expert panel on the commercialization of university research.* Ottawa: Government of Canada.

Atkinson-Grosjean, J., House, D., and Fisher, D. (2001). Canadian science policy and public research organizations in the 20th century. *Science Studies: An Interdisciplinary Journal for Science and Technology Studies, 14*(1), 3-25.

AUCC. (1999). *Trends: The Canadian university in profile.* Ottawa: Publications and Communications Division.

Bauman, Z. (1997). Universities: Old, new, and different. In A. Smith and A. Webster (Eds.), *The postmodern university: Contested vision of higher education in society* (pp. 17-26). Bristol: Society of Research into Higher Education and Open University Press.

Becher, T. (1989). *Academic tribes and territories.* London: Society for Research into Higher Education and Open University Press.

Becher, T., and Trowler, P.R. (2001). *Academic tribes and territories: Intellectual inquiry and the culture of disciplines.* 2nd ed. London: Society for Research into Higher Education and Open University Press.

Canada Research Chairs. (2001). University of Ottawa. www.chairs.gc.ca.

–. (2003). University of Ottawa. www.chairs.gc.ca.

Clark, B. (1987). *The academic life.* Princeton: Princeton University Press.

Currie, J., DeAngelis, R., de Boer, H., Huisman, J., and Lacotte, C. (2003). *Globalizing practices and university responses.* Westport, CT: Praeger.

Currie, J., and Newson, J. (Eds.). (1998). *Universities and globalization: Critical perspectives.* Thousand Oaks, CA: Sage.

de la Mothe, J., and Pacquet, G. (Eds.). (1999). *Information, innovation, and impacts.* Dordrecht, The Netherlands: Kluwer Academic Publishing.

Elzinga, A. (1985). Research, bureaucracy, and the drift of epistemic criteria. In B. Wittrock and A. Elzinga (Eds.), *The university research system* (pp. 191-217). Stockholm: Almqvist and Wiksell.

Fisher, D., and Atkinson-Grosjean, J. (2002). Brokers on the boundary: Academy-industry liaison in Canadian universities. *Higher Education, 44,* 449-67.

Fisher, D., Atkinson-Grosjean, J., and House, D. (2001). Changes in academy/industry/state relations in Canada: The creation and development of the Networks of Centres of Excellence. *Minerva: A Review of Science and Policy, 39,* 299-325.

Fisher, D., and Rubenson, K. (1998). The changing political economy: The private and public lives of Canadian universities. In J. Currie and J. Newson (Eds.), *Universities and globalization: Critical perspectives* (pp. 77-98). Thousand Oaks, CA: Sage.

Fisher, D., Rubenson, K., and Schuetze, H. (1994). *The role of the university in preparing the labour force.* Vancouver: Centre for Policy Studies in Education, University of British Columbia.

Gibbons, M., Limoges, C., Nowotny, H., Schwartzmann, S., Scott, P., and Trow, M. (1994). *The new production of knowledge: The dynamics of science and research in contemporary societies.* London: Sage.

Morrow, R.A., and Torres, C.A. (2000). The state, globalization, and educational policy. In N.C. Burbules and C.A. Torres (Eds.), *Globalization and education* (pp. 27-56). Critical Perspectives. London: Routledge.

Neave, G., and van Vught, F.A. (Eds.). (1991). *Prometheus bound.* Oxford: Pergamon Press.

Organization for Economic Co-Operation and Development. (1990). *Financing higher education: Current patterns.* Paris: OECD.

Readings, B. (1996). *The university in ruins.* Cambridge, MA: Harvard University Press.

Re$earch Infosource. (2001). Canada's top 50 research universities. www.researchinfosource.com.

Ringer, F. (1992). *Fields of knowledge: French academic culture in comparative perspective, 1890-1920.* Cambridge, UK: Cambridge University Press.

Shils, E. (Ed.). (1997). *The calling of education.* Chicago: University of Chicago Press.

Slaughter, S., and Leslie, L. (1997). *Academic capitalism: Politics, policies, and the entrepreneurial university.* Baltimore: Johns Hopkins University Press.

Slaughter, S., and Rhoades, G. (2004). *Academic capitalism and the new economy: Markets, state, and higher education.* Baltimore: Johns Hopkins University Press.

Stokes, D.E. (1997). *Pasteur's quadrant: Basic science and technological innovation*. Washington, DC: Brookings Institution Press.

Tierney, W. (2001). The autonomy of knowledge and the decline of the subject: Postmodernism and the formulation of the university. *Higher Education, 41,* 353-72.

Tierney, W. (Ed.). (1991). *Culture and ideology in higher education*. New York: Praeger.

University of Ottawa. (1995, 3 January). Yellow paper, strategic plan.

–. (1998a, 2 February). Minutes of senate.

–. (1998b, 18 April). Draft business plan.

–. (1998c, 26 May). Draft business plan.

–. (1998d). Performance report.

–. (2001, 7 December). Intellectual property policy.

3
The New Production of Researchers

Brigitte Gemme and Yves Gingras

The socialization of graduate students to research is an essential part of the reproduction of the faculty and of the renewal of any scientific community. Although only a minority of these researchers-in-training will eventually hold faculty positions, graduate degree programs are the central component of the academic research reproduction system. Besides standing as potential colleagues, graduate research assistants significantly contribute to the pursuit of faculty research, especially in the laboratory- and field-intensive disciplines. Their dual role as assistants of researchers and aspiring researchers makes them both witnesses and products of the current transformations of university research: their current occupations and future careers are or will be affected by the changes that some label as "revolutionary" (Etzkowitz and Webster, 1998). The growing number of ties between universities and other kinds of organizations, notably firms from the private sector, has impacts at the microscale on the research practices of individual academics (Slaughter and Leslie, 1997), current or aspiring.

Up to now, however, most of the research on the transformation of universities has focused on institutional structures or faculty members but not on graduate students. In analyzing the latter's experiences, we thus wish to contribute to a better understanding of the next generation of researchers. By examining the situation of a group of graduate students who received a scholarship dedicated to co-operative research in Quebec between 1999 and 2003, this chapter will explore how the training of graduate students is transformed by the premium placed on co-operative research and on collaboration with non-university organizations. After a survey of the recent transformations of the academic field, we will present the basic characteristics of the Quebec program of scholarships for research in context of application and analyze some aspects of the training of these master's and PhD students, like the origins of collaboration, the choice of research problem, the nature of the interactions students have during their research activities with their supervisors and other actors from outside their program, and the kind of research results they produce.

A Transformed Academic Field

For the scientific disciplines in Canada, research became part of the university mission in the first decades of the twentieth century. Until then, the training of graduate students mostly took place in the disciplinary context of university departments (Gingras, 1991). Given the relative homogeneity of disciplinary training across countries, Warren Hagstrom's classic analysis of the training of scientists, *The Scientific Community* (1965), provides a good point of reference for describing the changes that unfolded over the last quarter of the twentieth century. According to Hagstrom, students were expected to acquire during their training in-depth knowledge about the foundations of their discipline through coursework and preliminary examinations and then to master a specific topic through original research. The research-training portion of the PhD, which gradually became pre-eminent in the scientific disciplines, can be compared to the apprenticeship model, in which the student is expected to emulate his supervisor's practices, identify an appropriate research problem, learn to conduct experimental or field research, and share the results with the scientific community by submitting papers to peer-reviewed journals. In this model of graduate education, students identify with their supervisors and respect them deeply, while the supervisors nurture their students' sense of scientific independence and autonomy by avoiding the strict imposition of problems or methods.

In other words, what Hagstrom describes is the formation of scientific habitus defined by Bourdieu as "an acquired system of generative schemes objectively adjusted to the particular conditions in which it is constituted" (Bourdieu, 1977, p. 95). This socialization process results in a strong commitment to the implicit rules of the scientific field, and, in the words of Hagstrom, "these commitments are the outcome of a prolonged training process, lasting well into adult life, in which the student is effectively isolated from competing vocational and intellectual interests and in which he is extremely dependant on his teachers" (1965, p. 9). While the faculty members do need graduate assistants to help them work on problems in their research areas, students remain the most dependent, as "the graduate student at a crucial point in his career depends for recognition primarily on a single individual; his self-image as a scientist is dependent on the personal reaction of his advisers" (p. 136).

After they earn a PhD, the students who pursue a research career become autonomous and participate in the scientific life by submitting research results to the whole community and receive recognition in return. This symbolic reward system is at the core of the scientific field, in which scientists struggle to impose their scientific domination through the accumulation of scientific capital, which is at once, and inseparably, technical means (skills, tools, etc.) and social recognition (Bourdieu, 1975, 2001). Successful students – those who do acquire the scientific habitus – adhere to the guiding principles of the scientific field and play by its rules. Seeking other rewards, such as power or money, or recognition from outside the scientific field, would create conflict and alienate the scientist from his or her community. However, according to Hagstrom, one cannot argue that science could not progress in the hands of applied researchers, since he believed that "future developments in scientific theory and the organization of science [could] be initiated by such occupational types as the physicist in industry, the economist in a school of business, and the psychologist in a mental hospital." In cases where scientists are "strongly influenced by nonscientists," however, Hagstrom admits that he would need to make adjustments to his theory (1965, p. 294).

Since the publication of Hagstrom's book in 1965, there have been major changes in the organization of science due to the continuous struggle in and around the scientific field to define its boundaries and modify the criteria used to attribute symbolic capital to its members, whose position in the field is potentially contested and dependent upon the position of all other field members (Bourdieu, 2001). In Hagstrom's times, scientific institutions were managed mainly by scientists, and the dynamics he described, especially those leading to the segmentation of disciplines, were largely internal. However, although fairly autonomous from other fields – politics, religion, finance – for most of the twentieth century, science has depended upon the state to preserve its autonomy and could not help but be affected by the fiscal crisis that began in the mid-1970s. By constraining the resources available to the ever-expanding fields of science and, at the same time, by earmarking funds for specific research priorities (beginning with alternative energy sources following the first oil crisis of 1973; see, e.g., Dalpé and Gingras, 1990), the governments of industrialized countries and their research-funding agencies transformed the research practices of academic scientists. In this context, it seems likely that the criteria used to define membership in the community and to evaluate the quality of contributions to the field also changed. We thus expect to witness a difference in the formation of the scientific habitus between graduate students involved in "traditional" training (as described by Hagstrom) and those involved in training in this new context. Changing the rules by imposing new criteria of evaluation more attuned to external demands should affect not only the kind of research undertaken but also the kind of researchers trained.

Collaborative teamwork, which has been a central feature of scientific research since at least the 1950s (Gingras, 2002, pp. 32-33), also became a formal criterion for funding in many programs of granting agencies in the 1980s. Moreover, in a growing number of these programs, "collaboration" was defined to mean "participation of non-academic researchers." Co-operative research grants and matching funds initiatives, in which an agency agrees to contribute no more than half of the costs of a project, the other half being provided in money or in kind by the private sector, took university research closer to non-university, mostly industrial, preoccupations. Non-scientists and staff from non-academic organizations have also been appointed to committees to evaluate the relevance of grant applications (Gingras, Godin, and Trépanier, 1999; Vécrin, 2003). Even if untargeted research still rakes up most of the funds allocated to research in Canada (Godin, Trépanier, and Albert, 2000), a growing proportion of available monies is now dedicated to specific areas and to co-operative research, and this new situation has contributed to significant changes in the research practices of many faculty members (Slaughter and Leslie, 1997).

This trend also influences graduate students' research in both direct and indirect ways. First, students are likely to do research on a problem selected among those studied by their supervisors, and they are more likely to become part of a larger team instead of working in a dyadic relationship with a single faculty member. They may also be guided to work on a problem emerging from outside the scientific field and brought to the attention of their supervisors via the latter's contacts with industry, for example. In a more direct manner, graduate students may work as research assistants for professors and be assigned to co-operative research projects, related or not to their dissertation topics. A student may also have developed a co-operative research agreement of his or her own, notably in the context of a scholarship program[1] based on the student's capacity to secure co-operation and funding from a non-university organization such as a firm or government agency.

Other incentives originating from government policies and job market conditions also encourage students to turn to non-academic preoccupations in the planning of their research projects. The public restraints policies of the 1980s and 1990s resulted in a tightening of the academic job market, and until recently very few university positions were opened to new PhDs. Pursuing a career in academia more or less meant that one had to go through a string of postdoctoral fellowships and adjunct faculty contracts with little or no hope of landing a permanent, tenure-track position. As a consequence, many had to set aside aspirations to the scientific autonomy that such a position would offer. It is also likely that graduate students identified less with their faculty supervisors, as was the case when faculty positions were widely available and objectively attainable, and turned to other, non-academic professionals instead. Furthermore, during the information technology (IT) boom in the second half of the 1990s, and with the growing concern about "innovation" in firms, more industry positions became available for highly trained personnel.

From a long-term perspective, we can expect that these changes will affect the socialization process and its outcomes in the scientific field. For example, the researcher-apprentice will not only have to master the foundations of his or her discipline and the specialized knowledge of a specific research area but also have to develop sufficient command of the problems related to the context of application (Gibbons et al., 1994) and be skilled in the management of non-academic demands on academic research. The evaluation of the scientists' contributions, which used to be the prerogative of peers, is now opening to agents from outside the scientific field. The training and certification of at least some of the graduate students who contribute to the senior scientists' funded research also become influenced by outsiders. By transforming the parameters of the socialization of future researchers, these new processes may have deep effects on the scientific field in general and, consequently, constitute an interesting and important object of research. If Gibbons et al. (1994) are right in pointing toward the development of a new mode of knowledge production, then we should expect to observe the emergence of a new mode of production of researchers.

The FCAR Scholarship Program for Research in Context of Application

The FCAR scholarship program for research in context of application was set up by Quebec's Fonds pour la Formation des chercheurs et l'aide à la recherche (FCAR)[2] in 1998 with the following objectives:

- to encourage the training of highly qualified workers in priority research sectors;
- to facilitate the professional integration of graduates on the job market, especially in sectors where the recruitment of workers is problematic;
- to support the creation of university-firm collaborative networks to accelerate knowledge and skills transfer between universities and firms.

Graduate students registered full time in a master's or PhD program in Quebec universities were allowed to apply to the program and were required to undertake their research projects in close collaboration with organizations outside the university setting. The interested student had to conclude a research agreement with his or her university supervisor and a non-academic supervisor before or after registering in the program of his or her choice. The scholarship could be awarded for up to two years at the master's level ($13,000 per annum) and three years ($16,300 per annum) at the doctoral level and had to be supplemented by funds provided by the partner organization (an additional $7,800 for master's and $9,780 for PhD students).

Between 1999 and 2003, 168 students were offered a scholarship under the program. Within this group, 71 percent (119/168) were housed in the

Table 3.1

Comparison of the achieved sample with the target population of scholarship holders by gender, degree program, and disciplinary group

	Target population		Achieved sample		Difference
	%	N	%	N	%
Male	59	99	58	60	–1
Female	41	69	42	44	+1
Master's degree	61	102	72	75	+11
PhD	39	66	28	29	–11
Health sciences	12	20	13	13	+1
Natural sciences and engineering	71	119	72	75	+1
Social sciences and humanities	16	27	15	16	–1
Arts and letters	1	0	0	0	–1

natural sciences and engineering, 16 percent (27/168) in the social sciences and humanities, and 12 percent (20/168) in the health sciences, with only two students in the arts and literature. All were invited to participate in the study, and 109 responded to the questionnaire during the spring of 2003 (94 current students and 15 graduates). Five questionnaires had to be rejected because they contained too few answers, leaving us with a total of 104 respondents.[3] As Table 3.1 shows clearly, the gender distribution and representation of disciplinary groups in the achieved sample is very similar to that of the population. However, a discrepancy exists when one compares the achieved sample and the target population by degree objective. Students studying for a master's degree are over-represented, while doctoral students are under-represented. These discrepancies were due in part to the uneven pattern of enrolment across the four-year period.[4]

The applied fields, within the sciences, are the most widely represented, with a total of nearly 60 percent (59 percent or 61) of all respondents.[5] Notably, even if the program objectives explicitly mentioned university-*firm* collaboration, only 63 percent (65) of beneficiaries reported being involved with an organization from the private sector, as we can see in Table 3.2. Many others were involved with government agencies (39 percent or 41) or community organizations (10 percent or 10). Many students reported being involved with more than one type of organization, the most frequent arrangement being collaboration with a firm and a government organization.

Consistent with the characteristics of the target population, there are 58 percent (60) men respondents and 42 percent (44) women respondents. A majority of respondents are under the age of thirty and claim to have never

Table 3.2

Types of organizations involved with the scholarship holders

Type of partner organization(s)	%	N
Firm only	43	45
Government organization only	20	21
NGO only	5	6
Firm and government organization	15	16
Other arrangements	13	13
Total	100	104

interrupted their courses of study for more than a year since the end of high school, suggesting a continuous trajectory in higher education.

Origins of Collaborative Agreements

Apprentice-researchers in the FCAR program are, in a majority of cases, socialized in a structured, organized environment that, although more heterogeneous than the so-called traditional context of graduate studies, is far from foreign to the university culture. A majority of respondents have frequent contact with both university and non-university researchers and work in a mixed intellectual environment. Even when spending most of their time on non-university premises, students are likely to interact with university-trained staff, often PhDs and sometimes current or former postdoctoral fellows and professors.

The presence of students in non-university organizations is not an isolated event but often intertwined in a history of collaboration between university researchers and outside organizations. This suggests a complex socialization process. These collaborations in most cases pre-dated the scholarship award. The students' projects were often part of a larger collaborative effort between university and non-university researchers.

According to the students, the collaboration between their supervisor and the non-university organization had begun, in nearly half of the cases (46 percent or 48), before they arrived as graduate students. In eight out of ten cases (81 percent or 84), the outside organization had some contact with their supervisor or other university researchers before, which means that links had already been created between the two cultures. In about as many cases (86 percent or 89), the students claimed that their supervisor had been involved in some kind of collaboration with non-university organizations during his or her career. In many cases (42 percent or 44), he or she was identified as being the initiator of the collaboration between the student and the organization.

The training of graduate students benefiting from the FCAR scholarship is clearly part of a larger co-operative effort between university and non-university researchers. Only in a minority of cases did the scholarship program launch new co-operative projects. Rather, the scholarships complemented already established research programs and supported the costs of an additional researcher-in-training in pre-existing collaborations. Drawing from the language of symbolic exchange, Slaughter et al. (2002) compared the graduate students involved in university-industry relations to "tokens of exchange" between university professors and their industrial counterparts. According to the interviews of Slaughter's team with faculty members, supervisors would involve their graduate students in industry-related projects – providing their partners with the "gift" of a specialized, inexpensive worker and a channel of communication with academic knowledge – in order to receive, as counter-gifts, more resources for research (equipment, money, data, etc.). We prefer talking in terms of "mediators" since students are not merely passive "tokens." Approximately one-third (35 percent or 36) of the students affirm being part of the origin of the collaboration, thus creating a link between academia and a context of application. Graduate students thus seem to serve as a vehicle of knowledge transfer between university researchers and non-university organizations.

Problem Selection

Identifying adequate research problems may be the most crucial task of any scientific researcher and a challenge to most graduate students. The question of problem choice in science has usually been studied from the point of view of the scientist already active in the scientific field (Gieryn, 1978; Zuckerman, 1978). We approach the problem from the point of view of graduate students. From our data, we can go beyond the general information usually obtained through interviewing professors about the behaviour of students. Campbell, for example, reported, on the basis of interviews with faculty members from scientific disciplines, that "the responsibility for the selection of the research projects is assumed by the supervisor, as the student is not expected to be aware of the various criteria central to making the decision" (2003, p. 916). Furthermore, "the specific project to be undertaken by the student [is] integrated into the overall goals, objectives and ways of doing science that the supervising scientist is already engaged in" (p. 919).

The strong dependency of the student is confirmed by our own data on the FCAR program, which show that only 22 percent (22) of respondents claimed to have chosen their research subject before choosing their supervisor, while 48 percent (49) chose both at the same time and 30 percent (31) chose the supervisor before the subject.[6] Similarly, Bès (2004) noted in her study of doctoral students preparing "industrial dissertations" in France that students entering an already functioning partnership generally have little leeway for the choice of research problem, method, instrumentation, et cetera and are more likely to undertake work that has been, at least in part, "prepackaged" by senior researchers. Few students truly get to innovate, as they are mostly called to apply existing procedures to a slightly different problem. That being said, one may wonder if research in context of application would not allow, somewhat paradoxically, the training of less dependent and more autonomous researchers, as they have to develop ways to reconcile different perspectives and expectations in a single research project instead of following an established path traced by their university supervisor and previous graduate students.

Preliminary data from a survey of the general population of graduate students conducted with the same questionnaire clearly show that science students working in context of application are nearly twice as likely (18 percent as opposed to 10 percent) to have chosen first their research problem and have nearly 50 percent more chance (50 percent as opposed to 37 percent) of choosing both the problem and the supervisor at the same time. By comparison, science students with no collaborative links are twice as likely as scholarship holders in context of application to choose their supervisor before their subject (50 percent as opposed to 28 percent). This latter situation confirms Hagstrom's (1965) observation that only a minority of graduate students in science select their own research problems. In the social sciences, however, students are more autonomous since about a third choose

Figure 3.1

Scholarship holders involved in a wider project, including those where non-university organizations are present

"As far as you know, is your project part of a wider project directed by your supervisor or another person?"

No	38%	39
Yes	62%	64

"As far as you know, is a non-university organization (firm, government organization, NGO, hospital, etc.) involved in this wider project?"

No	13%	8
Yes	84%	54
Don't know	3%	2

their subject before their supervisor. Here also the counterintuitive effect of partnership is visible, although to a lesser extent: 40 percent of those working in collaboration affirm having first chosen their subject (compared to 33 percent of "traditional" students). However, whether the accrued initiative of scholarship holders reflects their specific personalities or the structure of the scholarship program could be established only through case studies of collaborative projects similar to those of Grossetti and Bès (2001) in France.

The tendency of students to be influenced by their supervisor in the choice of a research problem rather than only pursuing their own ideas is consistent with the finding that most students' research topic is embedded in a wider research program: 62 percent (64) of respondents reported that their project was part of a larger one, as we can see in Figure 3.1. More interestingly, among these "embedded" students, 84 percent (54/64) reported that this larger project received the participation of a non-university organization such as a firm, a government agency, or a community organization. These numbers clearly show that students participating in the FCAR scholarship program were, in the vast majority of cases, involved in research efforts wider than their own dissertation-related work.

Table 3.3 also presents data on the actors intervening in the definition of the student's research project and supports this finding. Unsurprisingly, the supervisor remains the main reference, cited by 92 percent (96) of respondents

Table 3.3

Involvement of different categories of people in the definition of the scholarship holder's research project, by disciplinary group

	Pure sciences and maths		Applied sciences and engineering		Health sciences		Social sciences and humanities		Total	
	%	N	%	N	%	N	%	N	%	N
Supervisor	85.7	12	95.1	58	91.7	11	88.2	15	92.3	96
Co-supervisor	71.4	10	65.6	40	75.0	9	35.3	6	62.5	65
Other professor(s)	14.3	2	16.4	10	16.7	2	35.3	6	19.2	20
Student peer	28.6	4	14.8	9	8.3	1	23.5	4	17.3	18
Employer (non-university)	21.4	3	39.3	24	41.7	5	23.5	4	34.6	36
Other non-university organization	50.0	7	36.1	22	41.7	5	52.9	9	41.3	43
Other person(s)	0.0	0	26.2	16	8.3	1	17.6	3	19.2	20
Total respondents		14		61		12		17		104

as involved in the definition of the research project, but other actors are also cited, notably the student's employer (outside the university) by 35 percent (36) of respondents and other representatives from non-university organizations by 41 percent (43) of respondents. Overall, at least 64 percent (66) of students interacted with someone unrelated to the university when defining their research project, which suggests that considerations other than strictly academic issues probably influenced the students' choice of problem and methodology.

The selection of an appropriate research topic for a dissertation could be subjected to a more specific study in which these processes could be observed as they occur instead of reconstructed *ex post* through retrospective questions in a survey. In the meantime, however, the data collected do indicate that students who received a scholarship designed to encourage co-operative research are effectively exposed to – and probably influenced by – non-academic issues when they select their research topic.

Interactions

Scientific skills, which rely at least as much on experience as on formalized knowledge, must be acquired not only through textbook education but also – and above all – by personal contact with skilled individuals (Polanyi, 1958). Graduate research training, which involves the student working with and/or under the supervision of other trained scientists, among them faculty members, postdoctoral fellows, and other graduate students, allows for the formation of the researcher's habitus and prepares the student to enter the scientific field. We can thus expect that the interaction of the graduate student with different kinds of researchers during his or her training might lead to a different kind of habitus being acquired. In other words, the relatively homogeneous space of actors implicit in Hagstrom's description of the scientific field, prevalent before the 1970s, has given way to a more heterogeneous space occupied by a set of more diversified actors with different interests.

The FCAR scholarship provided most of its beneficiaries with the opportunity to encounter these varied research actors. Three out of four of them (74 percent or 74), for example, used non-university facilities such as office space or a laboratory, and many of them also used an office or laboratory in the university setting. The possible combination of university and non-university space use is presented in Table 3.4. The physical presence of students on non-university premises certainly accounts for the frequency of their contacts with non-university organization personnel, which occurred at least once a week (and often daily) in 69 percent (70) of cases. These contacts appeared to be slightly more frequent than those with the students' supervisor, which occurred at least on a weekly basis in 61 percent (63) of cases. In fact, a moderately significant reverse correlation exists between frequency of meeting with the university supervisor and frequency of meeting with

Table 3.4

Scholarship holders' use of university and non-university research facilities (offices and laboratories)

Facilities used	%	N
University only	22	23
Non-university only	21	22
Both	53	52
Neither	4	4

non-university staff: the more often a student spends time with non-university staff, the less likely he or she is to see his or her supervisor on a daily basis. It must be noted, however, that about half of the students surveyed had access both to university and non-university facilities.

But what are the qualifications of the non-university staff members interacting with these students?[7] As Table 3.5 demonstrates, most of them are university trained and highly qualified: two-thirds (67 percent or 70) of students interact, in non-university organizations, with at least one PhD degree holder, one out of four (25 percent or 26) students interacts with at least one current or former postdoctoral fellow, and one out of ten (11 percent or 11) meets former university professors in the non-university setting. Only 15 percent (16) did not interact with people having at least some kind of university research training (master's degree or more) in context of application. Moreover, in 70 percent (71) of cases, at least a few of the non-university

Table 3.5

Level of qualification of non-university representatives interacting with scholarship holders, by disciplinary group

	Pure sciences and maths		Applied sciences and engineering		Health sciences		Social sciences and humanities		Total	
	%	N	%	N	%	N	%	N	%	N
No university training	28.6	4	24.6	15	0.0	0	11.8	2	20.2	21
Bachelor's degree	42.9	6	42.6	26	50.0	6	58.8	10	46.2	48
Master's degree	64.3	9	54.1	33	50.0	6	58.8	10	55.8	58
PhD and higher	71.4	10	72.1	44	75.0	9	41.2	7	67.3	70
Don't know	0.0	0	1.6	1	0.0	0	0.0	0	1.0	1
Total respondents		14		61		12		17		104

staff members interacting with students have research as their main task in the organization. Generally, two-thirds of the students (69 percent or 69) collaborate with organizations that have a structured, permanent research and development activity.

Obviously, the relations between scholarship holders and their contacts in non-university organizations are not strictly technical in nature. Consistent with the high qualifications and the level of research activities, we find that nearly two-thirds (64 percent or 67) of respondents report "intellectual advising" from the outside organization. Although the faculty supervisor remains the single most important source of support for the student in the preparation of his or her dissertation, being cited first by 65 percent (68) of students and in any position by 90 percent (94), non-university researchers are also cited by 56 percent (58) of respondents, and other non-university staff (technical or administrative) are cited by 32 percent (33) of respondents. Representatives from non-university organizations are also formally involved in the evaluation of the student's dissertation in nearly half of the cases (47 percent or 47), a proportion that tended to be higher when the student interacted with personnel holding a PhD. Involvement in assessment means that these "non-academics" are recognized by the university as having at least some scientific authority.

Output: A New Breed of Researchers?

The findings of our survey demonstrate that the students who received a scholarship to work in context of application are trained in a heterogeneous milieu where university and non-university researchers participate in the definition of research projects, interact with and advise the students, and set the more general research context of the dissertations. Does this new kind of research training lead to a different breed of researcher? The questionnaire offers a few hints on the subject through data on publications, commercialization, and future professional projects.

Table 3.6 presents the students' publication activity. Four out of five (81 percent or 84) students among our sample claimed having accomplished at least one type of research communication since the beginning of their program: 55 percent (57) had contributed at least one oral presentation or conference paper, 43 percent (45) had authored or co-authored at least one report, 41 percent (43) at least one article, and 39 percent (41) at least one poster. Among the eighty-one who had authored at least one publication of any sort, 82 percent (66/81) had at least one submitted to peer review (see Table 3.7), which points to the fact that students working in context of application are still internalizing the traditional values of the scientific field. When asked to rank the targeted groups of readers, three out of four (75 percent or 61) of these students who had published cited university researchers

Table 3.6

Types of publication authored or co-authored by scholarship holders, by disciplinary group

	Pure sciences and maths		Applied sciences and engineering		Health sciences		Social sciences and humanities		Total	
	%	N	%	N	%	N	%	N	%	N
Article	57.1	8	31.1	19	66.7	8	47.1	8	41.3	43
Book chapter	0.0	0	3.3	2	8.3	1	11.8	2	4.8	5
Book	7.1	1	0.0	0	0.0	0	5.9	1	1.9	2
Conference or publication	50.0	7	50.8	31	58.3	7	70.6	12	54.8	57
Poster	35.7	5	39.3	24	75.0	9	17.6	3	39.4	41
Report	42.9	6	42.6	26	33.3	4	52.9	9	43.3	45
Other	0.0	0	1.6	1	8.3	1	5.9	1	2.9	3
None	14.3	2	24.6	15	16.7	2	5.9	1	19.2	20
Total respondents		14		61		12		17		104

Table 3.7

Degree of scholarship holders' exposure to peer review, by disciplinary group

	Pure sciences and maths		Applied sciences and engineering		Health sciences		Social sciences and humanities		Total	
	%	N	%	N	%	N	%	N	%	N
Never published	14.3	2	25.4	15	18.2	2	6.3	1	20.0	20
All publications/ communications were peer reviewed	35.7	5	47.5	28	45.5	5	31.3	5	43.0	43
At least one was peer reviewed	21.4	3	15.3	9	36.4	4	43.8	7	23.0	23
None was peer reviewed	21.4	3	5.1	3	0.0	0	12.5	2	8.0	8
Don't know	7.1	1	6.8	4	0.0	0	6.3	1	6.0	6
Total respondents		14		59		11		16		100

as their primary readership, while non-university researchers occupied second place. Generally, university readership was considered, at any rank, by 86 percent (70) of publishing students, but 63 percent (51) did cite non-university researchers. More than a third (35 percent or 36) of respondents identified non-researchers as a potential readership for their contributions, while the general public was considered by only fifteen respondents, generally in the lower ranks. Submitting research results to the judgment of other scientists seemed important to most respondents, but it must be noted that one out of four (23 percent or 24) among all students reported being subjected to some kind of restriction in the publication of results. Unfortunately, none specified the type of restriction encountered. Further research should address this important question.

Although research results in the form of reports or articles and oral presentations are the main measurable products of the students' research activities, it could also be expected that at least some students would be involved in another kind of output since many work with industrial partners in applied research areas. Surprisingly, however, only ten respondents (10 percent) were involved in any kind of commercialization activity, either through production of secret industrial information (most frequent) or through patenting. Hence, it cannot be said that students working in context of application are particularly involved in the commercialization of research, although they probably have more opportunity than the "traditional" students to be part of such activities.

Professional Projects

The contribution of graduate students to the production of published research results is an important outcome of their training, but the most important is certainly the production of their selves as qualified researchers. After graduation, where do they plan to go? Table 3.8 sums up their answers. When forced to choose only one career option among different types of organizations, more than one-third (37 percent or 32/87) of those who were students at the time of the survey claimed that their preferred employer would be a firm from the private sector, while others preferred to work in a university (25 percent or 22) or in a government agency (23 percent or 20).[8] As expected, the proportion of students who wanted a university position was slightly higher among PhD students (29 percent or 17/56). However, in the write-in space of the questionnaire, some students added that they in fact wanted to hold "interface positions" in which they could keep working on applied scientific problems:

> Ideally I would like to have a position in a firm or in a research centre and be associated with a university in order to be able to link teaching (undergraduate and graduate level) with industrial research problems. (n. 20)

Table 3.8

Preferred sector of employment of scholarship holders (students only), by disciplinary group

	Pure sciences and maths		Applied sciences and engineering		Health sciences		Social sciences and humanities		Total	
	%	N	%	N	%	N	%	N	%	N
Firm (private sector)	30.8	4	40.7	22	40.0	4	16.7	2	36.7	32
University	30.8	4	14.8	8	40.0	4	50.0	6	24.7	22
Government organization	23.1	3	25.9	14	10.0	1	16.7	2	22.5	20
Non-government organization	0.0	0	0.0	0	0.0	0	0.0	0	0.0	0
Other	7.7	1	3.7	2	0.0	0	8.3	1	4.5	4
Don't know	7.7	1	11.1	6	10.0	1	8.3	1	10.1	9
Total respondents		13		52		10		12		87

> I want to work in management and research (integrating research and industry), counselling the firm. (n. 13, who chose "government organization" as the preferred employer)

On this matter, our respondents seemed to be slightly different from American science doctoral students. Among these students, Fox and Stephan (2001) observed that only 41 percent preferred non-academic employment,[9] while 64 percent (56/87) of our doctoral students had such plans.[10]

Graduate students trained in context of application are conscious of the different ways of doing and using research and of the cultural differences between the academic and non-academic settings. Many of them noted the tensions they experienced and the pressures they felt while working both inside and outside the university:

> What is hardest is that the firm wants tangible results as quickly as possible, while university research demands long processes of literature review and thinking. Industry people often find that the developments take a long time to come. (n. 57)

> The involved organizations have very different exigencies. Research asks for thought, deepening knowledge, rigour, coherence. The practical side wants results and performance, as soon as possible. (n. 21)

> It's hard to reconcile the sometimes very theoretical vision of the university with the "miracle solution" vision of the context of application ("milieu de pratique"). (n. 33)
>
> Sometimes, the company will not see the necessity of investing and making efforts to enhance the knowledge of some aspects that are, scientifically speaking, very important but that may seem, industrially speaking, very superfluous. (n. 59)

The necessity to acquire skills to cope with the demands of graduate research training and at the same time meet the expectations of different – and even sometimes conflicting – collaborators reflects the heterogeneous character of the context of application in which students are embedded. As a result, we can expect that the graduate students will continue to be required to fulfill the academic criteria of disciplinary broadness and original contribution to knowledge, while acquiring the capacity to adapt these skills to a specific context of application. We thus seem to be in a situation of an *addition* rather than a *substitution* of skills.

Conclusion

The students involved in co-operative research between university and non-university organizations are trained in a more heterogeneous context than the "traditional" graduate students who are isolated in university laboratories and offices. This diversity permeates all stages of research training, from topic selection to evaluation, both formally and informally. Successful graduate students are not only the ones who meet the expectations of their scientific peers from the university but also those who can interact fruitfully with actors who have different goals and interests but still contribute to knowledge production.

While students are still exposed to many of the norms of the academic community, submitting their work to peer review, for example, we must acknowledge the emergence of another kind of commitment. University positions, for example, do not seem to appeal as much to them as they do to "traditional" graduate students. A large proportion of students who obtained a scholarship for research in context of application insisted on "solving actual problems," doing "down-to-earth" research, and "exploring real-life problems," and they viewed this as an important advantage of being trained in a collaborative context. They did not seem to associate this "practical" aspect with usual university research training. This attitude may in fact preexist their entrance in the program and thus may reflect a circular relationship between a particular segment of the student population and the program description. Such programs certainly give an institutional basis for the stabilization of research trajectories non-existent twenty years ago. These programs open pathways to a new kind of researcher, more attuned to the trend toward research in context of application advocated by Gibbons et al. (1994).

Research training in context of application certainly contributes to the emergence of a new scientific habitus that differs from the habitus held by the scientists studied by Hagstrom in the early 1960s. The students' presence on non-university premises as well as their experience of a context of application with constraints and pressures to find solutions to actual, often pressing, problems contribute to the construction of a different perspective on scientific research. However, we cannot consider the training that aspiring researchers acquire outside the university setting as completely non-academic. As we have seen, the non-university staff members who provide the students with additional intellectual supervision are, in a majority of cases, university trained. We cannot simply state that their scientific habitus vanished when they became employed by a government organization or by a firm in the private sector. In a few cases, as the following comment shows, we may even think that the training partnership is considered by non-university researchers as a way to keep their own scientific skills sharp:

> [The non-university researchers got involved in my project] because they do not have the arguments ... to work on more theoretical projects [themselves]. I mean that although this project seems very practical to me (compared to what I would do in the university), for [the organization] it is not practical enough and they cannot justify to invest in the project. I certainly cost less than one of their employees! So it's more advantageous for them, because they can get to do their more theoretical research ... Otherwise, they would have to do without it because their administrators would not agree to finance such a project. (n. 69)

This comment clearly suggests that dichotomous oppositions such as "academic research versus industrial research" or "university versus industry" are too simple to describe the more complex landscape of contemporary research interactions between different kinds of institutions and actors. Between the obvious extremes, where "long-term pure research" and "short-term industrial research" can be easily distinguished, lies a vast spectrum of activities that makes possible the co-existence and collaboration of actors and institutions that find it useful (and in their self-interest) to work together. Given the very high level of satisfaction of the students involved in the program of research in context of application (Gemme, Gingras, and Milot, 2003), one can hardly look at it from the point of view of actors trained in a different state of the field and complain about the end of a golden era. One would do better to see these changes as another adaptation of universities to a changing society. The scientific field is dynamic, not static: its rules and accompanying socialization system are a product of history and, as we have seen, have changed. Such changes would not have surprised Hagstrom himself since, as we have seen in the introduction, he believed that science could be transformed by non-scientists. In such a case, he thought, his ideas about the sociology of science would have to be qualified (1965, p. 294). This time may have come.

Notes

The authors wish to thank Véronique Lépine and Lionel Vécrin, graduate students and research assistants, and Christelle Massé, junior intern, for their help in the collection and treatment of the data presented in this chapter.

1 Such scholarship programs include the National Science and Engineering Research Council of Canada (NSERC) "Industrial Postgraduate Scholarship" scheme and Quebec's Fonds pour la Formation des chercheurs et l'aide à la recherche (FCAR) program "Bourses en milieu de pratique," which we discuss in this chapter. We translate the official French name into "Scholarship for Research in Context of Application."
2 FCAR (replaced in 2001 by the Fonds québécois de recherche sur la nature et les technologies and the Fonds québécois de recherche sur la société et la culture) is a provincial research-funding agency that also offers regular scholarship programs for graduate students and postdoctoral fellows.
3 Most questions were answered by all 104 respondents. However, questions about the modalities of collaboration were answered by only 101 respondents. Some questions were not answered by one, two, or three individuals, which are not taken into account in the calculation of the percentages. Hence, the weight of an individual respondent, in percentage, may vary by more or less 1 percent between variables. All percentages are presented along with the number of individuals they represent.
4 At the time of the survey, 60 percent of respondents were registered at the doctoral level.
5 No distinction was made between pure and applied subjects within the health sciences.
6 We should keep in mind the possibility that students overestimate their autonomy in problem choice, while supervisors would tend to underestimate it. We have no reason to think, however, that the tendencies observed do not represent a real trend. On the difference of perception between students and faculty members on problem choice, see Berelson (1960, p. 178).
7 All of the following measures are based on the students' perception of their collaborators' qualifications and activities, which may not always be exact.
8 As for the few (15) who had finished their graduate program among our sample, half decided to pursue another degree or postdoctoral training after their experience, while the others were scattered evenly among different kinds of situations (firm, university, government, and unemployment).
9 Unfortunately, Fox and Stephan did not break down "non-academic" into more specific types of organizations.
10 Our preliminary data from a general survey of "traditional" graduate students (i.e., not involved in collaborative research with non-academic organizations) indicate that only 31 percent would prefer non-academic positions, while 48 percent would choose academe first.

References

Berelson, B. (1960). *Graduate education in the United States.* New York: McGraw-Hill.
Bès, M.-P. (2004). Connaissances et relations sociales des jeunes chercheurs. *Recherches sociologiques, 35*(3), 123-35.
Bourdieu, P. (1975). The specificity of the scientific field and the social conditions of the progress of reason. *Social Science Information, 14*(6), 19-47.

–. (1977). *Outline of a theory of practice*. Cambridge, UK: Cambridge University Press.
–. (2001). *Science de la science et réflexivité*. Paris: Raisons d'agir.
Campbell, R.A. (2003). Preparing the next generation of scientists: The social process of managing students. *Social Studies of Science, 33*(6), 897-927.
Dalpé, R., and Gingras, Y. (1990). Recherche universitaire et priorités nationales: L'effet du financement public sur la recherche en énergie solaire au Canada. *Revue canadienne d'enseignement supérieur, 20*(2), 27-44.
Etzkowitz, H., and Webster, A. (1998). Entrepreneurial science: The second academic revolution. In H. Etzkowitz, A. Webster, and P. Healey (Eds.), *Capitalizing knowledge: New intersections of industry and academia* (pp. 21-46). Albany: SUNY Press.
Fox, M.F., and Stephan, P.E. (2001). Careers of young scientists: Preferences, prospects, and realities by gender and field. *Social Studies of Science, 31*(1), 109-22.
Gemme, B., Gingras, Y., and Milot, P. (2003). *Formation à la recherche et milieu de pratique: Un portrait des étudiants et diplômés du programme "Bourses en milieu de pratique."* Note de recherche du CIRST 2003-05. http://www.cirst.uqam.ca/Portals/0/docs/note_rech/2003_05.pdf.
Gibbons, M., Limoges, C., Nowotny, H., Schwartzman, S., Scott, P., and Trow, M. (1994). *The new production of knowledge: The dynamics of science and research in contemporary societies*. London: Sage.
Gieryn, T. (1978). The problem of problem choice. *Sociological Inquiry, 48*(3-4), 96-115.
Gingras, Y. (1991). *Physics and the rise of scientific research in Canada*. Montreal: McGill-Queen's University Press.
–. (2002). Les formes spécifiques de l'internationalité du champ scientifique. *Actes de la recherche en sciences sociales, 142-43,* 31-45.
Gingras, Y., Godin, B., and Trépanier, M. (1999). La place des universités dans les politiques scientifiques et technologiques canadiennes et québécoises. In P. Beaulieu and D. Bertrand (Eds.), *L'état québécois et les universités: Acteurs et enjeux* (pp. 69-99). Ste-Foy: Presses de l'Université du Québec.
Godin, B., Trépanier, M., and Albert, M. (2000). Des organismes sous tension: Les conseils subventionnaires et la politique scientifique. *Sociologie et sociétés, 32*(1), 17-42.
Grossetti, M., and Bès, M.-P. (2001). Encastrements et découplages dans les relations science-industrie. *Revue française de sociologie, 42*(2), 327-55.
Hagstrom, W.O. (1965). *The scientific community*. New York: Basic Books.
Polanyi, M. (1958). *Personal knowledge*. Chicago: University of Chicago Press.
Slaughter, S., and Leslie, L.L. (1997). *Academic capitalism: Politics, policies, and the entrepreneurial university*. Baltimore: Johns Hopkins University Press.
Slaughter, S., Campbell, T., Holleman, M., and Morgan, E. (2002). The "traffic" in graduate students: Graduate students as tokens of exchange between academe and industry. *Science, Technology, and Human Values, 27*(2), 282-312.
Vécrin, L. (2003). *La naissance d'une triple hélice: Le programme des actions concertées du Fonds québécois de recherche sur la nature et les technologies*. Master's thesis, Université du Québec à Montréal.
Zuckerman, H. (1978). Theory choice and problem choice in science. *Sociological Inquiry, 48*(3-4), 65-95.

4
Public Policy in Ontario Higher Education: From Frost to Harris

Paul Axelrod

More than twenty-five years ago, with the certainty that comes from the pen of a freshly minted PhD graduate, I wrote that in the post-World War II period Ontario "universities were perceived, both by the individual and by society as a whole, as a critical element in the process of generating and accumulating wealth, and for this reason they were generously supported" (Axelrod, 1982, p. 214). Though now far less certain about most things, I have found little reason to alter my belief that the fate of higher education turns on the principle of perceived economic utility. Any number of current references would support this claim, though perhaps none resonates quite as powerfully, or as crudely, as the declaration in 1971 by the Ontario minister of university affairs that higher education should generate "more scholar for the dollar" (cited in Axelrod, 1982, p. 147).

All governments, whatever their political stripe, expect universities to contribute to economic growth and development. Since the end of the war, how did the Ontario government attempt to realize this result? What was the nature of the relationship between universities and government, and how did that relationship change?

At the conclusion of World War II, Canada's universities were coping with the temporary expansion generated by the flood of postwar veterans who took up university studies, aided by free tuition and financial support from the federal government. The Ontario government provided some unprecedented assistance to universities during the war, but when the last of the veterans passed through the system Ontario's three non-denominational, publicly assisted institutions (Toronto, Western, and Queen's) were physically and financially spent. For several decades, the universities were accustomed to appealing ritualistically to the premier for annual grants that would cover their deficits. These requests may or may not have been met. The "system" was simple, non-bureaucratic, and capricious. By the end of the 1940s, it was also inadequate and roundly condemned by normally unassertive university leaders. G.E. Hall, president of the University of Western

Ontario, earned Premier Leslie Frost's ire when he declared in the *Globe and Mail* in 1949 that "the presidents, deans and other officials in our universities have had to forsake education to become executive supersalesmen, leaders of delegations and beggars, so that universities may even remain in existence" (cited in Axelrod, 1982, p. 81). Even the premier's good friend, W.E. Phillips, chairman of the Board of Governors of the University of Toronto – which had always had special status among the small family of universities – denounced this "cap in hand" fund-seeking approach (McKillop, 1994, p. 558). He looked for a more sustained and reliable commitment of funds that would enable the universities to engage in some longer-term planning (Axelrod, 1982, p. 81).

Through most of the 1950s, the university-government relationship changed little in a province that was consumed more with highway building than higher learning. This system of benign neglect sustained the state of genteel poverty in which the universities languished, but for the most part it also kept the provincial government at bay and preserved the institutions' cherished autonomy (Monahan, 1998, 2004). R.C. Wallace, former principal of Queen's, had been appointed in 1951 as a part-time advisor to the premier on university matters, but he saw no reason either to infuse the system with significant funding or for the government to intrude into the institution's affairs (Axelrod, 1982, p. 83; Graham, 1990, pp. 247-50). As historian H.B. Neatby noted, higher education, accessible to a distinct minority, had a marked and traditional role in society: "[Universities] trained the children of the political elites; they served as finishing schools for their daughters and prepared their sons for admission to the liberal professions. These social functions were understood by governments and by university officials; there were no major confrontations over admissions, over course content or over student discipline because both groups shared the same social values. Cabinet ministers and members of the Boards of Governors might belong to different parties but they were all men of substance with similar views of the social order" (1987, p. 34). This comforting perspective changed, rather dramatically, in the 1960s. A strong hint of what was to come appeared in a report prepared for the National Conference of Canadian Universities by Edward Sheffield in 1955 (Sheffield, 1970, pp. 420-21). It anticipated that university enrolment would double in ten years, a prediction that was subsequently revised "upward" four times. In 1964-65, there were actually 178,200 students enrolled in universities across the country, 50,800 of whom were in Ontario. This expansion not only captured the flow through the educational system of baby boom youth but also signalled a belief in the importance of increasing participation rates in higher education. In 1950, one in twelve primary school students eventually entered university compared to one in six by 1965 (McKillop, 1994, p. 566). By 1970, more than 120,000 university students were registered in Ontario alone.

The federal government had addressed some pressing financial needs of universities by providing grants directly to the institutions beginning in 1951. Universities, increasingly, were recognized as engines of economic growth whose benefits flowed to individuals and society as a whole. In the words of the Royal Commission on Canada's Economic Prospects in 1957, universities "are the source of the most highly skilled workers whose knowledge is essential in all branches of industry ... It is incredible that we would allow their services to society ... to lapse or lag" (p. 452). Leslie Frost's explanation of Ontario's emerging approach to postsecondary education, articulated in 1958, echoed this utilitarian thinking: "The policy of the Ontario government towards higher education has always been the same ... to expand and improve the facilities for higher education in this province. I must admit, that although this policy was motivated to a great extent by our desire to assist young people to develop their intellectual potential and to develop into well informed citizens, it was motivated by our early realization that if this Province was to advance, it would need more than will, it would need brain power – and this perhaps is the world's most scarce resource" (Frost 1958). Notwithstanding such a commitment, the provincial government entered the 1960s with no clear mechanisms for facilitating university expansion. An informal advisory committee, later to become the Committee on University Affairs (CUA), was appointed by the premier in 1958 to evaluate university requests for funds and to recommend how the government should meet them. But the committee lacked the resources and staff to carry out this work effectively. Fearing an enrolment pressure that the province could not satisfy, the committee called a meeting in March 1962 of the presidents of Ontario universities and laid this challenge before them: could the presidents adequately plan for the future? Following the recommendations of a report by a president's subcommittee, headed by economist John Deutsch, the province adopted an enrolment-planning strategy to 1970. The Deutsch Report also endorsed the plan by the University of Toronto to create two satellite campuses and a proposal by community and business lobbyists to build two new universities in the Niagara region and Peterborough, recommendations soon accepted by the government (Axelrod, 1982, pp. 93-95).

The Deutsch Report provided a means to meet continuing student demand (though its initial projections significantly underestimated enrolment growth to 1970), but it left unresolved the question of university-government relations, which were becoming increasingly strained. In response to the enormous expansion of the higher education sector, the government created a separate Department of University Affairs in 1964 and secured the status of the CUA as an advisory (not a statutory) body, whose recommendations the department could accept or reject.

How did university autonomy fare through these changes? Essentially, quite well. Universities complained about the level of financial support that the department provided, which never seemed to be adequate, but funding overall continued to be enrolment driven, leaving universities with the ability to determine their own academic priorities, a process that was entrenched with the adoption of a formula-financing system in 1967 to be administered by the Committee on University Affairs. The minister, William Davis, had expressed concern about the duplication of programs that unconstrained university autonomy might generate (Davis, 1966, p. 33), and there were, to be sure, some limits to this autonomy. Through the creation of the Ontario Council on Graduate Studies, conditions were imposed on the establishment of new graduate programs in order to avoid inappropriate program duplication, and the CUA did not approve all professional program proposals that came before it. Furthermore, the government expected universities to provide spaces for all qualified applicants to undergraduate programs, and it firmly regulated tuition fees. But it rejected a proposal for a centralized, California-like University of Ontario, a suggestion that was uniformly denounced by the academic community. The minister himself (William Davis) agreed: "I feel ... the recommendation overlooked the very heterogeneous family of highly individualistic universities we have developed in Ontario" (Ontario Legislative Assembly, 1967, p. 4264). The universities, then, had responded to the expansion challenge, and "for most issues pertaining to the formula, the government appeared to defer to university representatives, reflecting what appeared to be a continuing faith in the university community" (Ontario Council on University Affairs, Task Force on Resource Allocation, 1995, p. 35).

The period from the early 1970s to the early 1990s was characterized by economic instability and uncertainty, featuring cycles of high unemployment, inflation, recession, and episodes of spectacular growth. The era witnessed rising levels of public debt, the emergence of the forces of continental free trade and globalization, and an undiminished public demand for higher education. Universities across Canada faced a common dilemma: the failure of government funding to keep pace with the real costs of higher learning. The unionization of growing numbers of university faculty was one result of this unanticipated economic turbulence (Tudiver, 1999, pp. 83-116).

Ontario's universities endured all of these pressures and more. After years of sustained growth, enrolment levels fell well short of expectations in 1972, and near panic occurred in the university sector. The levelling off of enrolment was short-lived, but the atmosphere of potential crisis appeared to linger. No fewer than five ministers presided over colleges and universities between 1971 and 1975, and no one held the post for longer than twenty months. By contrast, between 1959 and 1971, only two individuals (John Robarts and William Davis) occupied the education portfolio (which included colleges and universities), and both ministers subsequently ascended to the premiership. Economists who had enthused so recently over the substantial contribution of higher education to economic growth now questioned the "rate-of-return" on the university investment (Axelrod, 1982, pp. 141-78). The turbulent student movement of the late 1960s raised further questions about the value of higher education.

To reconcile the need for public accountability with institutional autonomy, the report of the Commission on Post-Secondary Education, published in 1972, had called for the creation of a "statutory intermediary body with some executive authority" that would be independent of both the universities and government. Instead, the government created the Ontario Council on University Affairs (OCUA) in 1974, whose role was "purely advisory" to the ministry. Its twenty members were all appointed by the government, and it was unable to "undertake system coordination and planning, except on terms decreed or confirmed by the Minister or consented to by the universities themselves" (Ontario Council on University Affairs, Task Force on Resource Allocation, 1995, p. 38).

Employing an innovative strategy, the new OCUA, under University of Toronto political scientist Stefan Dupré, secured from the government an explicit statement of its funding objectives for higher education, which included offsetting inflationary trends, maintaining existing levels of service, and accommodating expected enrolment increases. The OCUA then critically parsed these statements and added a goal of its own: the need "to maintain the financial viability of the university system" (OCUA, Second Annual Report, 1975-76, cited in Axelrod, 1982, p. 192). Next it costed each of these objectives and found the operating grant shortfall between 1974 and 1976 to be some $16 million. Demanding accountability from the universities, the government, if briefly, was hoisted by the OCUA on its own petard, and operating support for the universities rose significantly in the following two years, though not enough to meet the universities' demands. In subsequent years, the government returned to its customary pattern of rejecting the OCUA's advice on operating grants, and, significantly, it no longer articulated its objectives as clearly as it had in 1974 (Axelrod, 1982, pp. 191-92). By 1979, the fiscal problems were serious enough for the OCUA to title its annual report *System on the Brink*. It concluded that "the current financial situation and the funding outlook for the universities indicates a future of precipitous decline and turbulence as universities grapple with immense resource allocation problems" (Cameron, 1991, p. 245).

Several other initiatives during the 1970s merit mention: incremental tuition fee increases that were always politically difficult in light of the government's continuing commitment to a policy of accessibility to universities for all qualified students; the allocation of operating grants on the basis of a three-year average of a university's undergraduate enrolment, a strategy that protected institutions from the unpredictability of annual enrolment fluctuations; and a freeze, initiated by the OCUA, on enrolment-driven funding for graduate programs – a signal that the universities had failed to co-ordinate and rationalize successfully the expansion of graduate education in the province.

Finally, as part of its own program of spending restraint, the federal government altered the way in which it allocated funds for higher education, compounding the universities' fiscal problems. Established Program Financing, introduced in 1977, ended the fifty-fifty cost-sharing arrangement that the federal government had had with the provinces since 1967. Through this system, the more the provinces spent on universities and health, the more money they would receive from Ottawa. Under the new arrangement, provinces would receive equal per capita block grants for postsecondary education and health, but their governments were no longer under any obligation to spend this money on universities or health care, and the effects of this policy change were immediate. Between 1977-78 and 1982-83, "provincial funding per student in constant dollars fell ... by 20 percent in Ontario, and 12 percent in the rest of the country" (Davenport, 1987, p. 132).

The government responded to these mounting financial pressures by appointing the Committee on the Future Role of Universities in Ontario, headed by Harry Fisher, the deputy minister of colleges and universities. The Fisher Report, issued in 1981, called for increased funding to the system and a strengthened OCUA to facilitate more effective co-ordination among the universities. Notably, it pointed to the limitations of voluntary planning through the vehicle of the Council of Ontario Universities (COU). The COU "cannot easily adopt policies that are judged contrary to the interests of any of its members; and if it does adopt such policies, it cannot enforce them" (Ontario Council on University Affairs, Task Force on Resource Allocation, 1995, p. 27).

The report raised the prospect of closing some institutions, and it floated, once again, the idea of a centralized University of Ontario, which the universities, once again, denounced. The report's recommendations were ignored, as were those of the Commission on the Future Development of the Universities of Ontario, headed by retired business executive Edmund Bovey, who was joined by Fraser Mustard, president of the Canadian Institute for Advanced Research, and Ronald L. Watts, recently retired principal of Queen's University. The commission was mandated to recommend "a plan of action to better enable the universities of Ontario to adjust to changing social and economic conditions" in the context of the "Government's policy of fiscal restraint" (cited in Cameron, 1991, p. 248). It should consider assigning "different and distinctive roles" to Ontario universities but not propose the (politically risky) act of closing existing institutions. Reporting in 1984, the Bovey Commission ruffled other political feathers by calling for substantially higher tuition fees and a funding system that was less enrolment sensitive. It favoured a significant enhancement of university research capacity, though it refused to prescribe designated functions to individual institutions; instead, it sought to encourage innovation by compelling universities to compete with each other for a significant portion of public funds. It also called for a "renewal and adjustment fund" to facilitate the recruitment of younger scholars (cited in Cameron, 1991, p. 248). Like the Fisher Report, it recommended that a "reconstituted and strengthened OCUA be given responsibility for shaping the system; and that it have an enlarged monitoring function and specific regulatory powers to reconcile conflicting institutional ambitions in light of the needs of the system" (Monahan, 1998, pp. 358-59).

This agenda was swept away along with the Conservative regime in 1985 following the assumption of office by a minority Liberal government under Premier David Peterson. The new administration had no appetite for appearing to compromise the policy of accessibility to higher education by raising tuition fees or reducing enrolments. Nor did it follow the advice in a report prepared by John Stubbs, the president of Trent University, which recommended (echoing the recent commissions) that the OCUA should play a greater role in planning and co-ordinating the university system. In the words of one author, with respect to the structure of university-government relations, "nothing changed" (Monahan, 1998, pp. 358-59).

But some things were about to change, and the pace of change would accelerate. Instrumentalist policy initiatives, designed explicitly to link higher education directly to the economy, are largely associated with the "Common Sense Revolution," which began under the Mike Harris Conservatives in 1995. In fact, these tendencies were evident earlier, both under the Liberals, who governed from 1985 to 1990, and the New Democratic Party (NDP), which held power from 1990 to 1995.

Significantly, the Premier's Council reports of 1988 (entitled *Competing in the New Global Economy*) and 1990 (entitled *People and Skills in the New Global Economy*) stressed the important economic role of universities and colleges, particularly in the preparation of scientists, engineers, and technologists. The 1986 Ontario Centres of Excellence Programme (followed by a similar federal initiative) invited universities to compete for funds that generally favoured applied research projects in the sciences (Bell, 1996, pp. 322-49). The NDP's interest in the economic-education agenda was accompanied by an equity-driven social policy itinerary that was intended to include postsecondary educational institutions. It also sought to increase student transferability between colleges and universities and "to enhance [higher education's] role in the development of higher value-added skills and higher-achieving people" (Ontario Council on University Affairs, Task Force on Resource Allocation, 1993, p. 65). The University Restructuring Steering Committee, established by the minister of colleges and universities in 1992, was designed to make the university sector "responsive to the continuous or lifelong education, training and knowledge needs of a modern economy and democratic society, and ensuring the fullest possible response to the government's equity/access agenda within an environment of constrained public resources" (p. 68).

Some of the report's goals and accountability strategies were loudly resisted by the universities, fearing the further erosion of their autonomy, and a number of especially controversial policy initiatives were shelved. Instead, reeling from the recession and exploding deficit, the government introduced the Social Contract, which reined in spending throughout the public sector. As Glen Jones explains,

> [this] meant that the cabinet was not only deciding the level of operating support but mandating the ways in which the budget shortfalls would be handled. The impact was particularly dramatic in the university sector since the process of implementation served to shift the roles of various actors in the policy community. The Council of Ontario Universities found itself playing the role of management in sectoral discussion with the Ontario Confederation of University Faculty Associations. Negotiations between faculty and management were eventually delegated to the institutional level, but even here the provincial framework left little room for institutional autonomy let alone traditional forms of collective bargaining. Macro-level policy had suddenly shifted the locus of powers within the university sector. (1997, p. 154)

The overall impact of these policy changes, even before the Conservatives returned to power in 1995, can be captured in these statistics: "In 1985, 75 percent of university operating income and almost all of the government's operating grants were distributed by means of the funding formula. By 1993, only 60 percent of university operating income came through the funding formula. Much of the difference, representing 13 percent of total operating income, was allocated in the form of conditional grants from the government, which distributed grants to universities according to how well they met the government's prescribed program goals"; increasingly, through these grants, "the government ... rather than the universities ... was setting ... priorities" (George and McAllister, 1994, p. 8).

The Conservatives won the election of 1995, riding the wave of their commitment to the Common Sense Revolution, whose pillars included tax cuts, a shrinking of the public sector, the increasing privatization of government-funded programs, and, in the case of higher education, the assignment to universities and colleges of prescribed economic goals. In 1996-97, the overall operating grant to universities was reduced by 14.9 percent, or $1.55 billion (Council of Ontario Universities, 2002). This dramatic cut intensified the trend over the decade, which saw the percentage of total university funding covered by provincial grants drop from 55.1 percent in 1991-92 to 39.6 percent in 1999-2000, 7.4 percent below the national average (Council of

Ontario Universities, 2002). Fee increases, including the full deregulation of tuition for graduate and some professional programs, offset a portion of this lost public funding. At the end of the decade, as enrolments continued to rise, the financial needs of universities were palpable, and new funds were injected into the system. However, they came attached to very tight strings.

The conceptual framework of government policy drew in part from the December 1996 report of the Advisory Panel on Future Directions for Postsecondary Education headed by David C. Smith, principal of Queen's University, which recommended a "less regulated environment" for Ontario higher education, a greater degree of "accountability" by Ontario's autonomous universities and colleges, and clearer assessments of institutional "performance." The panel also pointed to serious "inadequacies in total financial resources" for postsecondary education and called for funding levels that matched those "comparable to the average for other Canadian provinces" and those of public universities and colleges in the United States. Among the report's most controversial recommendations was its proposal to permit higher educational institutions to set their own tuition fee levels as long as a significant proportion of this increase was used for student financial assistance. It called for more partnerships between public and private sector institutions, for easier transferability of students between colleges and universities, and for legislation allowing "privately-financed universities ... the authority to grant degrees." Finally, the panel recommended the creation of an "advisory body to provide sustained, arms-length analysis of post secondary education" (Ontario Ministry of Education and Training, 1996, pp. 1-12). While, as we shall see, a number of the report's recommendations influenced government policy, the latter did not. The Ontario Council on University Affairs was abolished soon after the Conservatives returned to power.

An equally important articulation of the government's market-driven approach to higher education was the 1999 report of the Ontario Jobs and Investment Board, which stipulated that "educational institutions and providers need to meet the needs and expectations of all their clients (learners, parents, and employers) by striving for excellence at all times, fostering entrepreneurship and innovation, and being responsive to the needs of the economy. To achieve these goals they should expand their partnerships with one another and with business" (Ontario Jobs and Investment Board, 1999, p. 17). The government believed that investment in technology and applied science was the road to economic prosperity; consequently, it implemented the Access to Opportunities (ATOP) program in 1998-99, which was designed to double the number of student places in computer science and engineering. Universities quickly adapted their program offerings to take advantage of these new funds. The Ontario Research and Development Challenge Fund provided support for applied projects that were able to secure private corporate sponsorship, mirroring the goals of the new federal agency, the Canada Foundation on Innovation (Fisher and Atkinson-Grosjean, 2002; Fisher, Atkinson-Grosjean, and House, 2001). To meet growing enrolment pressures, the government introduced the Fair Funding Program, which provided universities with financial incentives to increase student numbers, and it inaugurated the unprecedented Superbuild Program, which poured $742 million into selected capital projects (favouring technology and business areas) on the condition that an equal amount of financial support be raised from the private sector.

To encourage universities to be more accountable to the "taxpayer" and more responsive to the requirements of the labour market, the Ontario government, following trends elsewhere in Canada and abroad, introduced (in 2000-1) "performance indicators" (PI), a scheme that financially rewarded universities on the basis of institutional graduation rates and the employment records of graduates six months and two years after graduation (Axelrod, 2002; Bruneau and Savage, 2002). The province's formula, responsible in 2000 for the distribution of half of all new operating funds to universities, failed (and fails) to account for such factors as academic innovation, the quality of student scholarship, or the university's service to the community. Ann Dowsett Johnson, who oversaw *Maclean's* annual ranking of Canadian universities from 1991 to 2005, described the Ontario system as "bizarre" because its criteria were so narrow and incomprehensibly punitive. For example, two years after graduating in 1997, an average of 96.4 percent of ex-Ontario students were employed, and the differences between the success rates of those institutions that received PI funding and those that did not were, in a number of cases, statistically insignificant. Dowsett Johnson concluded that the system was "nothing but folly, parading in public as accountability," a critique, incidentally, that could be and has been made of the *Maclean's* rankings themselves, most recently by David Naylor, president of the University of Toronto (Dowsett Johnson, 2000; Naylor, 2006).

Increasingly, market-based values were shaping higher education policy in Ontario. In December 2000, the government passed legislation that allowed both non-profit and for-profit private universities to be established and to offer degrees. Such institutions would receive no capital or operating grants, but their students would be entitled to the same level of provincial financial assistance as those in publicly funded universities. A government memo in November 1999 explained that private universities "could be helpful in meeting student demand in addressing special situations in a manner that would not create fiscal pressures" (Ontario Confederation of University Faculty Associations, 2000, n. pag.). This suggests that private universities were foreseen as a mechanism for coping with expanding enrolments that would otherwise generate additional funding for public universities. The legislation also enabled the minister to permit Ontario's community colleges to offer bachelor of arts degrees and to become universities. The first of these, the oddly and frequently renamed University of the Ontario Institute of Technology (an outgrowth of a local community college), was designed explicitly to offer "market-driven programs" (Ontario Ministry of Finance, 2001). Thus, little-known private universities and vocationally oriented universities/colleges were able, potentially, to enhance their status by offering BAs, but the "flooding" of the market with such credentials would tend to (further) diminish the value and perceived distinctiveness of a liberal arts degree from traditional universities.

Some hoped that private higher education would lead to the establishment of "Harvards of the North" – that is, prestigious and well-endowed universities that would offer academic competition to the educational "monopoly" exercised by publicly assisted institutions. The former, at least, was highly unlikely, just as it was several years earlier when the Ontario Council on University Affairs (then headed by historian H. Vivian Nelles) investigated the issue, held public hearings, and rejected the private university option. It argued that "even a relatively wealthy jurisdiction like Ontario is not able to support high quality private institutions without recourse to some level of public assistance." It noted that, "in nearly half of the states in the United States, private institutions are given some help by state and local appropriations" (Ontario Council on University Affairs, 1996, p. 263), an outcome even more likely in the wake of World Trade Organization "fair treatment" trade rules (Griffin Cohen, 2000, pp. 123-41). The council, with some degree of accuracy, predicted that small religious colleges and business and technical institutions would be the first off the mark to seek authorization as degree-granting universities in Ontario. Several teacher education programs from American border colleges and from Australia had also sought recommendations for certification from the newly created Post-Secondary Education Quality Assessment Board (PEQAB), which received all such applications from educational institutions outside the province. Significantly, PEQAB could only *recommend* that new programs be approved or not. The minister of training, colleges, and universities had the final decision-making authority on this and on a growing number of postsecondary policy matters. In a period of such rapid and unprecedented policy change, the absence of a co-ordinating, intermediary body or "buffer," such as the Committee on University Affairs or the Ontario Council on University Affairs, was palpable. Those concerned about the traditional autonomy of the university would, in all likelihood, have questioned the process of policy making and the direction policy had taken in Ontario higher education.

Reflections

Since the late 1940s and early 1950s, public policy in Ontario higher education evolved from an informal approach directed to the needs of a select group to an interventionist one designed to integrate a huge postsecondary educational sector into the marketplace. There were some ironies here: an anti-government conservative government had proven to be the most directive in the history of the province with respect to public education (and other policy areas). Pinning its economic and educational sails to the winds of high technology, the government witnessed an unexpected foundering of the high-tech sector at the very moment colleges and universities were bringing new technology programs and buildings on stream. This was scarcely a case of rational, market-based, educational planning. The government, too, misread the demand side of higher education. In its original plan, too few university places were created for the double cohort that graduated in unprecedented numbers from Ontario high schools in 2003, leading to a new round of ad hoc and crisis planning, all occurring in the politicized context of an expected election campaign (Council of Ontario Universities, 2003).

Despite these pressures, university autonomy had not exactly disappeared in Ontario. Funding for the system was still, primarily, enrolment driven, and universities, in the main, mounted or closed academic programs on their own initiative. Tenure had survived. Indeed, in their administration of higher education, governments in other parts of the world (England, New Zealand, Australia, some American states) had proven to be more intrusive than in Ontario (Schuetze and Bruneau, 2004; Slaughter, 1998, pp. 45-70). Furthermore, the decades-old argument that universities were incapable of collectively taking decisions that impinged upon the interests of individual members within the Council of Ontario Universities still held sway. The COU could not simultaneously advocate for and police the activities of its members (Monahan, 2004, pp. 141, 147-49, 159, 209-12). Some oversight and accountability measures were indeed required, and governments of all political persuasions would be likely to continue to bring their own policy agendas to the higher education sector. Universities, in other words, were never to be left entirely alone, nor should they have been (Ontario Council on University Affairs, 1995).

The question is what form this external oversight should take. It was no mere coincidence that the various task forces on the future of higher education in Ontario over the previous three decades, however they differed, called for an intermediary body with teeth – an OCUA with statutory power to co-ordinate and regulate specific aspects of the university system such as the formula for allocating funds to universities and the authority to approve new institutions. Universities would retain their corporate and academic independence, but where self-interest prevented sensible collaboration (on enrolment targets, for example), the intermediary body would forge a system-wide resolution. It would be important for such an agency to have a large degree of independence from the government. The latter, as always, would determine actual funding levels, drawing advice from the intermediary body, but the *government's* reach into institutional life would be contained. By

2003, there was no clear limit on government authority, and there had been too many recent instances of narrowly conceived, ideologically driven, and evidence-free policy formulation. It remained to be seen whether the new Liberal government, elected in October of that year, would perpetuate or alter these decision-making patterns.

An answer to this question emerged gradually over the next several years. The Liberal government appointed former NDP premier, Bob Rae, to head an inquiry into the future of postsecondary education in Ontario. The commission released its report, *Ontario: A Leader in Learning,* in February 2005. In order to generate greater "accountability," "coherence," and "co-ordination" in postsecondary education, the commission recommended the creation of the Council on Higher Education. It would not be a "buffer body" or a "funding body" or a representative of educational "constituencies." Instead, it would "co-ordinate research on higher education, work with the sector and the government in establishing targets and measures for improvement and report on performance and outcomes" (Rae, 2005, p. 15). In May 2006, the government appointed Frank Iacobucci, former justice of the Supreme Court of Canada, and former interim president of the University of Toronto, to head the Higher Education Quality Council of Ontario. The council's mandate was to advise the minister on "targets to be achieved in improving the quality of post-secondary education, on the methods of achieving those targets and on the time frame for doing so, and on performance measures to be used to evaluate the post-secondary education sector." The council was also empowered to conduct research on "all aspects of post-secondary education" (Government of Ontario, 2005). While the council, then, might well encourage greater co-ordination and system-wide planning in postsecondary education, it would, in all likelihood, facilitate greater government intrusion into and control of Ontario universities through the introduction of new accountability and performance measures. The council's own performance would merit careful scrutiny by the university community in the years ahead.

References

Axelrod, P. (1982). *Scholars and dollars: Politics, economics, and the universities of Ontario, 1945-1980*. Toronto: University of Toronto Press.

–. (2002). *Values in conflict: The university, the marketplace, and the trials of liberal education*. Montreal: McGill-Queen's University Press.

Bell, S. (1996). University-industry interaction in the Ontario Centres of Excellence. *Journal of Higher Education, 67*(3), 322-49.

Bruneau, W., and Savage, D.C. (2002). *Counting out the scholars: The case against performance indicators in higher education*. Toronto: James Lorimer.

Cameron, D.M. (1991). *More than an academic question: Universities, government, and public policy in Canada*. Halifax: Institute for Research on Public Policy.

Council of Ontario Universities. (2002). Provincial operating grants 2.1. http://www.cou.on.ca/.

–. (2003). Universities now ready for 70,000 double cohort students in September. Online press release. http://www.cou.on.ca/_bin/newsroom/pressReleases.cfm#2003.

Davenport, P. (1987). Hard times and EPF: The funding and health of post-secondary education since 1977. *Canadian Issues, Canadian Society, and Culture in Times of Economic Depression, 8,* 119-46.

Davis, W.G. (1966). The government of Ontario and the universities of the province. In W.M. Cooper et al. (Eds.), *Governments and the university* (pp. 21-46). Toronto: Macmillan.

Dowsett Johnston, A. (2000, 17 April). A map to prosperity. *Maclean's,* 53.

Fisher, D., and Atkinson-Grosjean, J. (2002). Brokers on the boundary: Academy-industry liaison in Canadian universities. *Higher Education, 44,* 449-67.

Fisher, D., Atkinson-Grosjean, J., and House, D. (2001). Changes in academy/industry/state relations in Canada: The creation and development of the Networks of Centres of Excellence. *Minerva, 39,* 299-325.

Frost, L. (1958). Speech at Waterloo College, 3 December. Archives of Ontario, RG-2 P3.

George, P., and McAllister, J.A. (1994). *The expanding role of the state in Canadian universities: Can university autonomy and accountability be reconciled?* Toronto: Council of Ontario Universities.

Gilbert, S. (1999, spring). Performance indicators for universities: Ogres or opportunities? *OCUFA Forum,* 20-21.

Government of Ontario. (2005). Higher Education Quality Council of Ontario Act. S.O. 2005, c. 28. http://www.e-laws.gov.on.ca/DBLaws/Statutes/English/05h28_e.htm.

Graham, R. (1990). *Old Man Ontario: Leslie M. Frost.* Toronto: University of Toronto Press.

Griffin Cohen, M. (2000). Trading away the public system: The WTO and post-secondary education. In J.L. Turk (Ed.), *The corporate campus: Commercialization and the dangers of Canada's colleges and universities* (pp. 123-41). Toronto: James Lorimer.

Jones, G.A. (1997). Higher education in Ontario. In G.A. Jones (Ed.), *Higher education in Canada: Different systems, different perspectives* (pp. 137-59). New York: Garland.

McKillop, A.B. (1994). *Matters of mind: The university in Ontario, 1791-1951.* Toronto: University of Toronto Press.

Monahan, E.J. (1998). University-government relations in Ontario: The history of a buffer body, 1958-1996. *Minerva, 36,* 347-66.

–. (2004). *Collective autonomy: A history of the Council of Ontario Universities, 1962-2000.* Waterloo: Wilfrid Laurier University Press.

Naylor, David. (2006, 22 April). Measuring up: What university rankings do and don't tell us. *Ottawa Citizen.* http://www.canada.com/ottawacitizen/news/opinion/story.html?id=adc4a1df-d148-484f-a569-80c18039f7c6.

Neatby, H.B. (1987). The historical perspective. In C. Watson (Ed.), *Governments and higher education: The legitimacy of intervention.* Toronto: Higher Education Group, Ontario Institute for Studies in Education.

Ontario Confederation of University Faculty Associations (OCUFA). (2000, 23 October). Briefing note, Bill 132: Ministry of Training, Colleges, and Universities Statute Law Amendment Act, 2000.

Ontario Council on University Affairs (OCUA). (1995). *Some perspectives on academic freedom and accountability.* Toronto: OCUA.

–. (1996). A policy recommendation on freestanding, secular, degree-granting institutions in Ontario. In *22nd annual report, 1 April 1995 to 31 August 1996* (pp. 244-72). Toronto: OCUA.

–, Task Force on Resource Allocation. (1993). *Task Force on Advanced Training – no dead ends: Report of the Task Force on Advanced Training to the minister of education and training.* Toronto: OCUA.

–. (1995). *University-government relations in Ontario 1945-1995: A summary of selected initiatives and recommendations related to system coordination and planning.* Toronto: OCUA.

Ontario Jobs and Investment Board. (1999). *A road map to prosperity: An economic plan for the jobs in the twenty-first century.* Toronto: Ontario Jobs and Investment Board.

Ontario Legislative Assembly. (1967, 5 June). *Debates,* 4264.

Ontario Ministry of Education and Training. (1996). *Report of the Advisory Panel of Future Directions for Postsecondary Education: Excellence, accessibility, responsibility.* Toronto: Ontario Ministry of Education and Training.

Ontario Ministry of Finance. (2001, 4 October). Canada's newest university to meet the demand for market-driven degree programs: Province to invest $60 million in Ontario Institute of Technology. Press release.

Rae, Bob. (2005). *Ontario: A leader in learning: Report and recommendations.* Toronto: Ministry of Training, Colleges, and Universities.

Royal Commission on Canada's Economic Prospects. (1957). *Final report of the Royal Commission on Canada's Economic Prospects.* Ottawa: Government of Canada.

Schuetze, H.G., and Bruneau, W. (2004). Less state, more market: University reform in Canada and abroad. *Canadian Journal of Higher Education, 34*(3), 1-12.

Sheffield, Edward F. (1970). The post-war surge in post-secondary education, 1945-1969. In J.D. Wilson, R.M. Stamp, and L.-P. Audet (Eds.), *Canadian education: A history* (pp. 416-43). Scarborough, ON: Prentice-Hall.

Slaughter, S. (1998). National higher education policies in a global economy. In J. Currie and J. Newson (Eds.), *Universities and globalization: Critical perspectives* (pp. 45-70). Thousand Oaks, CA: Sage.

Tudiver, N. (1999). *Universities for sale: Resisting corporate control over Canadian higher education.* Toronto: James Lorimer.

5

How Fares Equity in an Era of Academic Capitalism? The Role of Contingent Faculty

Linda Muzzin

In this chapter, I critically examine the use of contingent (non-tenured) labour in Canadian academia. While much has been written on the dangers to the *academy* of the entrenchment of contingent faculty, I am more concerned with the injustices done to the contingent faculty themselves and what their treatment indicates about the inequitable nature of the university in an era of academic capitalism. My analyses and interpretation are based on site visits and interviews conducted in fifty academic departments in Canada, which gave ample evidence of inequities of various types. Thus, my argument rests on a large Canadian qualitative and ethnographic study that involved 160 interviews with contingent and tenured faculty and administrators on twenty-nine campuses (or about one-third of Canadian universities). Although the use of contingent faculty is often conceptualized as transitory, there had been no reduction in the contingent faculty complement in the preceding decade in these departments, even up to the most recent interviews in the spring of 2003.[1]

I use the term "exclusionary" as the superordinate term to describe these injustices, not just to suggest that particular bodies are less likely to be in the tenure stream. The term "exclusion" also refers to the "chilly climate" (Backhouse, 1995) toward minoritized groups on our campuses and the devaluation of knowledges these minoritized faculty bring (Ainley, 1990; Stalker and Prentice, 1998). In a study of twenty-six graduate students of colour, Margolis and Romero (1998) specified processes such as stigmatization, blaming the victim, cooling out and tracking (directing the woman of colour to a secondary career), stereotyping, and silencing as a few of the specific processes that exclude minoritized individuals in sociology departments. While all are present in my interviews with contingent faculty, the term "exclusion" serves as a way to summarize their experiences that labels these processes simply in the language used by study participants. The term "minoritization" deliberately refuses to locate the problem within contingent faculty themselves, instead locating it within academic processes that exclude particular groups and their knowledges. The use of this term allows the situation of women to be likened to ethnoracial minorities, even though women are in the majority in the Canadian population. It also avoids artificially forcing individuals into discrete sex or visible minority categories, instead focusing on the careers of those who are contingent in the academy to see how they differ from the permanent group.

My approach draws on qualitative rather than simple statistical research to show how exclusionary processes operate. This is the first report based on the aggregate results of our study that has been assembled. I relate the concerns about contingent faculty in the literature to particular political agendas. Then I turn to my main topic, which is how exclusion of contingent faculty in various ways works against sincere attempts to address issues of gender and racial equity. Since the scenario in each discipline is unique, I have chosen one area that has been hardest hit by retrenchment – sociology and anthropology – in order to contrast it with a discipline that has coped well – law – in order to reveal the gendered and racialized nature of academic capitalism.

The Permanence, Size, and Nature of the Contingent Faculty Cadre

As part of globalization,[2] universities in Canada engaged in significant restructuring in the 1990s. One of the strategies of restructuring has involved the use of contingent faculty, paralleling this trend in business, health, and welfare sectors in Canada as well as in the service sector globally. The use of contingent workers in business allows an organization to downscale or upscale depending upon fluctuations in the market without long-term salary and benefit commitments. In universities, similarly, fluctuations in "the market" (enrolment) and declines in the numbers of full-time faculty due to downsizing can be addressed using contingent faculty.[3] The higher the proportion of non-tenured faculty, the easier hiring and firing become.

The sociology and higher education literatures contain both historical and analytical accounts of the up-and-down growth of contingent faculty relative to tenured and tenure-stream professorial numbers since the 1970s. In the United States, contingent faculty have been called the "fastest growing sector" of the academic labour force in the 1990s (Nelson and Watt, 1999). Leslie (1998) termed it the "new majority" of all faculty, but the most recent studies calculate its size in the United States at just over 39 percent (Jacobs, 2004) and in the United Kingdom at 45 percent (Abbas and McLean, 2001). A Statistics Canada survey (CAUT, 2004) included only 1,694 "other faculty" among about 30,000 in a recent survey, which a CAUT spokesperson cautioned were only *full-time* non-tenured (Smallman, 2006). Canada does not collect statistics on part-time faculty, so the size of the cadre cannot be estimated. In the departments visited in my research, contingent faculty were not routinely listed on faculty websites, and I was often forced to sit with administrators and other full-time faculty with telephone lists to locate the part-timers. In the one field where I have spent years accounting for each person who teaches (i.e., the pharmaceutical sciences), 57 percent of 314 faculty are non-tenured (Muzzin, 2006). This is a high watermark based on the need for clinical faculty. The overall estimate for cognate departments such as sociology and anthropology is lower, perhaps 20 percent.

In terms of trends, one might anticipate that, once the restructuring of the 1990s eased, there might be a reduction or reversal of the policy of retaining significant numbers of contingent faculty. However, this is definitely not the case in American universities, where studies in the past ten years have indicated that faculty are either not being hired as a point of policy in research universities (Geiger, 2004) or that the proportion of contingent to tenured faculty continues to increase (Jacobs, 2004). These scholars have thus concluded that the "flexibility" provided by a contingent labour force has now become a *permanent* feature of the academy. Shumar (1997) argues that this phenomenon cuts across the entire labour force, such that all classes now contain cadres of contingent workers. In view of trends toward academic capitalism globally (Slaughter and Leslie, 1997; Slaughter and Rhoades, 2004), the permanence of this reserve army of labour can be predicted in Canada as well.

Contingent teaching is not new. It has been a permanent feature of some parts of the university historically in that law, nursing, and dentistry have traditionally invited practising lawyers, dentists, and nurses, respectively, to introduce students to the practice of their professions through part-time teaching in their upper years of study. Nursing education maintained practise-intensive hospital schools until well into the twentieth century. Reflecting their role in the "classical" university, Rajagopal's quantitative analysis of contingent faculty careers based on her Canadian data collected in 1992 calls this group of contingent faculty "Classics" (2002).[4] In the social sciences and humanities, which do not require preparation for professional practice, sessional teaching has also been traditionally undertaken by a few graduate students and new doctoral graduates intending to apply for tenure-stream faculty positions. These patterns have not changed. What *has* changed, according to Rajagopal and my more recent observations in specific fields, is the size of the cadre of contingent faculty in the second category (which she calls "Contemporaries"), especially in areas of retrenchment in the 1990s. These include nursing, the humanities, and the social sciences. Thus, while in law, for example, the effects of retrenchment have involved merely searching more diligently through the local community of practice and inviting all likely community practitioners to make contributions to professional education, in nursing, the humanities, and the social sciences retrenchment has been much more severe, and the contingent faculty have remained.

In these fields, a "teaching stream" of various sizes of full-time non-tenured faculty has been wedged into the traditional academy. As US data clearly show, this teaching stream is disproportionately feminized (National Education Association, 2001). The Statistics Canada survey cited above shows a similar feminization of the "other" category of faculty. My data show that, among the academic professions, those already feminized ("welfare state" professions) have been hardest hit by downsizing. In nursing, for example, where retrenchment hit both the profession itself and the academy, most of the curriculum in some schools was being taught by sessional and full-time contingent workers well into this decade. That is, in nursing, the tenure stream is dwarfed by the number of contingent academic workers. The humanities and social sciences are also hard hit. Rajagopal (2002) labelled its so-called part-timers "Contemporaries" because so many of them actually carry a full teaching load. This pattern of "part-timers" working over thirty hours a week can also be seen in the United States (Jacobs, 2004). In nursing and other academic professions, contingent faculty may supplement their "part-time" teaching with much better-paying outside jobs. In the humanities and social sciences, where positions are scarce in the downsized welfare sector, several part-time teaching positions may be strung together, with no benefits from any source, notably pensions. A group that Rajagopal (2002) originally termed "freeway fliers" teaches at several postsecondary institutions.

Freeway flying is encouraged when institutions impose limits on numbers of courses or try to restrict contingents from accumulating the number of courses taught that they need for permanent status. In our research, freeway fliers could be found across the country, combining work at a variety of local and not-so-local universities, colleges, and private educational institutions to maintain security and income. Our data show that those who are near graduating with a PhD often get caught for economic reasons, marking time until a local position might become available. They work tirelessly toward seniority for future security and eventually join the reserve army of academic labour. Historically, some in this situation have been faculty wives (Hannah, Paul, and Vethamany-Globus, 2002). Thus, my data show that the pattern of twenty years ago, of Classic part-timers holding secure jobs, has been joined by the now relatively permanent Contemporaries.

Reliance on Contingent Faculty: What's at Stake?

The results of US research studies focusing on different types of contingent faculty, the part time (Gappa and Leslie, 1993) and the full time (Baldwin and Chronister, 2001), raise a variety of concerns. What is at stake? In both US and Canadian writing, angst is expressed about the possibility of

(1) declines in "academic quality" in using contingent faculty (e.g., Puplampu, 2004);

(2) related radical changes in the nature of the university away from a "haven for scholars" (Newson and Buchbinder, 1986) that will kill curiosity-driven research, self-governance, and liberal education such that universities will become "giant training warehouses" (Axelrod, 2002, p. 51). The undermining of "academic freedom" is linked to tenured faculty no longer participating fully in decision making and contingent faculty, either uninvolved in university life or easily fired by managers, choosing to "play it safe" by lack of involvement. This concern also focuses on the relative lack of support for teaching as compared to research (as argued by Pocklington and Tupper, 2002); and

(3) the exploitation of permanent, highly trained, contingent academics drawn from groups traditionally excluded from the academy, who are not paid equitably and who, in many cases, do not receive benefits that have come to be expected by other workers. Non-tenured workers have unionized rapidly over the past few years, and labour conflicts on Canadian and US campuses are a related source of concern (Rhoades, 1996, 1998; Rhoades and Slaughter, 1997).

Is this vision of universities becoming low-quality, watered-down sweatshops run by non-academic managers justified? The first set of arguments regarding quality tends to be made by conservatives advocating the abolition of tenure in order to "weed out" the proverbial "dead wood" of non-productive faculty, thus making universities even more like businesses through the coercive use of merit systems. In a study of tenure-stream faculty in which I was a co-researcher with Sandra Acker, we were hard pressed to *find* any "dead wood" among the tenured faculty, so it is difficult to give credence to this argument. In addition, Jacobs' recent detailed analysis of faculty time (2004) shows that faculty work such long hours that they have little time for family or community. In the second category of arguments, established scholars for whom there had been an academic Golden Age, however brief, worry about what will become of the academy they knew and loved. In part, they are lamenting the relative decline of the privileges of the incumbent faculty, including self-governance, hard won through battles in the 1960s (Newson and Buchbinder, 1986).

This is not the kind of argument that comes from the contingent constituency. For this group, who in my research sometimes reported being excluded for half a lifetime from the privileges of the academy, there was no Golden Age. Given their scholarly credentials, their critique is well informed, incisive, and direct (Hannah, Paul, and Vethamany-Globus, 2002; Mysyk, 2001; Nelson, 1997; Nelson and Watt, 1999). These voices, however scholarly, have not yet been heard in mainstream debates about "quality," academic capitalism, and equity. In fact, unlike Classic part-timers, who are often highly regarded as content experts in their professions, our research found that

Contemporaries are more often regarded with suspicion. "Lip service" is given to including them in the academy, but typically little action is taken. Are faculty "in denial" about the transitory nature of the phenomenon?

Previous papers have reported results of an analysis of the experiences of the forty-two faculty of colour across our two studies of tenured and contingent faculty (Muzzin and Shahjahan, 2005) and revealed that tenured faculty and administrators are aware of the injustices done to contingent faculty but seldom took action to address them. I have chosen not to explore ethnoracial origins by field in this chapter partly because it is not so easy to place faculty in Statistics Canada categories. For example, how would I place a woman born in South America with a mix of three or four ethnoracial origins who cannot tell whether she is experiencing discrimination because she is a woman or because she is not White? The salient point is that this woman in academia feels that she has been marginalized during her whole career and that she and other contingent faculty report similar processes of exclusion based on the microdata of their everyday lives. Published writings and analyses by contingent faculty similarly detail the exclusionary practices of professional associations (Di Giacomo, 1999), administrators (Church, 1999), and academia as a whole (Mysyk, 2001).

At the same time, our results showed that not all the news is bad regarding equity initiatives in academia in the past few years. There *has* been some feminization and some racialization of the tenured and tenure-stream academy.[5] But there is also much bad news. After an examination of the historical context of the Canadian contingent faculty phenomenon, I will give examples of how gender and racial equity initiatives now being woven into Canadian campuses risk weakening and unravelling. Since I believe that a university in a declared democracy *must* model equity for the rest of the society, it is of paramount importance to examine how well we are faring in our efforts to address the substantial inequities that have developed among university faculty.

"Underfunding," Academic Capitalism, and Contingent Faculty

There is general agreement that what is called the "underfunding" of universities preceded the change in the contingent faculty cadre being discussed here (Blackmore, 1997; Geiger, 2004; Reimer, 2004; Slaughter and Leslie, 1997). This "underfunding" began soon after a commitment was made to mass education in the 1960s. Massification reflects the view that attention to educational equity would maintain the US hegemonic economic position in the world as well as address equity concerns in and of themselves. Wherever the emphasis is put in trying to understand this radical change in the constituency for postsecondary education, the important point to be made is that subsequently support for postsecondary education did not keep pace with enrolments, and the "welfare state" began to be dismantled (Amin, 1997; Teeple, 2000).

Economic retrenchment has been dealt with in various ways by post-secondary institutions. Large increases in tuition fees, mainly for professional programs, are probably the most publicly visible aspect of Canadian university fundraising efforts. However, there is also increased reliance on funds raised from government for strategic scientific projects, alumni canvassing, and other private sector sources. This kind of academic capitalism has led to a proliferation of coloured glass and girder construction university buildings with their donors' names enshrined as well as research chairs in fields of interest to corporations and/or providing free advertising of their philanthropy (Muzzin, 2001). A related strategy has been the importation of what Broadbent and Laughlin (1997) term "accounting logic" into the academic setting.[6] These practices mimic those found in business, where constant quantitatively based evaluation, such as in merit systems, is supposed to lead to "quality control." As suggested above, the "flexibility" of a "reserve army" of academic labour, as represented by contingent workers, is also viewed as good administration in that it allows rapid response to changing enrolments without long-term commitment to employees. As Rajagopal (2002, Chapter 4) has noted, the greater the size of the university, the greater these fluctuations, and the greater its need for contingent labour. Rajagopal documented that academic contingent labour, like contingent labour in general, contains more women and minorities than does the group of academic workers with secure positions. One might point to the representation by race of university teachers as compiled by the 2001 census as providing evidence that academia has reversed this trend and achieved good representation of ethnoracial minorities. But these numbers hide the distinction between contingent and tenured faculty and the intersections of gender, race, and other difference in the equation. We do not have statistics that would help to determine whether the feminization and racialization of contingent faculty have decreased in the past twenty years. My study suggests that they have not. For example, of the 57 percent of faculty who are non-tenured in the pharmaceutical sciences in Canada, over two-thirds are minoritized (women and/or people of colour).

A Story of Demographics, Faculty, and Equity Gone Awry

If this pattern holds across the university, we might ask why does the highly trained Contemporary cadre contain proportionately more women and minorities than the traditional cadres of the Canadian university? The answer can be found in the combination of White patriarchy and tenure that took hold in the 1960s. Many educational leaders may long to change (or may actually think they *have* changed) the White patriarchy entrenched in

Canadian academia as of 2006. But because of the historical combination of *en*trenchment followed by *re*trenchment that took place in that era, my data document how change toward a faculty that more faithfully reflects the more diverse student body of Canadian universities is coming painfully slowly. In hindsight, it can be seen that the hiring of young faculty in the relative prosperity of the late 1940s and early 1950s, combined with the 1990s retrenchment of universities, has slowed down gender and racial equity initiatives in the new millennium. New Canadian faculty were so scarce in the 1960s and early 1970s that they (mostly men) were often hired into the tenure stream with only the *promise* of finishing their doctoral dissertations. The United States was an important source of faculty in fields that had been traditionally male dominated, including the social sciences. There was such an acute shortage that even a few highly qualified Asian and Black professors were hired, though the academy in Canada had been virtually all White to this point, especially in the social sciences. My research revealed many of these individuals who either never made it through the tenure system or have lived out their careers as tokens of diversity in their departments, underlining the overwhelming White maleness of sections of the academy in Canada to this day.

In the social sciences, White women like me were also hired to teach during this time period. However, this was not typically in the tenure stream, since it was still expected in those days that we would marry and devote our time to our families, as had our mothers. While it might be expected that some of these permanent contingents might eventually be taken up by the academy, our study verified long-standing stigmas attached to long-time contract and sessional work, which gave new graduates "the edge" over the more experienced contingent cohort for tenure-stream positions. While we encountered contingent faculty who had attained permanency, taking up a tenure position after long-time contingency did not appear possible, unless one sought new credentials.

Participants in our research reflected the trends of the past few decades. For example, their accounts reflect how feminist influence on the academy began to be exerted politically in the late 1970s when a few women fought their way, using the courts and other means, to get tenure in traditional fields as well as to establish new fields such as women's studies. For example, one woman of colour in our study recalled that a colleague of colour who, in her words, "meets every standard I know ... ultimately *did* get tenured after a major pitched battle with the [faculty in this traditional field, but] ... it was tenure in a glove with a fork in it." And as Margolis and Romero (1998) point out, fields such as ethnic studies and women's studies arose when activist-oriented minoritized scholars were excluded from the social sciences. But in general, the tenure-stream positions we fought for were unavailable. The male professorial "baby boomer" cohort had matured, "frozen" these positions, and "raised the bar" for entry and tenure. Contingent faculty with good credentials were told that the "clock had been ticking" and that their "productivity" had not kept pace with the increasing standards of the university. Some of us made financial and other sacrifices to go back and complete our PhDs, managing to insert ourselves into the last few tenure-stream positions that were available just before retrenchment hit in earnest in the 1990s. Government subsidies were available for hiring women in that era. This made all the difference for some of the research participants in these hirings, since universities were starting to feel the constraints. Thus, there was *some* feminization of the faculty in the 1980s. According to their own accounts, others just became part of a "lost generation" of lifetime sessional workers or dropouts from academia. There are many such stories recorded in *Women in the Canadian Academic Tundra: Challenging the Chill* (Hannah, Paul, and Vethamany-Globus, 2002).

Voices of anti-racism also became louder in the 1970s, and a very few Black, Asian, Arab, and Aboriginal men and women began to broach the tenure stream. While the boomers have been locked into their academic positions, the ethnoracial diversity of Canada has increased markedly, as has the visibility of Aboriginal and Black peoples, due to their vigorous activism. In addition, Canada has recruited professionals and other highly qualified individuals from all over the world. Unfortunately, this diversity is still not reflected in the tenured faculty of most professional schools or in the humanities and social sciences departments that I visited in my research. As one contingent faculty member in my study commented, a chair in her department had "a fairly good equity record [with] sessionals because he looked at his regular faculty and saw not a single White person and mostly men. So he tried to hire equitable representation from the sessional pool." This crucial point might be easy to miss if we were just to take Statistics Canada data that show a decrease of White faculty from 83.9 to 82.4 percent from 1996 to 2001 and at least a slight increase in or maintenance of representation of all groups except Arab and Japanese faculty (CAUT, 2004). However, I have already emphasized that these data largely exclude contingent faculty, so the data hide any over-representation in the non-tenured cadre. Similarly, Statistics Canada data for university professors that show similar representations of particular ethnoracial groups in the academy as in the population cannot be taken as reassurance of academic diversity, since the contingent group is not broken out in these statistics.

I observed through site visits in my research that massification continues and that the *students,* especially in Vancouver, Toronto, and Montreal, have become increasingly diverse. But the tenured *faculty* entrenched in many areas of the academy remain essentially the same. For example, in academic pharmacy, 85 percent of 314 faculty in the nine schools are White. The remaining group exceeds the 12.7 percent of all workers that are listed in the

2001 census as "visible minority" (CAUT, 2004), which suggests that academic pharmacy is an ethnoracially representative discipline. However, among these 15 percent, it is worth noting that only *1 percent* are tenured or tenure-stream women of colour. Slightly less than one in ten White tenured or tenure-stream faculty is a woman, which shows that women of colour have to face the dual barriers of gender and race. As I have emphasized earlier, official statistics do not reveal nuances of this nature, which can be assembled only through site visits, careful interviewing that allows faculty to self-identify, and inclusion of *all* those who contribute to a curriculum.

Good News about Equity in the Social Sciences and the Professions

One senior sociologist whom I interviewed claimed that all the "retrenchment" that was taking place in Canadian universities today was "gendered" (and I might add "racialized") because it was mainly White men who were retiring. New hires, as much as possible, were women of colour. This is good news. The boomers are starting to retire! In almost every sociology and anthropology department that I visited, new positions filled in the past few years have favoured Black, Asian, and female tenure-stream applicants. In many cases, those scholars have been nurtured by one department and then actively recruited by a host of others. Thus, the consciousness that hiring for diversity in sociology and anthropology needs to be taken seriously is clearly there, and the will to be proactive has been demonstrated.[7]

Similarly, some good news can be found in law faculties. For example, over the decades, a few schools have feminized to the 50 percent level in the tenure track. (This was true only in a couple of sociology and anthropology departments that I visited.) Most importantly, some of these women law professors had made it into full professorships and/or high administrative positions. There, in most cases that I examined, their primary agenda had been to further the cause not only of gender equity but also of equity in *all* other regards by actively influencing the hiring of ethnoracial minority faculty, gay and lesbian faculty, and faculty with visible disabilities. Furthermore, largely due to the combined efforts of these senior White women, Aboriginal women, and other ethnoracial minority community members, many law faculties now have equity units for dealing with ethnoracial and gender issues across the board and/or socioeconomic and ethnoracial access programs at the undergraduate level.

In one university, law had linked with sociology through an equity program. This means that the program hires faculty to teach, for example, courses on Aboriginal law. Equity is fairly central in most law curricula due to our Canadian Charter of Rights and Freedoms. Some law schools are better known for being proactive in areas of equity compared to others, but all include such topics as part of their core curricula. Two equity-based units I visited are so independent of the original law school that they are no longer promoting "White man's law" exclusively and have provided a place for Aboriginal and Inuit law.

Bad News about Equity in the Social Sciences versus the Law Profession

There is good news and bad news with respect to the renewal of fields like sociology and anthropology compared to law. The bad news is that the majority of the sociology and anthropology departments that I visited are still White and androcentric – that is, there are *many* more senior White male tenured professors than female, Black, Asian, or Aboriginal tenured and tenure-stream professors. Further, more than in professional faculties such as law, these latter individuals are clustered into non-tenure-stream positions. In most cases, the positions are not even full time. Retrenchment has not allowed many of the positions left vacant by the slowly retiring White professors to be filled over the past few years. There was a net decline, in some cases precipitous, in the number of tenure-stream positions. This suggests that there were few opportunities to hire women and ethnoracially minoritized faculty.

As Geiger (2004) and Noble (2002) have pointed out, the sciences and science-based professional schools at research universities garner the lion's share of the resources, both internal and external, so that retrenchment has been particularly punishing in the humanities and social sciences. This reflects the strategic importance placed on Western science in the academy and the original reason for massification – to compete globally in the science race. Evidence from my research shows that not even law escaped the cuts of the 1990s and early 2000s, but law was better able to cope with the budget cuts and freezes mandated by central university administrations because it was able to draw on the traditional cadre of Classic part-timers who are practice-based specialists in local communities.[8]

Sociology and anthropology departments are less able to fall back on such geographically stable, Classic part-time faculty since the only "community practice" for most sociologists is part-time contractual teaching, activism, or positions in other fields as hired by government or other academic departments. In some locations, such as provincial capitals, full-time and contractual government positions can be combined to produce a Classic contingent position. In cities with community colleges, a full-time college professorship can be combined with a Classic contingent university position. As with the professions, this combination favours White men. In most places I visited, loss of retiring professors was followed by hiring Classic part-timers where they are available as well as by hiring more Contemporary part-timers. As I have suggested previously, these sessional and otherwise contractual employees are more likely, compared to the tenure stream, to be drawn from the female and ethnoracial minority groups that make up those who have no livelihood except the meagre stipends that universities offer. Thus, the non-tenured faculty in these social science departments are of at least two different groups, the insecure one more feminized and racialized than the secure one. There is truly an inequity here in that the insecure group is more likely to have a doctorate or be working on one, and these individuals are more likely to expect that they will be able to acquire a full-time position eventually. The Classics, on the other hand, are more oriented toward their full-time positions outside the universities, which provide them with good incomes.

Department heads in sociology and anthropology will openly acknowledge that Contemporary contingent faculty are being exploited. Contemporaries in sociology and anthropology tend not to teach in specialty areas as do Classic part-timers in the professions. Most faculty whom I interviewed had taught primarily courses in introductory sociology, Canadian society, and research methods, while hot new areas were taken up by tenure-stream and tenured faculty (consistent with discourses around globalization, information technology, and intellectual property). Teaching in an area different from your research is a real impediment to maintaining a research program in order to get a tenure-stream position. Administrators will acknowledge that these faculty are caught in a vicious cycle in that, with high teaching loads, they cannot keep up the publishing required to ever attain a tenure-stream position, should any become available. Thus, what was formerly a small cadre destined for the tenure stream has been replaced by a permanently exploited feminized (and somewhat racialized, though still mostly White) group supporting the still largely White male academic enterprise. As if it were not enough to be financially exploited, contingent faculty minoritized by gender, race, and other differences also face a chilly climate. As one contingent faculty member said simply, "I don't think it's a good place for minorities who are Black, especially since I think Black." Thus, although feminists such as Paula Caplan had earlier described the climate for women who found their way into the academy in the 1970s and 1980s as "chilly" (1993), Hannah, Paul, and Vethamany-Globus (2002) describe the climate for aging female Contemporaries, including those of colour, as a "tundra."

Mysyk's "Sessional Faculty as Migrant Labour" Theory

In theoretical terms, the geographical and interinstitutional mobility of contingent academic workers that is so strikingly characteristic of Contemporaries in sociology and anthropology has been linked to processes of globalization by Mysyk (2001). She likens the lives of these feminized, racialized Contemporaries to migrant farm labourers. A similar theoretical argument labelling the process "internal colonialism" has been made by Di Giacomo (1999). The data collected in my research illustrated these processes.

Specifically, many sociology and anthropology sessionals in our study, particularly those who were no longer graduate students, were trying to hold down sessional work at two, three, and even six or seven campuses where this was possible. By way of contrast, this phenomenon is rare in law, where there are only a handful of such freeway fliers. While some administrators expressed the view that this was largely an Ontario phenomenon because of the large number of universities there, I found it in all locations. For example, Nova Scotia has many more campuses per capita than other parts of the country, with the most institutions concentrated in Halifax. Where institutions had legislated a cap on the number of courses that could be taught by a part-timer, or where departments voluntarily limited this number, it was *necessary* for a Contemporary to work at more than one institution in order to make a living. These patterns were also found in Quebec and British Columbia as well as in Ontario, where individuals might use trains and buses to keep their appointed one-hour classes three times per week in widely dispersed locations. But many "part-time" workers are also migrant in the Prairies as well as on the West Coast and in central Canada, juggling snippets of sessional work at colleges, university colleges, private colleges, and universities. The careers of most freeway fliers are elaborate, marked by multiple moves often due to wives following their husbands as part of job transfers. Each move has been followed by exploration of the multiple openings for sessional work in each location. These careers indeed fit the description of feminized, migrant, exploited, Third World labour that is an important characteristic of globalization even if our interviewees insisted that they "loved teaching," as virtually all did. The phenomenon is clearer to see when one separates out the largely male Classic group of part-time faculty, who have a higher household income and who are relatively geographically stable.

Mysyk's (2001) theoretical analysis and interpretation of the situation in Canadian sociology and anthropology argue that migrancy includes those who work at a single institution for a year and then move on. Mysyk dismisses neoclassical equilibrium theories of migrant labour through which migrants, rationally calculating which employment "opportunities" will give them the greatest returns, seek out areas where capital is abundant and labour is scarce. Based on her experience of what she calls "becoming the phenomenon," she describes how the new contingent worker may fool herself into thinking that contingent work "is a temporary aberration in [her] meteoric rise to the top" (p. 81). The migrant contingent worker typically becomes disillusioned after multiple stigmatizations as "poor quality" because of her inability to get a tenure-stream position; the taking on of multiple unremunerated tasks to buy goodwill; the acquisition of the label "troublemaker" at the hint of a complaint; the backlash from male colleagues; and the year after year of "revolving door" jobs. The "merry-go-round" may revolve for some time, as it did for Mysyk. After financial and other sacrifices, as well as important intellectual contributions, a few, like Mysyk, may find a permanent position (see also Collinson, 2003). But the opportunities are rare. Mysyk's summary of the dynamics of contingent work are worth repeating: "Changes to Canada's postsecondary education system have occurred on the backs of sessional lecturers in the social sciences and humanities, many of whom, like their Third World counterparts, are forced to migrate back and forth across Canada from one limited-term position to another. And, like their Mexican counterparts who claim that they will become 'rich' by working as stoop labourers on Manitoba's vegetable farms but who seem to return year after year, sessional lecturers as migrant labourers are on a 'slow track to nowhere'" (p. 86).

"Regularization" of Contingent Faculty

A small number of contingent workers face a less dire but still compromised fate compared to the freeway fliers whom Mysyk describes. That is, within the tiny manoeuvring space within some social science and humanities budgets, some small inequities have been addressed. For example, most departments I visited had "regularized" at least one long-time sessional teacher in order to allow her to collect benefits such as pension and medical coverage after years and years of service. Other departments I visited were actively negotiating with central administration for the conversion of part-time to full-time positions that would then secure contingent faculty members some benefits. (In law, the conversion tended to be a quantum leap better in that the already-secure contingent faculty teaching and doing administrative work have, in a few cases, been converted to tenure-stream positions.) A few campuses had even arranged payment of benefits for those employed less than 50 percent, commensurate with the percentage of their contracts.

I am hesitant to attribute these developments exclusively to the equity-based motivations of sociology and anthropology department (and law school) heads for two reasons. First, interviewees described their very active involvement in union organizing activities over the past few years to secure these benefits for themselves (in some cases aided by their colleagues in law). Thus, it appears that contingent faculty in sociology and anthropology, like their colleagues in nursing, are largely responsible for their own gains. Second, in securing a full-time contractual non-tenured position, a department acquires some predictability over who is available to teach in the coming year, without the long-term commitment of a tenure-stream position (Mysyk, 2001). The "ameliorated" situation is thus arguably undertaken more for making the departmental staffing situation more predictable than for looking out for the security and nurturing of the contingent faculty themselves. All of those whom I met in this category were White women, and some were spouses of other academics, a much-abused group (see case studies in Hannah, Paul, and Vethamany-Globus, 2002; and Rajagopal, 2002, pp. 116-17). They recounted many situations in which full-time faculty treated them as second-class citizens despite their excellent teaching records.

Furthermore, my earlier positive comments about the equity initiatives in law and nursing need to be tempered. The faculty in so-called equity-based units (who tend to be poorly paid White women) clearly have "second-class citizenship" based on their long-standing non-tenured status. "Soft" money to support these initiatives from government or business is predominant, with incumbents often seeking their own funding and the funding of their units as a whole, while "hard" money still goes to tenured faculty and administrators who are researching, writing, and teaching about many corporate-relevant new areas such as intellectual property and manipulation of living organisms.

Conclusion

The research reported here on contingent faculty provides a minoritized rather than mainstream view of the university in an era of academic capitalism. Although Canadian statistics are not collected on part-time faculty, US and UK data show that non-tenured faculty comprise a substantial and permanent cadre within the restructured postsecondary sector. Joining Classic part-timers in the professions who have taught for decades at the academy is a new cadre of Contemporaries. Mainstream concerns have been expressed about poor-quality teaching and participation by this new contingent group, but my data are consistent with US data that show that contingent faculty work almost full time for token stipends and are typically retained over the long term because of their exemplary teaching. Furthermore, in the social sciences, many "freeway-fly" among multiple institutions, often with few benefits. Rather than being "failed academics," these freeway fliers describe themselves as scholars who are credentialed and ready for a tenure-stream position that has not materialized due to restructuring. This is particularly true in sociology and anthropology, where the opportunities have not been as great as in law. Thus, I conclude that sociology and anthropology have been limited in their ability to accommodate minoritized groups because of restructuring. This is ironic since equity is part of a sociological mandate. So how fares equity? The continuing exploitation and marginalization of contingent faculty are well known and perhaps ignored by administrators and tenured faculty as "the price of doing business." I have suggested here that the situation in law is marginally better, with space being made for equity centres and for Inuit and Aboriginal law in the curriculum. This has to do with the availability of Classic part-timers, unlike in sociology, less restructuring in the 1990s, and targeting of the field by activist minoritized groups, including Aboriginal scholars and women of colour.

But this good news about law needs to be tempered. My data suggest that the contingent cadre includes more gender and ethnoracial minoritized faculty than the tenured group. Participants in my research described being attracted to positions such as running equity offices only to discover that such positions are contingent and not considered a stepping-stone to the tenure stream. Incumbents also face a chilly climate often created unintentionally by tenured faculty and administrators (in what Scheurich and Young, 1997, have called "epistemological racism"). The good news, I have argued, is that the contingent cadre has provided a tenuous foothold for Aboriginal and Black faculty in the academy, mostly due to their own vigorous activism rather than the efforts toward equity of their administrators, however sincere they are about a mission of social justice. But the price has been unacceptably high. As one Aboriginal scholar remarked, "I watched them all. They've all dropped out because of the continued intellectual and cognitive harassment."

Except for a few important publications on contingent faculty noted here, mainstream Canadian academic literature on the university is strangely silent about the cadre of university faculty who are contingent. Data are not routinely collected on them, and not much of the debate about the future of Canadian universities is focused on contingent faculty. The research on contingent faculty that my colleagues and I have conducted over the past few years supports arguments that the increased hiring of contingent workers at the university is an equity issue that cries out to be addressed. Doing away with tenure, as suggested by some advocates of globalization, would not solve the equity problem in that senior White men who dominate the academy are not "dead wood," at least not in the traditional sense of the term. In some cases, they would be essential for the advancement of biotechnological and other research and teaching that is of such importance in academic capitalism. Furthermore, it is hard to see how other solutions, such as providing secure positions for teaching faculty, might solve the equity problem. Given the privileged position that research holds in the university, this solution would just entrench a feminized and partly racialized stream in second-class positions, perpetuating the status quo. Finally, reflecting the reach of Western science, a permanent contingent group now characterizes areas such as the humanities and social sciences, whose input to the global economy is not entirely clear. In fact, one could argue that the humanities and social sciences produce significant activism *against* discourses of globalization. Thus, to the extent that academic capitalism that privileges the sciences and androcentric professions continues to unfold on our campuses, the problems that these areas are facing will probably deepen. And contingent faculty, a Third World caught within the First World, will hold this unjust system in place.

Notes

1 Departments varied in the extent to which they relied on contingent faculty, with one sociology department in 2003 reporting less than 20 percent and one nursing department reporting more than 75 percent contingent faculty. Included in our study were fields considered to be central to academic capitalism through their involvement in biotechnological research such as health professions (pharmacy, dentistry, optometry) as well as those not ostensibly engaged with academic capitalism (sociology and anthropology, law, nursing). Departments were chosen to reflect the national diversity within the fields studied. The funding for this project was obtained from SSHRCC, and it involved multiple site visits from 1999 to 2003, with at least one school in each field in each province. In addition to conducting 160 individual face-to-face interviews and analyzing the transcripts and fieldnotes to determine how administrators and faculty constructed their careers and curricula, we critically examined printed and Internet materials on each program. This research was preceded and informed by a study of about 200 non-tenured but tenure-stream and tenured faculty and administrators in professional education. I use the word *my* to refer to the research because, as a tenured academic, I had the opportunity to do most of the interviewing and analysis that led to this chapter. However, the involvement of contingent faculty researchers in my team was indispensable to the project, including Vicky Nygaard, Avis Mysyk, Maria Wallis, and Cheryl Albas. Discipline experts, including Marcia Boyd (dentistry), Marlee Spafford (optometry), and Frances Gregor (nursing), also opened professional fields to us. Finally, involvement of my graduate students has been important in my writing, especially about minoritized faculty. They include Riyad Shahjahan, Jackie Limoges, Kimine Myazumi, and Begna Dugassa.

2 The doctrine of globalization is not just economic, though its ideological justification often appears so. Critical scholars have labelled globalization as "neocolonial" in its forcing of White technologies and economic and political systems on other parts of the world over the past decade (e.g., Dhruvarajan, 2004; Shiva, 1995). Since the US invasion of Iraq, globalization can be seen as unmistakably military, just as it was during the original dividing up of South and North America, Africa, and Asia among the European powers in the 1500s and beyond. Dissenting territories are occupied militarily. While contemporary populations may not be captured and sold as slaves, they are moved geographically and forced to adopt dominant White ideologies, both within their own countries and within the "overdeveloped" countries to which they have migrated. That is, there are "third" and "fourth" (Amin, 1997) worlds in both the "first" and the "second" (now annexed to the "first") worlds. Canadian academic contingent workers, as Roxana Ng pointed out to me in a classroom discussion in 2001, are part of the Third World, even if they are located in the overdeveloped world.

3 Since I am critical of discourses of globalization, I place words that I wish to question or problematize in quotation marks.

4 Rajagopal's data cannot be used as a base for the arguments in this chapter since they were collected before the deepest retrenchment of the 1990s. However, her theoretical analysis is valuable, which is why I cite from her book here.

5 A reviewer pointed out that the CAUT article cited above shows that the overall percentage of "visible minority" professors matches almost exactly this percentage in the overall population, varying somewhat by ethnoracial group, with Aboriginal faculty almost nonexistent. However, as I have pointed out, neither the CAUT nor Statistics Canada data distinguish between tenured and contingent faculty. My contention, based on my research, is that these aggregate data mask an over-representation of White males of all ethnicities in the tenure stream and an over-representation of racially minoritized women in the contingent group. This is illustrated in my accounting of the pharmaceutical sciences, where 15 percent of faculty are ethnoracially minoritized. This compares quite favourably with the 2001 census of 12.7 percent visible minority workers. However, 61 percent of all pharmaceutical sciences tenured faculty are White men, while only 2 percent are minoritized women, and 38 percent of non-tenured faculty are White men, while 8 percent are minoritized women. I also located the "missing" Aboriginal faculty in the non-tenured group,

almost all in law and nursing. Although I have not completed a census of fields outside pharmacy, clearly law is more diverse in that we were able to include nine racially minoritized faculty members (more than one-third of the group) in our study, whereas in nursing we could locate only four (10 percent), and in sociology and anthropology less than 10 percent.

6 Broadbent and Laughlin define accounting logic as "the view that it is possible to quantify outputs and outcomes and link them to financial inputs" (1997, p. 37). The danger of such a view is that such representation will appear neutral and fair despite the distortion required to "operationalize" complex processes using rationalistic or positivistic methods. Bensimmon (1995) has critiqued these practices from a feminist poststructural theoretical perspective.

7 It is technically true that each position taken by a formerly excluded group excludes a White person, but since there are already so many entrenched White men it is really only White women, not White men, who remain seriously underrepresented in the tenure stream. But see Sokoloff (1992) for the difficulties involved in making these types of arguments.

8 They will teach for almost nothing at the university, providing a two-sided cost savings (in that a full-timer doesn't have to be hired, and the part-timer doesn't have to be paid). Such teaching has a certain degree of cachet for these lawyers and their firms. As non-tenured part-time professors, they have both the expertise in law practice required to teach students wanting to become lawyers and a good salary, so they are often willing to forgo even a small honorarium or stipend, turning it back into the university coffers. To the extent that these individuals are teaching the corporate philosophies of their firms, there is an obvious danger of academic capitalism in these retrenchment arrangements. Historically, law practitioners who taught in law schools ran small businesses, just as dentists continue to do today. Now lawyers who teach in universities tend to be representatives of corporate firms.

References

Abbas, A., and McLean, M. (2001). Becoming sociologists: Professional identity for part-time teachers of university sociology. *British Journal of Sociology of Education, 22*(3), 339-52.

Ainley, M. (1990). *Despite the odds: Essays on Canadian women and science.* Montreal: Véhicule Press.

Amin, S. (1997). *Capitalism in the age of globalization: The management of contemporary society.* London: Zed Books.

Axelrod, P. (2002). *Values in conflict: The university, the marketplace, and the trials of liberal education.* Montreal: McGill-Queen's University Press.

Backhouse, C. (1988). *Women faculty at the University of Western Ontario: Reflections on the employment equity award.* London: University of Western Ontario, Faculty of Law.

Baldwin, R., and Chronister, J. (2001). *Teaching without tenure: Policies and practices for a new era.* Baltimore: Johns Hopkins University Press.

Bensimmon, E.M. (1995). Total quality management in the academy: A rebellious reading. *Harvard Educational Review, 65*(4), 593-611.

Blackmore, J. (1997). Disciplining feminism: A look at gender-equity struggles in Australian higher education. In L. Roman and L. Eyre (Eds.), *Dangerous territories: Struggles for difference and equality in education.* New York: Routledge.

Broadbent, J., and Laughlin, R. (1997). "Accounting logic" and controlling professionals. In J. Broadbent, M. Dietrich, and J. Roberts (Eds.), *The end of the professions? The restructuring of professional work* (pp. 34-49). London: Routledge.

Canadian Association of University Teachers (CAUT). (2004). Closing the equity gap: A portrait of Canada's university teachers, 1996-2001. *CAUT Education Review, 6*(2), 1-4.

Caplan, P. (1993). *Lifting a ton of feathers: A woman's guide to surviving in the academic world.* Toronto: University of Toronto Press.

Church, J. (1999). Laboring in the dream factory, part II. *Qualitative Studies in Education, 12*(3), 251-62.

Collinson, J.A. (2003). Working at a marginal "career": The case of UK social science contract researchers. *Sociological Review, 51*(3), 405-22.

Dhruvarajan, V. (2004). Colonialism and capitalism: Continuities and variations in strategies of domination and oppression. In P. Tripp and L. Muzzin (Eds.), *Teaching as activism: Equity meets environmentalism* (pp. 134-48). Montreal: McGill-Queen's University Press.
Di Giacomo, S. (1999). The new internal colonialism. *Qualitative Studies in Education, 12*(2), 263-68.
Gappa, J., and Leslie, D. (1993). *The invisible faculty: Improving the status of part-timers in higher education.* San Francisco: Jossey-Bass.
Geiger, R. (2004). *Knowledge and money: Research universities and the paradox of the marketplace.* Stanford: Stanford University Press.
Hannah, E., Paul, L., and Vethamany-Globus, S. (2002). *Women in the Canadian academic tundra: Challenging the chill.* Montreal: McGill-Queen's University Press.
Jacobs, J.A. (2004). The faculty time divide. *Sociological Forum, 19*(1), 3-27.
Leslie, D.W. (1998). *The growing use of part-time faculty: Understanding causes and effects.* San Franciso: Jossey Bass.
Margolis, E., and Romero, M. (1998). The department is very male, very white, very old, and very conservative: The functioning of the hidden curriculum in graduate sociology departments. *Harvard Educational Review, 68*(1), 1-32.
Muzzin, L. (2001). Powder puff brigades: Professional caring vs. industry research in the pharmaceutical sciences. In E. Margolis (Ed.), *The hidden curriculum in higher education* (pp. 97-120). New York: Routledge.
–. (2006, July). Diversity in the Canadian pharmacy professoriate. Paper presented at the Social Pharmacy Workshop, University of Nottingham.
Muzzin, L., and Shahjahan, R. (2005, April). Privileged vs. subjugated knowledges in university-based professional education. Paper presented at the annual American Educational Research Association meetings, Montreal.
Mysyk, A. (2001). The sessional lecturer as migrant labourer. *Canadian Journal of Higher Education, 31*(3), 73-92.
National Education Association, Higher Education Research Center. (2001). Part-time faculty. *National Education Association Update, 7*(4). http://www.nea.org/he/heupdate/images/vol7no4.pdf.
Nelson, C. (Ed.). (1997). *Will teach for good: Academic labor in crisis.* Minneapolis: University of Minnesota Press.
Nelson, C., and Watt, S. (1999). *Academic keywords: A devil's dictionary for higher education.* New York: Routledge.
Newson, J., and Buchbinder, H. (1986). *The university means business.* Toronto: Garamond.
Noble, D. (2002). *Digital diploma mills: The automation of higher education.* Toronto: Between the Lines.
Pocklington, T., and Tupper, A. (2002). *No place to learn: Why universities aren't working.* Vancouver: UBC Press.
Puplampu, K. (2004). The restructuring of higher education and part-time instructors: A theoretical and political analysis of undergraduate teaching in Canada. *Teaching in Higher Education, 9*(2), 171-82.
Rajagopal, I. (2002). *Hidden academics: Contract faculty in Canadian universities.* Toronto: University of Toronto Press.
Reimer, M. (Ed.). (2004). *Inside corporate u: Women in the academy speak out.* Toronto: Sumach Press.
Rhoades, G. (1996). Reorganizing the faculty workforce for flexibility: Part-time professional labour. *Journal of Higher Education, 67*(6), 626-59.
–. (1998). *Managed professionals: Unionized faculty and restructuring academic labour.* Albany: SUNY Press.
Rhoades, G., and Slaughter, S. (1997). Academic capitalism, managed professionals, and supply-side higher education. *Social Text, 51,* 9-38.
Scheurich, J.J., and Young, M. (1997). Coloring epistemologies: Are our research epistemologies racially biased? *Educational Researcher, 26,* 4-16.
Shiva, V. (1995). *Monocultures of the mind: Perspectives on biodiversity and biotechnology.* London: Zed Books.

Shumar, Wesley. (1997). *College for sale: A critique of the commodification of higher education.* London: Falmer Press.

Sokoloff, N. (1992). *Black women and White women in the professions: Occupational segregation by race and gender, 1960-1980.* New York: Routledge.

Slaughter, S., and Leslie, L. (1997). *Academic capitalism: Politics, policies, and the entrepreneurial university.* Baltimore: Johns Hopkins University Press.

Slaughter, S., and Rhoades, G. (2004). *Academic capitalism and the new economy: Markets, state, and higher education.* Baltimore: Johns Hopkins University Press.

Smallman, V. (2006). Personal communication.

Stalker, J., and Prentice, S. (1998). *Illusion of inclusion: Women in post-secondary education.* Halifax: Fernwood Press.

Teeple, G. (2000). *Globalization and the decline of social reform: Into the twenty-first century.* Aurora, ON: Garamond.

6
Reclaiming Our Centre: Toward a Robust Defence of Academic Autonomy

Janice Newson and Claire Polster

Members of the academic profession have become increasingly alarmed about growing infringements on their autonomy. Some believe that these infringements threaten the survival of the profession as "self-governing and self-determining" and undermine its distinctive values, its historically based practices, and the broad social purposes that it serves (Halsey, 1992; McGregor, 1993; Reading, 1996; Vidovich and Currie, 1998). Several developments are blamed for this deteriorating situation. Among them are the displacement of collegial self-governance by managerialism in universities; the application of information technologies to core activities of the academic profession such as teaching and learning; privatization; globalization; neoliberalism and neoconservatism; the growing political power and influence of private sector corporations over government policies; and the economic power of transnational corporations that is embodied in regional trade agreements such as NAFTA and GATT (Currie and Newson, 1998; Newson and Buchbinder, 1988; Polster, 1994; Slaughter and Leslie, 1997; Soley, 1995). Our purpose here is not to scrutinize how these developments contribute to the erosion of the autonomy of the academic profession, important as this may be. Rather, our purpose is to make a strategic intervention into the consideration of how to respond to infringements on academic autonomy in ways that will preserve and strengthen the notion and practice of autonomy itself.

We first assert a version of academic autonomy that is strongly rooted in the idea of serving the public interest. We believe that this notion of autonomy can generate effective strategies that create space in the current context for academics to exercise judgments in keeping with their professional commitments as well as respond to (rather than merely defend from) the pressures, demands, and realignments that are undermining their publicly oriented mission. We then focus on several specific examples to display how the erosion of academic autonomy is taking place at local, national, and international levels. We show that multiple, complex, and often mutually reinforcing pressures rather than a single cause or uniform process underlie the erosion of academic autonomy. Next we discuss both collective and individual strategies employed by academics in response to the lessening of their autonomy. We show how these responses help to construct, at least implicitly, an impoverished and weakened conception of academic autonomy because they fail to articulate with the profession's role of serving the public interest. Finally, to illustrate though not exhaust our call for more effective responses, we propose a basis for constructing alternative strategies that exemplify the conception of academic autonomy that we advance at the beginning.

We are not proposing that academics should or can function under conditions of absolute freedom and control over their own domain of activities. Instead, we view academic autonomy in relative terms as a condition of practice that is shaped by the configuration of social relations, societal pressures, and expectations in effect at specific historical moments. Consequently, rather than viewing academic autonomy as an abstract ideal, we focus on the social relations that support and sustain it. The growing infringements on academic autonomy suggest that these social relations are undergoing changes. We are concerned with how these changes in social relations reposition academic workers and what they imply for the meaning and exercise of academic autonomy.

Toward a Robust Conception of Academic Autonomy

It could be argued that we should support our claim that academic autonomy is being eroded before we assert a more "robust" conception of academic autonomy as the basis for responding to this erosion. To give it centrality, however, we decided to advance our conception of academic autonomy before outlining the problems to which it could be a solution. For one thing, our case does not stand or fall because academic autonomy is currently under threat. Claims to academic autonomy have always been contested to some degree or another, given that they reflect particular configurations of social relations. More importantly, claims to autonomy by definition need to be robust, or they negate and contradict the very values and commitments on which they are based.

We believe that a robust conception of academic autonomy must be firmly rooted in a concern for the public interest. In the closing decades of the twentieth century, as the remantling of the state put into question the continuation of public sector activities of all kinds (Pannu, 1996), professional autonomy was often viewed as nothing more than a self-interested claim to work-related privileges for highly educated workers who, at public expense, exercise a monopoly over the services they provide. This critique demands more than abstract and rhetorical responses. Instead, the extent to which professional autonomy serves and preserves the public interest must be made specific, concrete, and visible.

In asserting the professional claims of academics, the public needs reminding that their own interests are served by the continued exercise of academic autonomy in a myriad of ways. The public's reliance on academic commentary in news reports, uncompromised assessments in drug approval protocols, independent public policy analyses, and scrutiny of political and powerful corporate actors all attest to the importance of a strong and robust exercise of academic autonomy. Moreover, academic knowledge is increasingly being directed toward developing marketable products in areas such as information processing and biological engineering technologies on the grounds that these products can bring about unprecedented improvements in health, human reproduction, quality of life, environmental challenges, and the like. It is therefore vital that the public has access to adequate and uncompromised assessments of these products and promises. In other words, the public needs to understand how infringements on autonomous academic judgment concretely endanger their own interests.

A conception of academic autonomy that strongly preserves and sustains this mission requires the following conditions of practice: the time and space necessary for reflection, evaluation, and judgment based on professional criteria and considerations; a position of disinterest or open-mindedness in which the inquirer is neither guided by preconceptions of the results of the inquiry nor beholden to individuals or groups whose particular interests may be served by research results; and active responsiveness to the public interest.

Unlike other professions that offer services to the public, the academic profession does not have a codified agreement with the state to mediate its relationships with government, industry, local communities, social movements, various types of associations, and the public in general. Rather, the university mediates these relationships to a considerable degree. Consequently, certain kinds of institutional arrangements need to exist inside the university, as well as between the university and its various external constituencies, to practically accomplish the conception of autonomy we have proposed. These arrangements include collegial self-governance within universities to allow academics to develop and apply to their activities criteria of evaluation that are commensurate with their academic/disciplinary/professional judgment; unconditional (i.e., untied) funding (probably therefore "public" funding); active and politically effective professional associations (including learned societies) to enable academics to continually develop, sustain, and preserve their traditions, crafts, skills, and intellectual vitality, to expose themselves to diverse points of view and nurture new ones; and mechanisms that facilitate two-way interchange with, and accountability to, a broad range of publics.

On the surface, our conception of academic autonomy and the conditions required for its practice do not depart from understandings of autonomy that are commonly advanced by academics themselves. We do not claim to be advocating a conception that departs significantly from these taken-for-granted understandings per se. Rather, the distinction lies in our emphasis on practices rather than on states of mind, on concrete social arrangements required to support such practices, and on mechanisms that effectively institute two-way interchange between academics and a diverse public. More importantly, although academics' sense of their autonomy may resonate with the conception we have proposed, this sense is being less realized in practice because the actions and social relations that make it possible are being significantly changed. We will show in the next section how academic autonomy is being narrowed by these changes.

Infringements on Academic Autonomy

Descriptions of infringements on academic autonomy and their implications are available in our own work and in articles and books by other scholars from a number of countries (Currie, 1996; George and McAllister, 1995; Jones, 1996; McGregor, 1993; Newson, 1992, 1994; Polster, 1994, 1996, 2001; Polster and Newson, 1998; Slaughter and Rhoades, 1993; Tapper and Salter, 1995; Vidovich and Currie, 1998). Our concern here is more with the process of erosion, and we use a range of examples, drawn primarily from the Canadian experience, to illustrate several important features of it. First, we show that the erosion of academic autonomy results from multiple causes with multiple effects, which interact with and often reinforce each other. Second, infringements often take place at more than one level (local/institutional, national, and international) sequentially, inter-relatedly, or at the same time (Polster and Newson, 1998). Third, the academic practices being undermined or replaced with new ones are essential practices for exercising the robust conception of academic autonomy that we asserted above. And fourth, the erosion of academic autonomy is not taking place simply because of a consciously co-ordinated power play on the part of university administrators, government bureaucrats, politicians, and industry leaders, even though these agents exercise increasing influence over the practices of academic workers. Rather, the examples reveal that the process of erosion is incremental, consequential, and contingent. It includes micro-practices adopted by individual academics as they "manage" their careers and intellectual commitments as well as the collective practices of academic units and whole institutions as they shape and reshape priorities in their research and teaching programs. Slowly but steadily, changes accumulate and begin to constitute substantial and significant transformations.

The Erosion of Academic Autonomy at the Institutional Level

Inside the university, various practices are being put into place that undermine collegial relations and prevent academics from charting the course of their own work. Our examples focus on ways in which institutional managerialism increasingly substitutes for collegially based methods of decision making.

Modes of Decision Making

Documentary modes of decision making are displacing collegial forms of decision making in universities (Cassin and Morgan, 1992; Newson, 1992). For example, rather than developing university plans and mission statements through traditional channels such as the senate committee structure, proposals are circulated among and responses are solicited from the campus community. On the surface, these new forms of decision making appear to accommodate essential features of academic autonomy: for example, they allow – indeed invite – not only responses based on academic judgment but also responses from interested public constituencies. However, the proposals that are circulated typically originate with the university administration, often in response to initiatives advanced by external bodies like government ministries and funding agencies. Their broad objectives are presented as givens, with little if any opening for academics or public interest groups to shape them or make ultimate decisions about whether such objectives should be pursued at all. Instead, the most that is granted either to academics or to public constituencies is "input" into decision making. Control over the parameters of the debate, the attention given to particular inputs, and the final resolution all rest in the hands of a small, less accessible group of decision makers comprised mostly if not wholly of institutional managers. Moreover, the relatively opaque process precludes open debate and bypasses the more participatory political process that used to be exercised in collegial bodies.

While normal collegial practices are being displaced by new forms of decision making, collegial bodies such as senates, faculty councils, and academic departments are also being bypassed altogether in order to accommodate new "exigencies" of the times, such as reaching out to corporate sponsors for the funding that governments either no longer provide or provide through matched grant programs requiring private sector funding partners. These new forms of university-industry partnerships and contracts are managed by central administration offices and often are negotiated in secret, ostensibly to enable administrators to protect proprietary information and/or seize opportunities that they would miss if they used "cumbersome" collegial processes.[1] Classifying certain issues (e.g., deals that provide companies with exclusive drink sales contracts on campus) as "strictly administrative," so that collegial involvement is deemed unnecessary, is another way of bypassing collegial structures.[2]

New public funding sources like the Canada Foundation for Innovation (CFI) and provincial counterparts like the Ontario Challenge Fund, which promote product-relevant research partnerships, have contributed in additional ways to the erosion of collegial processes in local institutions. Without specifying procedures for allocating and distributing the monies, substantial public funds have been placed in the care of these newly appointed bodies rather than established public granting agencies, which have a long tradition of supporting collegial mechanisms in local institutions. Pressed by the desire to compete effectively with other institutions, many administrations have invented their own approaches to and procedures for selecting areas of emphasis and engaging their researchers in applying for these funds. For example, at some Canadian universities, decisions about the areas to be targeted for CFI support were made by hand-picked committees without widespread consultation of the collegium.

Performance Indicators

The adoption of performance indicators (PIs) by institutions is a second significant way that academic autonomy is being eroded. These indicators introduce new considerations into academics' decisions about what work they will do and how they will do it. In order to acquire the necessary resources and legitimacy for doing their work, academics direct their activities to the performance requirements embedded in these indicators. Individuals and academic units are thereby encouraged, if not forced, to adopt an increasingly calculating, instrumental, and individualized orientation to their work (Taylor, 1999). Rather than embarking on a five-year research project like a book, thus leaving an empty space on the annual evaluation form for four years, an academic may decide to write one article for each of five years. Alternatively, academics may be less inclined to engage in activities that are not readily accountable through performance measures or are not assigned scores that are high enough to make the effort worthwhile. Newer faculty are particularly susceptible to this micro-management of their work activities because they are getting careers under way and cannot easily afford to give up the benefits associated with institutionally rewarded performances, particularly if they have yet to face assessments of their work for a tenure file.

The realignment of the approaches that academics take to their work in response to PIs may jeopardize both their own and the university's ability to serve the public interest. Performance-based measures can undermine the development of a productive and supportive institutional culture and thus prevent the institution from responding effectively to some of the public interest demands that are being made on it. When the acceptable "rate" of performance over a given time period is used as a feedback mechanism, productivity can be impeded as much as enhanced. In order to withstand or to negotiate some degree of control over work pressures, academics individually and collectively are motivated to adopt strategies for controlling their performance rates so that they will not set themselves up to perform at an equal or even greater rate at a future point. These strategic responses to performance indicators also intensify fractiousness and competition among colleagues and academic units precisely at a time when more collaborative, co-operative, and interdisciplinary ways of working, which are believed to be more suitable to producing socially beneficial knowledge, are being called for.

Finally, performance indicators also debilitate academics' morale, which, along with the divisiveness and competitiveness mentioned above, undermines their ability to work together to resist infringements on their autonomy and to convince the public that such infringements pose a threat to the public interest. Measuring their performance and linking their motivation to concrete rewards suggest both to academics and to the public that, unless they are continually called to account for what they do, academics cannot be trusted to do worthwhile work, or judge what is worthwhile and of high priority to do, or even work at all without the promise of particular rewards. In a subtle way, the use of these indicators invites the public to doubt the basis for granting academic autonomy at the very time that academics need the support of the public to help challenge the actions of governments and other bodies that are preventing them from pursuing their public mission.

The Erosion of Academic Autonomy at the National Level

Many of the changes that have led to infringements on academic autonomy can be traced to the underfunding of universities and academic research by governments at both national and provincial levels. In Canada, for example, the share of total federal spending on transfers to postsecondary education has fallen by 50 percent since 1979-80 (Ministry of Advanced Education, Training, and Technology, 1999). Underfunding in itself, however, does not necessitate that limitations be imposed on academic autonomy. Instead, it is a condition that permits, or is coincident with, related developments that in turn bear on the exercise of academic autonomy. Here we use examples to illustrate two such developments at the national level: new ways of intervening "from the outside" in the internal affairs of local universities, and the reduced effectiveness of national bodies that have historically helped to preserve and sustain academic autonomy.[3]

Targeted and Partnership Funding

While both direct and indirect government support for researcher-initiated research is diminishing, support for targeted research is expanding (Kurland, 1997; Polster, 1994). As a consequence, academic researchers are less able to do the kind of research that they want to do and are compelled to orient their research to issues for which funding has been targeted. The increased emphasis on partnership research in both federally and provincially funded programs has similar implications for the exercise of academic autonomy. Not only are external groups (mostly governments and corporations) shaping the general areas in which research will be supported, but they are also defining the parameters of entire research projects, imposing upon academics what research will be done as well as deciding the conditions under which it will be done. It is increasingly common for industrial partners to oblige academics to work in secret, to delay publication while intellectual property rights are secured, and even to obtain permission from the funder to publish the research at all (Zinberg, 1991).

In addition, partnership research limits the practice and scope of academic autonomy in a number of other ways. Partners and the academics working with them often acquire new kinds of leverage within university structures (e.g., on hiring and curriculum committees), giving them greater institutional power than they might otherwise have in collegially governed bodies (Newson, 1993). Evidence of this kind of "purchased leverage" is hard to come by because signed contracts between universities and corporate clients are routinely classified as "proprietary" and thus confidential, a practice that in itself points to the erosion of institutional democracy, since such arrangements would once have been publicly debated in collegially governed academic bodies.

Also, while it is argued that partnership funding encourages universities to initiate research that is relevant and responsive to societal issues, it in fact encourages universities to focus more narrowly on the needs and interests of the business community and other financially well-endowed potential partners. Universities create linking mechanisms such as industrial liaison offices to attract and sustain partners that almost exclusively focus on partnering relationships with industry – and not with social groups that have less access to financial resources. At the same time, academics who wish to respond to the needs and interests of other groups are inhibited from doing so because there are less institutional resources to support this kind of work.

Both targeted and partnership research erode academic autonomy in the longer term as well by limiting the kinds of training available to graduate students, especially in the natural sciences, where they apprentice with faculty members who have sufficient research grants to support graduate assistants. The restriction of their training in turn restricts their "choices" of the kind of work they will do when they become academics. Perhaps more importantly, it also shapes their emerging professional identities as "entrepreneurial" academics with an eye to profit making rather than as public-serving intellectuals (Crouch, 1990, 1991).

Professional Associations

Strong professional associations are key to academic autonomy. Among other things, they are important forums within which the profession can talk to itself and thus sustain a conception of its mission and develop strategies to accomplish and protect it. Increasingly, however, the financial and political support for these organizations is being eroded. Government funding for them is diminishing. Indeed, in 1995, the Social Sciences and Humanities Research Council of Canada announced that it would be phasing out all core funding for individual scholarly associations as well as for national associations of the humanities and social sciences (SSHRCC, 1995, pp. 7-8). As well, because service to these organizations tends to count for relatively little in academic performance reviews, fewer academics are taking the time, or feel that they can afford the time, to work on them. Both because of financial pressures and less active and involved memberships, collective resistance to the erosion of academic autonomy is not being exercised. Even if they are aware of the attendant dangers and should wish to do otherwise, these associations are increasingly focusing on their survival in the face of decreased funding rather than on more complex issues affecting their members, such as performance indicators and intellectual property regimes. This shift contributes to declining commitment on the part of academics to these organizations, and their strength deteriorates further.[4]

Government is not only reducing or eliminating the funding of these organizations but also reducing their role in its own policy-making processes. In fact, a startling difference in the way that governments now formulate policies bearing on universities compared to two decades ago is that groups like professional and learned associations are marginalized if not excluded from the process, while other groups, such as those that represent the corporate sector, have moved into an "inside track" (Polster, 1994, Chapter 2).

The Erosion of Academic Autonomy at the International Level

Many of the incursions on academic autonomy that we addressed above are happening not only within Canada but also within many other countries. Although the same processes are taking place in many countries (and the actual forms that these incursions take, such as performance indicators, are also being developed and refined through international discussions (Lingard and Rizvi, 1998; Polster and Newson, 1998), their main impetus is through circumstances or forces that are national in scope. Increasingly, however, the ability of academics to autonomously define the course of their own work is being limited through developments that are international in scope. Below we provide two examples.

Intellectual Property Regimes

The development and extension of international (and national) intellectual property regimes (IPRs) are increasingly restricting academic autonomy. As more knowledge becomes the private property of individuals and organizations, access to the resources that academics need to do their work is reduced, and their means for gaining that access further restrict their autonomy. For example, it is becoming more common for corporate owners of intellectual property (IP) to allow academics access to that IP in exchange for previews of their research findings or first rights of refusal on the intellectual property resulting from their research (Marshall, 1997). Not only are traditional academic practices (e.g., freely disseminating research results) and academic autonomy in general thereby curtailed, but the privatization of knowledge, which renders academics vulnerable to the demands of IP owners in the first place, is further advanced as well.

The development and extension of IPRs also increase pressures on, and incentives for, academics to produce intellectual property of their own. These pressures and incentives may reduce academic responsiveness to social interests and needs, particularly if the latter appear to have no "intellectual property potential." They also open up the potential for all sorts of abuses of the public trust and betrayals of the public interest (Noble, 1993). Accordingly, the basis upon which academics claim autonomy becomes less credible, and that autonomy is further imperilled. In the long term, the development and extension of IPRs may threaten academic autonomy even more fundamentally. The very mission of the academic profession is the free pursuit and dissemination of knowledge. No public knowledge means no academic profession and by association no liberal university, at least as we know it today.

It is worth noting that IPRs are connected to and may intensify some of the specific incursions on academic autonomy previously discussed. For example, the development of IP is weighted – some would argue disproportionately – as a significant factor in performance assessments by universities and government funded bodies. In some protocols, obtaining a patent is one of the most highly scored measures of performance (Taylor, 1999). University efforts to promote the development of IP also help to undermine collegial decision making, insofar as the contractual and legal arrangements for licensing and patent agreements are undertaken by a special arm of the central administration, often under the cloak of confidentiality. Moreover, large sums of money from overstretched university operating funds are being allocated to technology transfer offices and legal fees that necessarily accompany IP development, monies that might otherwise be used to embark on activities that respond to a more broadly defined sense of the public interest than the advancement of private businesses.

Information Technology

The implications of information technology (IT) for the university and the academic profession are multiple and far reaching (Newson, 1995). A few points regarding its implications specifically for academic autonomy are worth noting. First, even though the implications for the academic profession and academic autonomy are declared to be potentially transformative, in most countries the wiring of universities has been presented by administrators as necessary if not inevitable rather than as an option to be debated and discussed. In addition to the politics of how it is being inserted into academics' work practices, the application of IT to academic work also erodes autonomy in several respects. For instance, the pressure on academics to make themselves available to students online reduces their ability to organize and control their working lives: it effectively places them permanently "on call." Perhaps of greatest concern is the rapid expansion of online education, which involves the delivery of prepackaged, mass-produced courses. This development erodes academic autonomy by removing from individual academics control over course content and teaching methods (Noble, 1998a).

Second, and more troubling, is the potential of online education to further fragment or to tier the academic profession, producing an underclass of academics who are not directly involved in the production of knowledge, only in the transmission of knowledge produced by others. While the more dire consequences may fall to academics belonging to this new "underclass," this fragmentation is potentially harmful to all academics, regardless of their place in this emerging hierarchy. Further fragmentation of the profession may intensify conflicts of interest between various classes of academics, which may reduce the profession's ability to collectively and effectively resist further incursions on its autonomy.

And third, the intense competition taking place among institutions to offer their own version of online or virtual university programs escalates the effects of other threats to academic autonomy that we have discussed. On the one hand, universities are making themselves, and their resources of knowledge and skills, even more accessible to corporate sector "partners" in the software and communications industries in order to acquire and maintain the expensive technological equipment that their tight budgets cannot afford.[5] These partnership agreements cede much control over the content and methodology of teaching to the corporate partners, if not directly then through the constraints imposed by the technological formats: academics are reduced to being "talking heads" or tour guides of multimedia mazes. On the other hand, universities are also engaged, either as partners of private corporations or as educational corporations of their own, in converting courses, course designs, and course materials into intellectual property. Some university administrations are aggressively asserting their ownership of academic teaching materials, while in response academics are seeking to retain control over the use of their own course materials by resorting to copyright (Noble, 1998a, 1998b). The "technology turn" is thus dramatically upping the ante in the struggle to define ownership of intellectual property, which in turn transforms academics' exercise of their autonomy.

Responses to the Erosion of Academic Autonomy

Important as it is to understand the multiple ways in which academic autonomy is being infringed upon, it is equally important to consider the effects of the strategies that academics are employing to respond to these infringements. We mean neither to question the motives of the academics who employ these strategies nor to be disrespectful of them. On the contrary, we are concerned that, in spite of their good intentions, the academic profession is being pulled off its centre by engaging in these strategies and is intensifying the threat to its autonomy.

As already illustrated, individual responses to specific infringements often become steps in an accumulating series of actions and counteractions that further restrict their choices and limit the exercise of their professional judgment. More significantly, the overall effect of many responses is to construct a weakened conception of academic autonomy, which is less if at all responsive to the public interest. To demonstrate our points, we examine several examples of actions being taken, first by organizations and collective bodies that represent the interests and perspectives of academics, and second by academics individually.

Institutional/Associational Responses

Guidelines and Model Clauses

One strategy pursued by organizations that represent the professional interests of academics has been to develop guidelines and model clauses for responding to such things as corporate-university partnerships, performance-based assessments, and online and technologically enhanced instruction. This strategy specifies the "conditions of practice" that should prevail as these new relationships and methodologies are put in place in local institutions. They help academics and their faculty associations to determine on a case-by-case basis whether a particular development infringes or does not infringe on academic autonomy, and they specify the arrangements that would have to be negotiated to ensure that infringements do not take place.

Although the stated intention is to protect academic freedom and university autonomy, this approach often sidesteps important elements of a robust conception of academic autonomy. It tends to narrow the scope of academic freedom and autonomy to individual cases and individual academics rather than affirming that academic freedom requires conditions of practice that apply to the overall context in which academic work is carried out. For example, guidelines on university-corporate collaborations that focus on particular instances and on the relationship between the corporate client and the particular academics who are directly involved in the partnership fail to address implications of the specific partnership, or of corporate-university partnerships in general, for entire academic units, institutions, and the academic profession as a whole.

Yet the implications of partnership contracts are not limited to the individual academics involved. Rather, they have complex and far-reaching consequences for other colleagues and the institution as a whole. They set precedents with which other academics will be expected to comply. In a collective bargaining context, they may also become the "past practice" that sets the standard for assessing the rights and obligations of all bargaining unit members. Funds that are allocated to manage these partnerships are not then available for other activities, and collegial practices may be compromised, as in the case of funded chairs where the corporate funder acquires a role in hiring. Moreover, because these contracts are often confidential to those directly involved, the broader implications may not be known to those whom they effect. As such, the latter have no way of addressing issues that may limit their academic freedom and autonomy.

Most importantly, the guidelines and model clause strategy encourages an individual rather than collective conception of academic freedom and autonomy almost by definition. After all, the conditions of practice that they specify apply to a process in which the arrangements between the academic researcher and the corporate clients are customized through a specific contract. These contracts "contract out" from arrangements that collective bodies have developed and believe to be necessary for the exercise of academic autonomy as well as from collective agreements negotiated on behalf of the faculty as a whole.

In fact, guidelines and model clauses may actually facilitate and even legitimize developments such as university-corporate partnerships, performance-based assessments, and online teaching that have far-reaching implications for the academic profession. Insofar as their checklists of conditions can serve equally well as a "how to" as a "not to" prescription, they as much permit such developments to proceed as they prevent excesses and protect "bottom line" concerns. Rather than addressing whether or not these developments should be supported under any conditions, they instead concede that they may proceed as long as the professional interests of the academics involved are preserved. They thereby fail to give practical force to the notion of the public interest that may be at stake in these developments and thus reinforce the perception that the academic profession is concerned only with protecting the particular rights and privileges of its own members.

Although the guidelines and model clause strategy is arguably a stop-gap measure in the short run, it surrenders to a conception of academic autonomy that is impoverished in several ways. It undermines collective processes of defining and protecting academic autonomy. It is permissive toward the larger processes that are threatening academic autonomy. It also accepts secrecy in negotiating arrangements that affect the professional, as well as public, interests that academic autonomy serves.

Maintaining Institutional Balance

Some university administrations and collegial bodies are promoting the principle of "institutional balance" as a means of addressing some of the threats to autonomy that we described in the previous section. It is based on the assumption that academic autonomy can be effectively preserved if such things as corporate funding and online instruction are kept within limits and the other, more traditional, means of supporting and delivering university activities are retained to at least an equal degree.

On the surface, institutional balance appears to provide universities and academics with a reasonable and prudent approach to protecting academic autonomy because it allows them to be responsive within limits to government and private sector initiatives. Important elements of academic autonomy, however, are in danger of being undermined or sacrificed by adopting this strategy. Maintaining an appropriate "balance" between activities that serve the purposes of private sector donors and those that serve more traditional purposes typically involves a calculation of the aggregate number of corporate funded projects or the total corporate funds that support activities in a specific department, faculty, or institution. What is not assessed are the specific implications of each project individually for autonomy. Funding relationships that bring in small corporate donations can have consequences for academic autonomy that are as great as, or greater than, those of much larger donations. (The fact that the "loan" of state-of-the-art performance equipment to McGill University in Montreal was secured in exchange for a position for the donor on the curriculum committee of the Faculty of Fine Arts illustrates the point; see Newson, 1998.) Moreover, "institutional balance" does not take into account that marginal financing can secure considerable "leverage" over university affairs, as Gareth Williams has noted. In arguing that lower levels of government funding will not eliminate the government's ability to influence the direction of university activities, Williams emphasizes that "relatively small amounts of expenditure can exert powerful leverage if they are strategically used and sharply focused" (1992, p. 23). Although he fails to acknowledge that the same argument about leverage applies equally well to private sector funding of universities, his point clearly challenges the assumption that maintaining "balance" in funding arrangements protects universities and academics from infringements on their autonomy. Similarly, "institutional balance" is by no means a feasible response to the threats to autonomy posed by the increasing application of technological enhancements in university teaching. To offer even a few online courses, expensive and extensive technological adaptations are necessary, thus disproportionately drawing limited funds away from more traditional forms of instruction. Moreover, once having made the investments, cash-strapped universities will attempt to recover and justify these costs by encouraging even more online courses.

Finally, the assumption is problematic in itself that balance per se ensures that academic autonomy will not be unduly compromised. If even a handful of academics serve as "hired hands" for corporate sponsors or as entrepreneurial professors appropriating public funds to advance their own financial interests, the credibility and effectiveness of the more publicly oriented activities carried out by other academics are undermined. In fact, the very policies that have encouraged academics and universities to pursue mutually lucrative university-corporate partnerships have, at the same time, served to justify the increased monitoring and auditing of academics' activities by administrative and external bodies. In the United States, the activities of a minority of university administrations and researchers ultimately led to congressional hearings and the imposition of "conflict of interest" guidelines to ensure that the public trust would not be violated. The potential for some academics and some institutions to adopt overly self-interested and profit-oriented motivations and practices has encouraged the view that the academic profession as a whole is either unable or unwilling to protect the public interest and has resulted in further infringements on the autonomy and judgment of all academics and all institutions.

Thus, like the guidelines and model clause strategy, the principle of institutional balance contributes to a diminished version of academic autonomy: quantitative and technical judgments substitute for academic and professional judgments; the protection and preservation of the public interest are no longer seen to be secured through unconditional funding; and the concession is made that academics are unable to govern themselves and to be publicly accountable.

Sanctuaries

A third organizational response to the multiple infringements on academic autonomy is creating spaces – either programs, subsets of programs, colleges, faculties, or entire institutions – that allow some academic work to proceed under the social relations and conditions that prevailed before the changes we have been describing took place. In fact, proponents of sanctuary programs often boast that faculty members are guaranteed "academic autonomy" unaffected by the infringements. For instance, internal decisions about course offerings, academic objectives, and pedagogies are apparently based on uncompromised collegial processes.

This response also fails in a number of ways to address the underlying pressures that contribute to the narrowing and erosion of academic autonomy. Perhaps more than the other responses, it also helps to legitimate them. First and most obvious is the elitist and exclusionary effects of this strategy: by definition, only a limited group of students and faculty members are able to participate in it. But more insidious than exclusiveness itself is the implication that both the faculty and student participants enjoy academic autonomy by "special arrangement" rather than conceiving of autonomy as the normative condition under which all academic work is accomplished.

Moreover, creating special preserves that maintain the traditional conditions and social arrangements for doing academic work in the public interest abandons the rest of higher education to the many private uses that we have described. Regardless of intentions, this give-away of a publicly funded resource in itself represents a profound betrayal of the public trust on which academic autonomy is based. Perhaps most alarming is that this strategy encourages blindness toward what is happening in the rest of the institution or system of higher education as well as toward the limitations to which even sanctuaries are subject. Although the preserved space may be empowered to determine its internal practices, it does not have the ability to prescribe the parameters under which it continues to function. The sanctuary approach thus helps to institutionalize an ineffective and impoverished conception of academic autonomy, even more because proponents often represent themselves as taking a strong and uncompromising stand toward the developments that pose threats to academic autonomy.

Individual Responses

As well as through collective organizations, academics are individually changing their practices and adopting a range of personal strategies in response to infringements on their autonomy. To illustrate, we briefly elaborate on three types of individual responses to separate but related infringements, each of which mutually reinforces the others.

Retreating from Collegialism

Because of the decreasing institutional influence of collegial mechanisms (Newson, 1992; Taylor, 1999; Vidovich and Currie, 1998), the investment of time and energy in collegial bodies and activities is being viewed by many academics as yielding diminishing returns. Rather than revitalizing these mechanisms, they are retreating into a more limited conception of their work, such as concentrating on research, teaching, and other projects (often entrepreneurial) over which they feel they have more control. These choices, however, further diminish their autonomy because the space in which they carry out their more narrowly defined activities is very much shaped by decisions taken in the "bureaucratic sphere" that they abandon. Hence, their ability to do the kinds of teaching and research work that they want continually diminishes in proportion to their abdication of collegial mechanisms that are the means available to them to shape the broader contexts of their work. Moreover, as academics try to acquire additional resources for their work by putting their energy into projects that administrations or corporate sponsors wish to promote (e.g., the development of online courses in exchange for a "reduced teaching load"), less of their energy and fewer resources are available for the collective projects of collegial units.

Adjusting to Declining Resources

As argued previously, declining levels and reallocations of government funding as well as intellectual property rights that increase private ownership of knowledge are reducing access to the knowledge that academics need to conduct their research. Rather than collectively resisting these trends, many academics are accommodating them. For example, they are tailoring their research interests to the needs of external sponsors or making deals with the owners of knowledge (e.g., signing over their own rights to the knowledge resulting from their research) in order to gain free access to the knowledge they need. While these strategies may enable selected academics to do research in the short term, they do nothing to halt the overall reduced access to resources that would allow them to autonomously define and conduct their work. Instead, such strategies further promote changes in the social relations through which funding and knowledge resources are being distributed, and they advance the privatization of knowledge that impedes the free pursuit and dissemination of knowledge.

Proving One's Value

Growing demands on academics to demonstrate that they are producing value for money is a third manifestation of their declining autonomy. Rather than resisting and critiquing the narrow, utilitarian conception of academic work inherent in these demands, many individual academics are accepting, even promoting, the use of performance indicators as a legitimate means of "proving" their worth and showing that they deserve financial support. However, compliance with performance indicators acquiesces to and reinforces a weakened conception of academic autonomy. Performance indicators introduce external and limited criteria into the evaluation of academic work (Polster and Newson, 1998). They may also reduce the quality of the work that academics produce by encouraging them to undertake projects and approaches because they are more likely to produce tangible outcomes or deliverables rather than because they are intrinsically important or valuable (Taylor, 1999). As well, academics may become less responsive to social groups and social needs that are more difficult to meet or are less recognized as having value. As academics increasingly orient what they actually do to what they can show they are doing, they undermine justifications for their autonomy that are based on the quality of their work and their responsiveness to the public. Thus, once again, rather than protecting their autonomy, their responses as individuals open it up to greater challenge and further erosion.

Conclusion

Many of the current responses to the multiple infringements on academic autonomy are problematic for a number of reasons. They tend to shift the focus of academic autonomy from the collective to the individual. They concede that judgments and evaluations of academic quality and content can be based on other than intellectual, professional, or publicly oriented criteria. They also promote a model of academic autonomy, which tends to represent academic freedom and university autonomy as professional entitlements failing to make visible how academic autonomy serves the public interest. Even though they may have some short-term utility, these responses constitute a weak and politically ineffective response to the pressures that actually underlie infringements on academic autonomy. At the same time, they reflect, reinforce, and may even generate pressures that lead to the further lessening of autonomy and public trust.

But perhaps most significant is that these responses proceed from a fundamentally defensive position. Rather than being rooted in a robust conception of academic autonomy, the responses we have described are reactive, fragmented, and aimed at the symptoms of the erosion of academic autonomy rather than the underlying processes through which it is being accomplished. An analogy to chess may clarify why this is problematic. As chess players know, if they play simply in response to their opponents' moves, they are ultimately destined to lose the game. In contrast, when their play is centred on a clear vision of what they want to accomplish, they have a basis from which to respond effectively to their opponents' moves in an integrated way and to work creatively toward the achievement of their own goals.

How might we then begin to develop offensive responses to replace the more defensive ones that we have examined? We do not intend to answer this question with a program for action that lists specific rules or recipes to follow in specific cases or formulae that help to determine the appropriate responses to particular kinds of infringements. We have several reasons for not answering in this way.

First, rules and formulae cannot be created to cover all the particulars of specific situations. Second, defined responses to particular kinds of situations tend to require specific and legalistic definitions of academic rights and responsibilities and of the specific conditions to which they apply, thus inadvertently limiting the scope of academic autonomy. Third, whether by administrations and governments that wish to promote developments that lead to infringements on autonomy or by professional associations and individual academics who are trying to limit and contain these infringements, the increasing proliferation of rules that segmentalize, regulate, and micromanage academic workers' activities only contributes to deepening the crisis around academic autonomy. In other words, we believe that attempts to protect academic autonomy through regulation will only further erode it. Far more desirable and effective would be for individuals and groups to be able to "customize" their own responses to the particular cases in which they are involved, based on a collective sense of academic autonomy that they share with professional colleagues as well as the public that they serve. To have such a sense requires not rules, codes, and guidelines but a living academic culture that consistently supports and advocates commitments, values, and practices that are commensurate with the profession's purposes and mission. This is not to say that universities and academics should never produce rules, codes, and guidelines to inform their actions. It is rather to say that such objectified forms of consciousness (Smith, 1987) cannot substitute for, or sustain by themselves, the vibrant academic culture that we have in mind. Indeed, such rules, codes, and guidelines may only serve academic and the public's interests if they develop from within, and are continually transformed by, a vibrant academic culture. To have such a culture means that the culture that academics currently share must be revitalized to face the many pressures that currently threaten its survival. Such revitalization must also involve a refinement of the academic mission in relation to the pressing issues of our times. We have not been able to address the issue of the academic mission in any detail here, although our conception of academic autonomy clearly implies a particular conception of that mission as well. One urgent focus is to collectively revitalize the conception of academic autonomy and to move from a more robust conception to resist the multiple incursions being made into it. This is the first and most important strategic move that the academic profession must make. Once we are clearly and firmly rooted within such a conception, the specific steps that we need to take to defend our autonomy in our particular institutions will become clear.

The trick is to agree on and to remain grounded in a conception of academic autonomy that guides our collective and individual responses to its erosion. Toward that end, we offer two suggestions. First, as academics, we should not let ourselves off the hook and push this issue aside in order to deal with the many other demands we have upon us, which stem in large part from our continually putting this issue aside. Instead, we must spend time thinking and talking with colleagues as well as interested and concerned members of the public, wherever we find them, about what a more robust conception and practice of academic autonomy would involve. Second, academics need to engage in more collective thinking and action on this issue, perhaps through initiating discussions on academic autonomy in various professional associations that, in turn, could begin to generate among academics and their associations, in as many national and local contexts as possible, a shared conception of the principles and conditions that are basic to the practice of a sufficient and necessary degree of autonomy. This would be valuable given that the problems we have addressed in this chapter are rapidly becoming endemic to academic experiences across the globe. Academics must not underestimate the importance, indeed the urgency, of this mobilization. Unless we take the time to seriously address these issues, the university as an institution may continue to survive, but academic autonomy and the academic profession itself may not.

Notes

This chapter is reprinted with permission from *Science Studies, 14*(1) (2001), 55-75.

1 The attempt in the early 1990s to locate the International Space University at York University was an illustration of this (see Newson, 1998). More recently, controversy and political dissent have also emerged at long-established institutions like the University of Toronto and McGill University because of uncollegial and secretive decisions taken by university administrators to accept funds from corporate donors.

2 It is worth noting that such deals erode university autonomy in a number of respects. Two examples illustrate the point. Recently, at a conference at McMaster University in Canada, a student who hosted a program on the campus radio station reported that he was engaged in an on-air critical discussion of the practices of a particular fast-food corporation that had a licence to operate food outlets on campus. The discussion was interrupted by his producer, who informed him that he needed to be mindful of that particular corporation's commercial relationship with the university, which might preclude him from being critical. As it turned out, no such formal prohibitions existed, but it is noteworthy that the producer thought that they should act on this presumption. Controversy has also arisen in a midwestern university in the United States concerning a commercial agreement with Nike that precludes public criticism of its sports products. The implications for academic autonomy are obvious if and when universities engaged in such arrangements also conduct research in relevant areas such as, in these cases, food safety and kinesthetics.

3 In addition to the example we provide below, the imposition of national codes of conduct on academics, such as the Tricouncil Code of Ethics with which Canadian academics and universities are now forced to comply on pain of sanction, is a relatively new, and potentially significant, form of restricting academic autonomy "from the outside."

4 Our comments are primarily based on the annual meetings, policy initiatives, and committee reports of our own Learned Society as well as those of the newly merged Humanities and Social Sciences Federation of Canada.

5 One example involves the entire California State University system, with four large multinational high-tech software and communications companies that have been willing to "foot the bill" for the CSU system's technological upgrade in exchange for an astounding degree of control over and ownership of intellectual property. The deal has been contested as monopolistic and contrary to public interest and has even involved legislative intervention (as reported at the Digital Diploma Mills? A Second Look at Information Technology in Higher Education conference, Harvey Mudd College, 23-26 April 1998).

References

Cassin, M., and Morgan, J.G. (1992). The professoriate and the market-driven university: Transforming the control of work in the academy. In W.K. Carroll (Ed.), *Fragile truths: Twenty-five years of sociology and anthropology in Canada* (pp. 247-60). Ottawa: Carleton University Press.

Crouch, M. (1990). Debating the responsibilities of plant scientists in the decade of the environment. *Plant Cell, 2,* 275-77.

–. (1991). Confessions of a botanist. *New Internationalist, 217,* 21.

Currie, J. (1996). The effects of globalisation on 1990s academics in greedy institutions: Over-worked, stressed-out, and demoralised. *Melbourne Studies of Education, 37*(2), 101-28.

Currie, J., and Newson, J. (Eds.). (1998). *Universities and globalization: Critical perspectives.* Thousand Oaks, CA: Sage.

George, P.G., and McAllister, G.A. (1995). The expanding role of the state in Canadian universities: Can university autonomy and accountability be reconciled? *Higher Education Management, 7*(3), 309-27.

Halsey, A.H. (1992). *The decline of donnish dominion.* Oxford: Oxford University Press.

Jones, P. (1996). Time for charters of collegial autonomy. *Campus Review,* 8.

Kurland, C.G. (1997). Beating scientists into plowshares. *Science, 276,* 761-62.

Lingard, R., and Rizvi, F. (1998). Globalization, the OECD, and Australian higher education. In J. Currie and J. Newson (Eds.), *Universities and globalization: Critical perspectives* (pp. 257-74). Thousand Oaks, CA: Sage.

Marshall, E. (1997). Need a reagent? Just sign here. *Science, 278,* 212-13.

McGregor, G. (1993). On the nature and scope of university autonomy: Minimal, precarious, and vital. *British Journal of Educational Studies, 41*(1), 46-55.

Ministry of Advanced Education, Training, and Technology. (1999). Federal spending on post-secondary education. http://www.aett.gov.bc.ca/policy/.

Newson, J. (1992). The decline of faculty influence: Confronting the effects of the corporate agenda. In W.K. Carroll (Ed.), *Fragile truths: Twenty-five years of sociology and anthropology in Canada* (pp. 227-46). Ottawa: Carleton University Press.

–. (1993). The service university. *Our Schools/Our Selves, 4*(2), 40-44.

–. (1994). Subordinating democracy: The effects of fiscal retrenchment and university-business partnerships on knowledge creation and dissemination in universities. *Higher Education, 27,* 141-61.

–. (1995). Technopedagogy: A critical evaluation of the effects on academic staff of computerized instructional technologies in higher education. *Higher Education Policy, 7,* 37-40.

–. (1998). The corporate linked university: From social project to market force. *Canadian Journal of Communication, 23,* 107-24.

Newson, J., and Buchbinder, H. (1988). *The university means business: Universities, corporations, and academic work.* Toronto: Garamond Press.

Noble, D.F. (1993). Insider trading – university style. *Our Schools/Our Selves, 4*(2), 45-52.

–. (1998a). Digital diploma mills: The automation of higher education. *Firstmonday, 3*(1), 1-13.

–. (1998b). Digital diploma mills: Part 2. *CAUT Bulletin, 45*(8), 5, 8.

Pannu, R. (1996). Neoliberal project of globalization: Prospects for democratization of education. *Alberta Journal of Educational Research, 42*(2), 87-101.

Polster, C. (1994). *Compromising positions: The federal government and the reorganization of the social relations of Canadian academic research.* Unpublished doctoral dissertation, York University, Toronto.

–. (1996). Dismantling the liberal university: The state's new approach to academic research. In R. Brecher, Q. Fleischmann, and J. Halliday (Eds.), *The university in a liberal state* (pp. 106-21). Aldershot, UK: Avebury Press.

–. (2001). How the law works: Exploring the implications of emerging intellectual property regimes for knowledge, economy, and society. In K. Adhikary and A. Sales (Eds.), *Perspectives on knowledge economy and society: Sage Studies in International Sociology monograph issue, Current Sociology, 49*(4), 85-100.

Polster, C., and Newson, J. (1998). Don't count your blessings: The social accomplishments of performance indicators. In J. Currie and J. Newson (Eds.), *Universities and globalization: Critical perspectives* (pp. 173-92). Thousand Oaks, CA: Sage.

Reading, W. (1996). The university in ruins. Boston: Harvard University Press.

Slaughter, S., and Leslie, L. (1997). Academic capitalism: Politics, policies, and the entrepreneurial university. Baltimore: Johns Hopkins University Press.

Slaughter, S., and Rhoades, G. (1993). Changes in intellectual property statutes and policies at a public university: Revising the terms of professional labor. *Higher Education, 26,* 287-312.

Smith, D. (1987). *The everyday world as problematic: A feminist sociology.* Toronto: University of Toronto Press.

Social Sciences and Humanities Research Council of Canada. (1995). Budget cuts affect SSHRC's programs. *SSHRC News, 7*(8), 7-8.

Soley, L. (1995). *Leasing the ivory tower: The corporate takeover of academia.* Boston: South End Press.

Tapper, E., and Salter, B. (1995). The changing idea of university autonomy. *Studies in Higher Education, 20*(1), 59-71.

Taylor, J. (1999). *The impact of performance indicators on the work of university academics: A study of four Australian universities.* Unpublished doctoral dissertation, Murdoch University, Perth, Australia.

Vidovich, L., and Currie, J. (1998). Changing accountability and autonomy at the "coalface" of academic work in Australia. In J. Currie and J. Newson (Eds.), *Universities and globalization: Critical perspectives* (pp. 153-72). Thousand Oaks, CA: Sage.

Williams, G. (1992, 14 July). What price market forces in the quality stakes? *Manchester Guardian,* p. 23.

Zinberg, D. (1991). The changing university: How increased demand for scientists and technology is transforming academic institutions internationally. Dordrecht, Netherlands: Kluwer Academic Publishers.

7

"Gender at Work" in Teacher Education: History, Society, and Global Reform

Jo-Anne Dillabough and Sandra Acker

Throughout his working life, the French sociologist Pierre Bourdieu remained dedicated to an understanding and elaboration of "the constancy of the structure of the relation of domination between men and women which is maintained beyond the *substantive* differences in conditions linked to moments in history and positions in social space" (2001, p. 102). Bourdieu's commitment to an analysis of the "constancy of the structure" has most typically been labelled by sociologists as a critical modern concern associated with the reproduction of social inequality in state institutions (e.g., the academy) where Bourdieu relies substantially upon a class and labour theory of the state. In the years before his death, he not only widened this theoretical remit but also returned (after some years of avoiding any discussion of gender) to questions about gender and their cultural manifestations in institutional life. In so doing, he gave particular attention to some of the enduring symbolic and ritualistic elements of inequality associated with the gendered division of labour under the dynamics of global change. In this chapter, we focus upon both the enduring features of gender relations in higher education and some of the newly reconfigured elements of the gendered division of labour as a cultural response to global reforms, with a particular focus on women teacher educators.

In so doing, we wish to identify the various invested sites of meaning that women academics attribute to their work in periods of substantial global reform and change, which can be seen here as both enduring and quite new (see Skeggs, 1995). We also wish to explore how broader neoliberal ideals (e.g., notions of the autonomous worker) – as central to the global reform movement – insinuate themselves into academic women's lives, experiences, and accounts of a professional "self" in what Bourdieu (1998) calls the "social work"[1] disciplines/professions. We are principally concerned with the part played by gender in mediating the effects of such regulatory controls cross-nationally and their impact on the construction of female work in a professional discipline with a history of institutionalizing female labour, in this case teacher education. Accordingly, we reiterate Bourdieu's (1998) commitment to theorizing globalization as both a social process and a structure, which is manifest in the operational and discursive practices of professions themselves (Adkins, 1997; Dale, 1997; Reay, 2000). We also wish to understand how transnational reforms regulate and reproduce the gendered division of labour over time and serve as one "strategic nexus" (Bourdieu, 1992) and enduring symbolic apparatus that ultimately support the development and successful execution of global reforms in higher education.

We focus on both macro- and micro-elements of contemporary change in the academy. This dual focus is pursued by drawing upon the localized experiences of a sample of women academics working at different levels of the professional hierarchy in faculties of education in the United Kingdom and Canada as well as by addressing macro-elements of institutional change that influence their work. For example, we consider the impact of public sector regulation[2] on women's experiences of work and professionalism to be a response to larger, global restructuring trends. Our particular concern is with features of academe such as intensified research cultures, assessments of professionalism, and fiscal restraints and their role in shaping contemporary female work in teacher education. The central question we address is what do women's accounts of work in changing teacher education contexts reveal about the relationship between women's position as workers and "professionals" and the institutional processes that are currently impacting upon them? In particular, we wish to identify the processes through which women are repositioned and reconfigured as gendered workers in a globalizing/marketizing academy. We also consider how we might theorize differently about women's labours in the feminized professions as a response to larger cross-national neoliberal restructuring trends. In so doing, one can witness the differentiated impacts of institutional processes on women's work in teacher education as ultimately "more than local and less than global."

Our main argument is that teacher education serves as a key site where complex and contradictory tensions surrounding the definition of the female worker are often played out (Maguire, 2000). Teacher education is a sector of work where successive reforms have been implemented cross-nationally but that also maintains specific historical and local patterns of work for women (Edwards, 2001; Openshaw, 1999). It is therefore an instructive context in which to examine a prime professional and deeply symbolic representative of the "social work" disciplines.

Global discourses that circulate in teacher education and faculties of education have created recurring conditions for women academics. Particularly prominent among these discourses is the image of the rational expedient worker (Dillabough, 1999). Such an image, together with its attendant expectations, has been projected with increasing force upon women's working lives. While women are often held accountable to narrow expectations that are generated by such an image, their variegated experiences of working life in times of change are by no means always in accord with them.

This chapter begins with a brief description of why teacher education is a key site of restructuring, monitoring, and heightened research pressure in the academy. Social developments that have been shaped by a powerfully gendered history are identified within teacher education as a prime example of the state's traditional private/public split and an enduring and contested site of meaning for women workers. We argue that such developments explain, in part, why women workers are particularly affected by such currents of international change. We then draw upon interview data from three different studies of women teacher educators and focus on a cross-national analysis of women's accounts of working life during times of increasing state regulation and aggrandizing market cultures.

Teacher Education as a Vulnerable Professional Discipline in the Academy

Teacher education and faculties of education have been at the centre of the restructuring debate in universities in many national contexts (e.g., Australia, New Zealand, Canada, the United States). According to Hartley (2000), one characteristic of the restructuring movement internationally is that teacher education is depicted as a platform for enhancing national economies. At the same time, such reforms are often put forward by policy makers as initiatives to promote the development of efficient and highly perfected "citizens." The result has been what Mahony and Hextall (1997) have identified "as a managerialist restructuring of a public profession" that articulates a concern over such issues as citizenship but ultimately accords greater power to performance cultures. Uniquely important about these restructuring processes, which often emerge under the guise of accountability mechanisms within and outside the university (e.g., the Teaching Training Agency in the UK), is that they are not isolated within any one national context. Such market reforms are present in the UK, Australia, New Zealand, and certain provinces in Canada. These reforms have entered the complex maze of both the university and the broader public sector of many countries (Blackmore, 1999a, 1999b; Blackmore and Sachs, 2007).[3] A primary reason that cognate reforms emerge cross-nationally lies in their competitive market value globally (Sassen, 1998). It may also be that cognate reforms emerge disproportionately in those disciplines that are often classified as "public welfare" or "social work" professions. Such professions are often inhabited by women and/or identified with low-status, service work (see also more recent work on female "worker subjectivities") (Davies and Peterson, 2005).

Historically, "low status" is entrenched in the teaching and teacher education professions. As Gardner (1995) has suggested, the marginal status of teacher education – particularly in relation to the elementary/primary sector

– is rooted in conceptions of teaching and, therefore, teacher education, as something anyone can do: that is, as founded upon the exercise of general or non-specific skills. While "working-class" men were among the earliest teacher apprentices in the UK (Maguire, 2000), the profession of teacher education later became dominated by the perception that elementary/ primary teachers and associated teacher educators should be women (Edwards, 2001). Teaching was a role to which, apparently, women could "easily" and "naturally" commit until they took up their "proper" roles as benevolent keepers of the family (Gardner, 1995). As Edwards (2001) has suggested, women were also favoured for financial reasons as they characteristically earned substantially lower salaries than men. In this context, "it was difficult for women to see themselves as workers" (Edwards, 2001, p. 37). Indeed, the recognition of women as teachers in such professional contexts was likely to signal a decline in status for affiliated professions such as teacher education.

Gendered perceptions of this kind – founded upon circulating and highly symbolic ideas of the public and private worker – permeated teaching and teacher education in the UK and elsewhere (Dillabough, 1999). Until relatively recently, women in teacher education were confined by stereotypical roles related to curriculum functions, found in subject areas such as domestic science and girls' physical education (see Rich, 2001) or, where they existed, in single-sex and often religious teachers' colleges. Women teacher educators were doubly subject to marginal status because they worked in the male academy and were affected by the dominant myths circulating about female work at the time. As Edwards (2001) suggests, such mythical accounts of female work were dualistic in character. On the one hand, women were held in low regard as poorly paid workers in the public space of social life. On the other hand, they also embodied the romantic myths of "mother made conscious" in the classroom (Steedman, 1986).

Educational historians generally agree that, until the late 1970s, the goal of teacher education policy in most Western countries was to support the ideals of social progress of teachers and students rather than to entrench teacher education in broader economic and political aims (McCulloch, 1997). At least in the UK, it seemed that this approach was premised partly upon a historical awareness that teacher education policy should be connected to public welfare, public consciousness, and professional autonomy, even if such moralizing conceptions of "the good" were heavily regulated by gender ideals or the gender binary. Nevertheless, competing elements of globalization discourse were also present in the 1970s (Robbins, 1998).

The competing elements of change have sometimes been contradictory and incompatible in different national contexts. Over the past three decades, there has been widespread recognition that governments see teaching and teacher education as appropriate sites for endorsing quasi-market forces through, for example, increased accountability, the rise in the research culture, and mass testing of teachers. Urgently required, however, is an exploration of ways in which these changes impact on women workers who are variously located in the labour structures and processes of teacher education and who come to understand themselves as workers through such processes.

Our goal, then, is to illuminate how such reforms – as they relate to globalization in the macro sense – function to regulate and govern the localized, cultural, micro conditions of women's work. We also highlight how they might represent the reproduction of social inequality in women's working lives on a wider scale. In so doing, we hope to expose institutional processes that not only regulate worker conditions in teacher education but also reproduce a historical vision of women as highly sexualized "service" providers in the academy rather than professionals on their own terms. We suggest that these historical processes are mediated by contradictory and gendered notions that circulate about the "rational" competitive worker in teacher education and form, at least in part, the foundation of what Bourdieu (2001) saw as the "constancy of the structure" as it operates in modern social institutions such as the academy.

Methodology

The data we present are derived from three qualitative studies of women's work in teacher education and faculties of education conducted between 1996 and 2006. A primary goal of each study was to examine the role that contemporary gender hierarchies play in shaping the conditions of women's work in faculties of education during times of global restructuring. As researchers working independently on related projects with overlapping goals, we decided that data from each project could appropriately be drawn upon to reveal the tensions among the personal, social, economic, and cultural commitments of service embodied in symbolic representations of women as "servants to the state" and women's broader struggle for inclusion as workers. In each study, a key approach was the use of semi-structured, in-depth interviews. We thus illustrate our argument about the symbolic aspects of gender, professional identity, selfhood, and change through accounts of women's working lives.

The first study, conducted by Jo-Anne Dillabough between 1996 and 2006, entitled "Women's Labours in Teacher Education," involved in-depth interviews as part of a longitudinal cultural ethnography of one teacher education department in the UK. The interview data were collected from a sample of women teacher educators and contract researchers (variously positioned by race, class, gender, and sexuality) in a teacher-training college in a major urban concentration in England, located in a sprawling, culturally diverse sector of the city. In common with other education institutions in a period of intense policy reform and budget cuts, the college was experiencing significant changes, including pressure on faculty to conduct more externally funded research, the loss or restructuring of many of its programs, and substantial budget constraints (see Dillabough, 1999; 2000).

The second study, entitled "Traditions and Transitions in Teacher Education," was conducted in Canada with Sandra Acker as the principal investigator and co-investigators Elizabeth Smyth, Thérèse Hamel, Diane Hallman (now Miller), and Jo-Anne Dillabough. The objective of this study was to track the rise of the research culture through accounts of academics working (and/or retired) as deans, program directors, and other faculty in teacher education (see Acker, 2003; Acker and Weiner, 2003). In this chapter, we draw on a sample of seventeen interviews with women and men in eight institutions in one Canadian province.

The third study, "Gender, Leadership, and Change," compares the experiences of women academic managers in faculties of education in Canada, Australia, and Britain. The first phase of this project drew upon eight interviews from an earlier project in Canada and nine conducted in Australia (see Wyn, Acker, and Richards, 2000). The second phase, conducted by Sandra Acker with the assistance of Michelle Webber, Johanna Wyn, and Mary Fuller, extended the research coverage to Britain and broadened the definition of manager/administrator to include women who are in what might be called "lower middle management" (e.g., associate chairs of departments, program directors) as well as more senior managers such as deans. This research also focused more directly on experiences of restructuring and change in the globalized university and included between eight and twelve women participants in each country (see Acker, 2005). For this chapter, we utilize data from interviews conducted in Canada and Britain.

Women Academics' Accounts of Work in Teacher Education: Themes and Issues

As we have argued elsewhere (see Acker and Dillabough, 2007), the problems inherent in the gendered premises of global reforms and their structural links to women's work may, at first glance, seem unrelated to teacher education or to higher education more generally. However, as international research demonstrates (see Maguire, 2000), the teacher educator has been redefined in many nation-states to reflect a strain of rationality that privileges global economic policies of worker accountability but may also honour masculinized or "heteropatriarchal" (Alexander, 1997; Cavanagh, forthcoming) visions of social change and policy formation. Therefore, as we apply feminist sociological critiques of the "rational worker" (see Dillabough, 1999) to the cross-national study of women teacher educators, we find that they are raising new social concerns.

The Uneasy Alliance between "Research Culture" and "Professional Accountability" in Women Teacher Educators' Work

One of the most common difficulties women identify in their own accounts of work centres on the tensions stimulated by economic rationalism and the pervasiveness of the "research culture" circulating in the academy. As the women in our three projects indicate, this tension represents a subtle but powerful institutional process implicated in the gendered division of labour, alongside the formation of conceptions of a professional subjectivity or "selfhood," particularly as they relate to the assessment of women's academic work and, more recently, research productivity. This tension, moreover, serves to regulate the cultural reproduction of gender conflicts in institutional life. In other words, the idea of heightened research productivity does not simply operate to regulate the historical conditions of female work as an invested site of meaning that operates in the present. It also sets the stage for the appearance of a quite novel set of gender relations and highly symbolic gender conflicts operating in the culture of teacher education that might be traced, at least in part, to the structural elements of global reform. While it is clear that men also experience such regulative pressures, it would seem, according to the women interviewed cross-nationally, that the men are somewhat cushioned by their historically superordinate place in the academy.

Before detailing the links between gender, social conflict, and the general rise of the research culture, we begin with an account by a full professor of education ("Carter"; all names are pseudonyms) about the rise of this new culture in a Canadian university. At a descriptive level, his comments reveal one accountability mechanism that has reshaped the conditions of teacher educators' work – the separation between the "haves" and the "have nots" of the research culture and the elevation of research productivity to accord with a "research intensive" university focus: "So that all happened in the early '80s, ... and it became necessary for the dean to remove some people from the list of graduate faculty, and that was called the [local name for the event], and everyone who was [removed from the list] has retired now, so we're calm after that, but that was really unpleasant. Parenthetically, I don't think the graduate program has looked back. I think it's been strong ... It was partly in the spirit of the university's attempt to be a research intensive university."

As these remarks indicate, the 1980s may have been the time when the rise of the research culture emerged as significant throughout some teacher education sites (Robbins, 1998) as they struggled to gain status in the context of the research university. As Irene, another full professor, observed about this trend in the province we studied in Canada, "[in the mid-1980s] the new dean ... had to deal with what was the old crowd of people ... They weren't all old, ... but they were the previous era of people, ... and there weren't a lot of retirements out at the time, so he was really talking, and he started the debate and dialogue on research." For many teacher educators, their own research training has been constructed as a positive form of professional development (see Hamel and Larocque, 2001). However, in an increasingly demanding climate of change, professional programs that carry forward the historical memory of their own vulnerability are also likely to be deeply ambivalent about the pressures of a research culture. Indeed, a greater emphasis on research cultures and related productivity demands could serve to mask the latent position of the teacher educator researcher in the wider university context as a global economic asset.

In Canada, the interest in research culture/productivity identified by our participants also emerged at a time when some provincial governments were substantially cutting university budgets. Due to variations among Canadian provinces, the national impacts of these trends are difficult to track. Nor are they necessarily straightforward. Indeed, as many women in the three studies suggest, the effects vary, with some senior academics benefiting from the new "free-market" frame and others suffering a great deal. In women's accounts, "suffering," in the form of heightened levels of professional fear and "anxiety," often emerged as gender conflicts between senior male and junior female faculty, particularly in escalating the general "climate of competition." As Karina, a Canadian academic, remarked about her own tenure review process,[4]

> I was actually afraid. That's why I was very careful going to tenure to prepare things and to be sure that I had quite a list, an extensive list across the country of people who could be approached for letters and so on because I didn't know whether there might be a few of them (men) who would write and say "she's difficult. She's a bitch. She can't get along with her [male peers], or she doesn't, she's not a team player." ... And I was with some people, but I wasn't in other cases, and I had been very angry about my workload.
>
> I think it was a bit of a "good girl" to "bad girl" shift ... which partly happened because they so absolutely stonewalled any concerns I had about my situation. I was there to do the work none of the rest of them had wanted to do, you know, and that was the price of admission.

This account suggests an underlying element of unequal gender competition as well as the assertion of a particular moral economy of female work. Some of this competition may be linked to a professional hierarchy in faculties of education where senior males tend to be decision makers or full professors and women are more often junior faculty. With this gender structure operating as a form of political hierarchy, male faculty may inadvertently possess "social assets" (Robertson, 2000) in a later stage of their professional careers. This scenario seems likely when one considers that the rise in service and research commitments in teacher education, alongside larger economic shifts in university life, has coincided with the hiring of increased numbers of junior women academics. More significant, however, is that Karina implies that gender conflicts that may be linked to current employment structures and work intensification in the university mediate and indeed worsen the impact of accountability (e.g., tenure review). What is therefore meaningful beyond the obvious gender conflicts present is the symbolic and highly moralizing manifestations of gender inequality ("good girl," "bad girl," disproportionate amounts of service work) embedded in Karina's account. The presence of these historical and dialectically formed gender codes may indeed heighten the cultural role played by gender and other social formations in mediating women academics' working relationships to teacher education. They may also generate what Nixon et al. describe as "different and incompatible" structures of work where performance cultures are central to the "habitus" of academic life: "While the economic power of senior academics has been increased by the current climate in competition, others feel deprived of the significance to which they are thinking their academic status should entitle them: ... They work at a pace dictated by external pressures ... The result is that different and often incompatible structures are emerging within different groups occupied in different tasks and often pursuing different interests" (2001, p. 230).

Similarly, one teacher educator working in the UK, Marie, described the gendered nature of the service demands on her time and a consequent inability to conduct research after a period of relentless reform in her program (see also Dillabough, 1999). Noteworthy is that Marie made this comparison as a response to the gender hierarchy of male management in her own institution and the burden of being female in a teacher education program that is entrenched, both symbolically and practically, in a history of women's institutionalized labours in the private sphere: "I was asked to be a year tutor ... A year tutor is like everybody's mother. You'll be stuck with everything. It's difficult to cope with ... I just didn't realize how I became everybody's dogsbody ... So I did that for two years, and I wouldn't do it anymore. It stopped me from doing any research." In certain contexts, the professional requirement to conduct research may indeed complicate women academics' working conditions and create another layer of social inequality in what Maguire (2000) names the "traditionally feminized vocational context": "The pressure to publish and satisfy academic and political pressures sits uncomfortably alongside the need to teach and support vocational/professional development. This pressure may well be particularly acute in the 'traditionally' feminized 'vocational' contexts such as nursing studies or teaching studies" (p. 152). Rita, a professor in Britain, spoke directly to these concerns at the point where her own promotional status and research performance in the late 1980s became central to the economic mandate of the university. In this context, professional promotion is equated with research, not necessarily as something arising from intellectual interest but as an indicator of accountability:

> What I was told was that although my teaching was fine and my admin was fine, I wasn't doing enough research, and what that actually meant, though I didn't realize and know it at the time, was that I wasn't getting enough external funding for research. The university was looking for indicators of external funding for research. They weren't interested in, really, in your ability to kind of get the research done on the cheap and in your own time. I was told that I needed to have more of an indication of external, that's to say, international recognition of my work.

If we look beyond promotional considerations, parallel institutional pressures to conduct research across sites suggest the emergence of novel, yet still hidden, gender conflicts as structural markers of accountability. The key, according to women participants, is not that men are outside the impacts of these conflicts and related pressures. Rather, it seems that men are burdened with less service work as a function of their inherited position in the institutional hierarchy (see Acker and Feuerverger, 1996, for supporting evidence). It may also be the case that men carry a greater competitive edge in heightened neoliberal cultures due to the ongoing female support that many male academics have in the home and the cultural interpretation of their role in the institution (including the cultural politics of gender relations in the academy). Rebecca, another full professor in the UK, referred to a specific example of heightened neoliberal pressures, the Research Assessment Exercise (RAE), whereby collective research performance, assessed every five years by panels of peers, determines allocations of financial resources:

> I think that universities have become, as a result of the RAE, ... much more pressurized places for people to work in ... I have a sense that people in research at the universities work fantastically hard because you do everything yourself in the universities ... You do the administration. You do all the technical work. You do the typing and producing of your ... papers, OHTs [overhead projector transparencies], books, or whatever. So you do an awful lot, and everything comes down to yourself and your, almost, entrepreneurialism ... So people who can hack that do okay, do quite well, but people who can't have a very tough time. So I think people do get much stress. There's sometimes quite a lot of unhealthy competition.

Rebecca's comments are suggestive of differences in the globalizing processes of accountability; on the one hand, there is what might be described as "arm's length" assessment, while on the other there is a process that might be experienced as more direct, personal, and potentially humiliating. In the remarks that follow, Rebecca seemed to highlight more generally the regulatory elements shaping the cultural and arguably moral "field" of research as it takes form in various sites: "The theme of publish or perish is ... even clearer now, you know, that you have a choice of doing that and doing well or not doing that ... but feeling that you're ... having your neck breathed down all the time or else being kicked out fairly unceremoniously. There's lots of, not in my own institution but in other institutions, you hear about kind of naming and shaming exercises, you know. One place I heard of where they have a chart on the wall with the number of papers that people have published." Here we begin to see how competition and rising pressure to conduct research reconfigure the very notion of academic work and scholarship in teacher education. However, as we have emphasized, it must be recognized that such pressures are experienced differently in different locations. Women workers are therefore differentially affected by such changes depending on the levels of status and security they may hold in their jobs as well as on the countries and institutions in which they work (Robertson, 2000).

This differentiation notwithstanding, heightened accountability and the corresponding rise in the research culture cannot be taken at face value as a neutral professional indicator across the range of disciplines in the university. Instead, in teacher education, such academic requirements may often emerge as a symbolic and structural reconfiguration of working life, particularly because of its own history as a powerfully gendered profession or as a profession that has institutionalized women's labours. Women workers may be particularly susceptible to such forces and conflicts since the requirements cannot necessarily be met on equal terms by differently positioned women and men. As Morley (1999, 2004) argues, heightened quality assurance of academic performance reveals a fine line between women's "liberal" opportunity structures and discursive practices of exploitation. In this context, even liberal feminist visions of "success" (see Rose, 1999) are accompanied by rather disturbing and highly moralizing images of the female worker. As Rebecca stated, "I'd actually brought in all these grants and managed to keep them going, and I thought, God, they expect me to carry on working at this rate, and I had thought I was working too hard already, just in terms of having to be a good girl all of the time." Rather than accruing cultural capital, women workers may therefore be seen as "objects," "commodities," or puppets of a larger research culture in which economic and cultural shifts in a new global order are translated indirectly into working practices that transform the gendered division of labour. This transformation in labour processes may occur with little recognition of the barriers women face institutionally or is masked by the forms of self-surveillance and governance required in a larger macro-structure of constancy and change.

The changing nature of academic work described by women in the three studies highlights the gendered tensions that women teacher educators experience when they are positioned inside a regime of contradictory choices: for example, the rational worker and the subordinate benevolent keeper whose professional subjectivity may be regulated in part by the enduring symbolic elements of the now contested private sphere. The emphasis placed on such contradictions in women's accounts implies a need to understand quite new labour processes and structures in market cultures and their impacts on the organization of female work. There can be little doubt that men in teacher education are also affected and marginalized by such issues. But if we wish to account for the historical symbolism of women teacher educators' work and the hidden structural barriers to social equality for differently positioned women in institutional life, and the residual surplus meanings circulating about women teacher educators as "mother made conscious" (Steedman, 1986), then gender as a mediating force in marketized educational cultures must be accorded particular significance. And if we go one step further and combine these concerns with the "real" effects of workplace restructuring and the culture of research directly, then the mediating force of gendered expectations for such work processes, output, organization, and performance become even more clear, as Rebecca noted: "We can all understand why women may not be in a position to write enough or bring in as much money, ... but if you compete with the boys you'd have a better chance of being judged equally on those terms, although you don't alter the terms on which you're being judged." And, as Karina reminded us, the gender hierarchy of institutional life may mediate women workers' engagement with the research culture, not only by creating a particularly gendered image of the teacher educator, but also by constraining, in real terms, one's ability to conduct research:

> Some people seem to manage to make it a very unstressful life. Many of those are men. Many of them are of another generation, I think. I think it's changing ... It's not really as if the other parts of the work go away just because everybody's now supposed to also be a heavy hitter researcher ... bringing in the external funds, and of course every time you get funded that's another layer of work too, 'cause then you've got that work to do, you know, and some people ... are beginning to discover that. They may have gotten the grant, but doing anything with it is, you know, beyond their wildest dreams.
>
> The women who were hired at that time and having these heavy workloads because, of course, then there were all these cutbacks and major retirements, and the senior people certainly weren't going to soak it up, and the rehirings were being done in a ratio of one for every three retirements, so there were

just huge amounts of work to do, ... and of course the senior guys stayed very much protected.

Within this image of the university resides the subtle implication that the female worker must conform to the symbolic ideal of the traditional male citizen – the "autonomous rational agent" (Braaten, 1997, p. 144; see also Dillabough, 1999). Such a figure is seen as free to compete as an unfettered agent, needing only to call on the state when it is necessary to protect his or her rights as a worker. This "heteropatriarchal" or heteronormative image of female work (Alexander, 1997; Cavanagh, forthcoming), as one residual effect of globalizing reforms, cannot confront neoliberal expectations that are embedded in the research culture that may tacitly assume that women are equal to men in their ability to achieve the status of "real citizen worker."

Fiscal Restraints and Gender Conflicts in Teacher Education

The reconfiguration of female work is not determined solely by increased pressures to conduct research or as a form of accountability for the tallying up of annual publications. We should also see the movement of global economic reforms as an element of restructuring in a more obvious economic sense. And it is here – at the level of financial responsibility and broader global demands around economic efficiency in the professional hierarchy of teacher education – that women workers are facing particularly difficult ethical dilemmas and increased gender conflicts. For example, women do not, it seems, possess "exchange/social assets" (Robertson, 2000), which may be central to transforming their own and other women's professional circumstances beyond current conditions. Budget restraints may therefore affect women disproportionately seriously. The remarks offered below by Hester, an associate professor of teacher education in Canada and a program director, reveal such economic constraints. Yet she did not have the same level of power as a dean or provost of the university. Hester's lack of "exchange assets" thus made it more difficult for her to contest the terms and conditions of her working life:

> Obviously one of the changes has been the huge reduction in allocation of resources coming into different faculties from the central administration, kind of off-loading of the cutbacks that have occurred from the reduction in federal grants and provincial grants ... This is maybe the case because we are not respected in the university for the research we generate ... At the faculty, we're ... always being leaned on to accept more students. It's just an easy way to fill up the university coffers. I remember making the comment to the dean ... that I'm not going to, you know, we're not the campus

> ATM machine, and I'm not going to be treated that way. You know, the [name of administrator] just pushes the button, and we take a bunch more students. No problem, no more resources to handle it. I think it's obscene, but anyway there's been a big movement in that direction within the faculty of education.

While her comments do not point immediately to a gender issue, Hester went on to discuss how university fiscal restraints undermine her position as a female worker. In the following passage, she implied that women are constructed outside the rational paradigm of public work in globalizing times: "I don't think that the women are taken seriously as thinkers ... The kinds of ways that feminists would understand, you would see the workings, but it's not always obvious, the old boys' network, the ways in which the decisions get made. Who gets called on to make the decisions, and, you know, the women get called in to do the cleanup work." In her view, they are "used" as an "exploitable resource" (Ozga and Deem, 2000). Her commentary echoes the statements by Karina quoted earlier about women's symbolic labour and related concerns about who does the "cleanup work."

It is not easy to escape the enduring symbolic and historical demands of female service in teacher education. Indeed, such impositions seem to heighten the overall effects of global demands. At the same time, increased competition and the imposition of "capitalist scripts" (Mohanty, 1997) onto teacher education have meant that productivity pressures undermine more than a century of feminist struggles in education – including the representation of conditions of equality for women's paid work and broader issues of equity in higher education. Pearl, a full professor in Canada, noted that, "as an administrator, I am confronted daily with dilemmas which are ethical dilemmas. For instance, I need to earn 13 percent of the budget. Well, and I really want to preserve the autonomy of the university as equity, accessibility, etc. etc. But I still have to find an ethical way to develop some components of my faculty, like continuing teacher education, in order to make money." Carrie, a teacher educator from Britain, expressed similar sentiments as she observed how public sector regulation and accountability influenced the behaviour of her female manager after the onset of heavy inspections by the Office for Standards in Education, Children's Service, and Care (OFSTED), the education inspection agency in the UK. Her observation highlights how the organization of working life altered as a consequence of such regulatory mechanisms, which in turn heightened conflicts among women in the workplace:

> Well, if there were pressures on her to make us work harder, ... she said you've got to do it. So you accepted it, you disliked it, but she didn't talk down to

> you. She was under considerable pressure from her underlings, who were subverting her, and from the male hierarchy above, and when she got the chance to get out she did. That left us in the lurch because we were left with a whole term when we were meant to be inspected. This is the way the university works. It doesn't replace for a term, and it saves money. That's all very well, but if you're going to be inspected you need a management person in place. They didn't put one in place ... Yet there is something bloody dodgy in these men's minds that somehow it's not their fault. I was so angry.

The omnipotence of fiscal restraint in the academic workplace raises larger questions about the economy and the part it plays in regulating the conditions of female work and gender relations. It is here that images of the instrumental worker in teacher education emerge most powerfully as a particularly constant yet subtle element of institutional structure – what Bourdieu might name as a form of doxa or symbolic violence (as a taken-for-granted or even accepted form of social inequality that has substantial historical resonance; see Bourdieu, 2001). Speaking of herself, Hester remarked, "I've lost touch with the person a little bit because the job makes you lose touch with that person. It's just like you're under this constant shellfire, rat-a-tat." Ultimately, then, where gender dominates above all is in the emphasis on global practices of economic restraint that serve as "rational" markers of institutional success that fail to recognize their effects on marginalized groups. Cultivating a collaborative, meaningful, feminist response in such a context is extremely difficult, as Pearl noted:

> We lived through a very serious process of reorganization. Departments were merged ... I strongly opposed this ... I stood up ... many times. The director of [unit name] was a woman ... She insulted me, but I had a mandate. Quite often women were used for that. Women with little experience were hired in the name of equity, and that was not a favour to anybody. Then they were very obedient to central administration because they didn't have the authority of experience.
>
> The changes were hegemonic ... with this aura of "common sense" or "universal" or "has to be." But it isn't a coincidence that they didn't pay attention to experience when hiring female administrators.

Such political moves reveal the corrosive nature of institutional regulation; in some cases, control over the nature of female work will be direct (through cuts), and sometimes it will be indirect and more discursive in form. And such forms of control do not emerge without conflicts. As Smyth et al. argue, "in a marketized education system [workers and managers] are often divided against each other as they seek to grab a share of the same education market"

(2000, p. 52). In this context, women workers cannot, by virtue of their gender and history in the profession, be viewed as conforming to the ideal model of the "autonomous" professional, as indicated by Hester:

> The job is too big for one person. Our program has tripled in size in the last three or four years ... Several years ago there were two full-time secretaries for the co-ordinator. Now there's one full-time secretary for the co-ordinator. Several years ago the co-ordinator did not teach ... Now the co-ordinator teaches two courses.
>
> Of course, in teacher education there are different structures at work. It's a bit of a pink ghetto. There are not males who are inhabiting positions of leadership within teacher education here. So those dynamics aren't working so much, perhaps, to affect me in this job but in the larger structure within the faculty where I'm working with the graduate sector as well. And by the men who not only inhabit the power position there but the men who are the power mongers there.

Now perhaps more than ever women's close relationship to capital has exacerbated the forms of exclusion and alienation they have always felt as a result of the deeply entrenched gender hierarchies in education:

> Women who are in the teacher ed. management positions are knocking themselves out. [They] are being completely destroyed by these kinds of economic measures. (Hester)

> [The women] were very stressed and very tense, in common with all teacher training. It is the same everywhere ... [Many have] actually left, they have not been able to cope. (Carrie)

Conclusion: Globalization and the Regulation and Reproduction of Female Work

> A genuine understanding of the changes that have occurred ... in relations between the sexes can, paradoxically, be expected only from an analysis of the transformations of the mechanisms and institutions charged with ensuring the perpetuation of the order of genders. (Bourdieu, 2001, pp. 84-85)

In this chapter, we have identified some of the social and cultural mechanisms associated with global restructuring that are implicated in the gendered divisions of labour in teacher education. We have also explored the more general impact of public sector regulation on women teacher educators' working lives cross-nationally and the forms of symbolic control and work organization to which they are exposed as a result of both macro and micro processes of globalizing academic cultures (Smyth et al., 2000). The key practices we have referred to are the sometimes contradictory yet ultimately structural gendered effects of the rise of the research culture for women, the role of inspections and assessment exercises, the impact of economic constraints on teacher education, women's symbolic, historical entrenchment in the public/private split of working life, and the mediating role of gender in accountability practices. The accounts we have drawn upon suggest that women workers in the UK and Canada report similar trends in the organization of their working lives as well as increased pressure to conduct research in a sometimes conflictual, heavily regulated, and competitive academic climate. This climate is characterized by deeply symbolic gender conflicts and related work intensification practices, which take various forms and represent both enduring sedimented gender relations and quite new social divisions.

It is significant that not all trends are parallel in form across sites, and there are indeed local effects. What seems to be dissimilar is the form of state regulation over working practices. For example, in the British context, women report pressures and emerging gender conflicts from national arm's-length assessment exercises such as the RAE, work intensification, and more general reform initiatives. By contrast, in Canada women report pressures from (individualized) tenure review processes, institutional service expectations, gender conflicts associated with fiscal restraint, and gendered employment structures, along with the insistent pressure to publish. Dissimilarities are probably due to cross-national differences in some policy practices, a national (UK) versus provincial (Canada) structure for supporting teacher education, specific economic, social, and cultural circumstances in both sites, and state arrangements that concern the historical development of the profession, as well as the local forms of gender relations in each site. What seems to be common, however, is the role of accountability (research culture, service work, intensification) in the regulation of new kinds of gender conflict, the degree of associated stresses, and the ongoing symbolic regulation of gender ideals as mediating the effects of global restructuring, as well as the larger economic imperatives of university life (Blackmore and Sachs, 2007). While some women may benefit from these changes, they are clearly creating unpalatable conditions of work for many/most women in teacher education.

This trend is further complicated by the gendered history of teacher education as a low-status profession (one of Bourdieu's "social work" disciplines) in the university and women's historically "inferior" position in the academy.

Women's accounts therefore suggest that contemporary cultural processes are at work in the production of different and indeed gendered patterns of labour in teacher education internationally. Such processes seem to be related to the nature and timing of research intensification and fiscal restraint in teacher education as well as the increasing status of research in the larger context of the university. Indeed, such social conditions are not only economic; discursive struggles and invested sites of professional meaning are manifested in local cultural contexts that always represent more than simply material effects (Skeggs, 1995).

It may also be that, while public sector regulation appears rather indirect in the university, its direct effects take the form of competition among faculty members. Such competition emerges around the forms of accountability in place for evaluating academic work, with academics competing on unequal social grounds. In this context, one might argue that both regulation and reproduction operate simultaneously. For example, economic restraints or the heavy weight of research in tenure and promotion means that accountability, in some form or another, regulates the very conditions of women's (and men's) working lives. Yet such rational forms of accountability function also to reproduce social and gender inequality for women. As Bourdieu (2001, p. 91) writes, "the most striking example of this permanence in and through change is the fact that positions which become feminized are either already devalued or declining, the devaluation being intensified [through intensified work cultures]."

We thus begin to see how women's professional identifications and academic work in teacher education are shaped by broader material, cultural, and social forces, which are indeed gendered and linked to globalization at a macro level. At the same time, it is important to recognize that economic globalization – as it appears in relation to research productivity, fiscal restraint, and accountability – does not have universal and undifferentiated effects. We therefore view the category of globalizing work in the service professions as one of many elements at work in the localized reproduction of the gendered division of labour. Our cross-national work suggests that macro processes of educational change are manifested differently and therefore mediated by differently positioned women in diverse social locations. At the same time, it is problematic to perceive local stories as mere details of a unique working life; clearly, these details speak to change, conflict, and continuity experienced by women in the larger structures of the social order. They also tell us something about the relative constancy of the social/gender order itself in particular spheres of working life. We also suggest here that we have identified, in part, underlying dialectical frames of the gender order and their relationship to larger aspects of social change, only one of which can be identified – as different scales of globalizing reform. As Bourdieu (2001) says, "given that [women's] interests are [sometimes] bound up with the left hand of the state and with social positions in the bureaucratic field ... there is every reason to expect that they will be the main victims of neo-liberal policy [p. 92] ... The constancy of habitus that results from this is thus one of the relative constancy of the sexual division of labour: because these principles are, in their essentials, transmitted from body to body, below the level of consciousness and discourse" (p. 95).

In closing, we suggest that it is unacceptable to divide the symbolically entrenched practice of gendered or domestic servicing in the "social work" professions from contemporary forms of globalizing change in teacher education. In fact, the effects of domination that are asserted through novel globalizing processes and structures in the academy are but one of many sites where female work is both regulated and reproduced. It is through the empirical documentation of these processes that feminist sociologists will no doubt, with the assistance of "contradictions in the social system" (see Bourdieu, 1998), contribute to a greater understanding of female work and its configuration in such dislocating times.

Notes

This chapter is a revised and updated version of earlier work by Dillabough and Acker (2002, 2003) used here with permission from *International Studies in Sociology of Education* and *Tidskrift för lärarutbildning och forskning* (*Journal of Research in Teacher Education*). We wish to extend our gratitude to all the individuals who participated in each of the respective studies. We are grateful to Barbara Soren and Michelle Webber for assistance with data collection and analyses respectively and the members of the Canadian research team for intellectual and practical support on the Transitions and Traditions project (Elizabeth Smyth, Thérèse Hamel, Dianne Hallman (now Miller), Michelle Webber, and Nicole Sanderson). We also wish to thank Kathy Bischoping and Phil Gardner for providing comments on an earlier version of this chapter. We gratefully acknowledge the financial support of the Social Sciences and Humanities Research Council of Canada and the Connaught Research Fund at the University of Toronto.

1 We borrow Bourdieu's (1998) idea of a "social work" profession or discipline to explore the working lives of those who have been seen as cultivators of the "public good," rather than simply suggesting that teacher education is a straightforwardly *feminized profession.*

2 Policy analysts often refer to such international reforms as *public sector regulation* because they are characterized by the multi-bureaucratic permeation of market ideology into particular forms of institutional life (Hood and Scott, 2000). Such *regulative ideology* appears to drive increasing international competitiveness, institutional restructuring (e.g., amalgamations), academic monitoring, fiscal restructuring, and the rising demands for research and professional accountability.

3 In Canadian universities, restructuring has taken the form of departmental amalgamations and financial cutbacks. In Australia, by contrast, it has emerged in the form of institutional mergers, leading sometimes to redundancy and departmental closures. In both Australia and the United Kingdom, heightened performance indicators have been a striking feature of contemporary institutional operations.

4 After a prescribed period of time, anywhere from approximately three to seven years in the university, depending on the institution – longer in research-intensive universities – an academic prepares an extensive dossier of accomplishments in applying for tenure. If tenure is not granted, even after an appeal, she or he will have to leave the position.

References

Acker, S. (2003). Canadian teacher educators in time and place. *Tidskrift för lärarutbildning och forskning (Journal of Research in Teacher Education), 3-4,* 69-85.

–. (2005). Gender, leadership, and change in faculties of education in three countries. In C. Reynolds and J. Collard (Eds.), *Leadership, gender, and culture* (pp. 103-17). Maidenhead: Open University Press.

Acker, S., and Dillabough, J. (2007). Women "learning to labour" in the "male emporium": Exploring gendered work in teacher education. *Gender and Education, 19*(3), 297-316.

Acker, S., and Feuerverger, G. (1996). Doing good and feeling bad: The work of women university teachers. *Cambridge Journal of Education, 26*(3), 401-22.

Acker, S., and Weiner, G. (Eds.). (2003). Special issue on traditions and transitions in teacher education (in English) of *Tidskrift för lärarutbildning och forskning (Journal of Research in Teacher Education), 3-4.*

Adkins, L. (1997). *Gendered work: Sexuality, family, and the labour market.* Buckingham, UK: Open University Press.

Alexander, M.J. (1997). Erotic autonomy as a politics of decolonization: An anatomy of feminist and state practice in the Bahamas tourist economy. In M.J. Alexander and C. Talpade Mohanty (Eds.), *Feminist genealogies, colonial legacies, and democratic futures* (pp. 63-100). New York: Routledge.

Blackmore, J. (1999a). Localization/globalization and the mid-wife state: Strategic dilemmas for state feminism in education? *Journal of Educational Policy, 14,* 33-54.

–. (1999b). *Troubling women: Feminism, leadership, and education.* Milton Keynes, UK: Open University Press.

Blackmore, J., and Sachs, J. (2007). *Performing and reforming leaders: Gender, educational restructuring, and organizational change.* Albany: SUNY Press.

Bourdieu, P. (1992). The practice of reflexive sociology (the Paris Workshop). In P. Bourdieu and L. Waquant (Eds.), *An invitation to reflexive sociology* (pp. 218-60). Chicago: University of Chicago Press.

–. (1998). *Acts of resistance: Against the tyranny of the market.* New York: New Press.

–. (2001). *Masculine domination.* Stanford: Stanford University Press.

Braaten, J. (1997). From communicative rationality to communicative thinking: A basis for feminist thinking. In J. Meehan (Ed.), *Feminists read Habermas: Gendering the subject of discourse* (pp. 139-61). New York: Routledge.

Cavanagh, S. (Forthcoming). Sex in the lesbian teacher's closet: The hybrid proliferation of queers in school. *Discourse, 29*(3).

Dale, R. (1997). The global economy, the state, and the politics of education: An analysis of the state-education relationship. In A.H. Halsey, H. Lauder, P. Brown, and A. Stuart Wells (Eds.), *Education: Culture, economy, society* (pp. 273-82). Oxford: Oxford University Press.

Davies, B., and Peterson, E. (2005). Neo-liberal discourse in the academy: The forestalling of (collective) resistance. *Learning and Teaching in the Social Sciences, 2,* 77-98.

Dillabough, J. (1999). Gender politics and conceptions of the modern teacher: Women, identity, and professionalism. *British Journal of Sociology of Education, 20,* 373-94.

Dillabough, J., and Acker, S. (2002). Globalization, women's work, and teacher education: A cross-national analysis. *International Studies in Sociology of Education, 12,* 227-60.

–. (2003). "Gender at work" in teacher education: History, society, and global reform. *Tidskrift för lärarutbildning och forskning (Journal of Research in Teacher Education), 3-4,* 109-34.

Edwards, E. (2001). *Women in teacher training colleges 1900-1960: A culture of femininity.* London: Routledge.

Gardner, P. (1995). Teacher training and changing professional identity in early twentieth century England. *Journal of Education for Teaching, 21,* 191-217.

Hamel, T., and Larocque, M.J. (2001, September). Legitimacy and universitarisation of teacher training in Quebec: Emergence of a research culture in the Faculty of Education of Université Laval from 1939 to the present. Paper presented to the European Education Research Association, Lille, France.

Hartley, D. (2000). Shoring up the pillars of modernity: Teacher education and the quest for certainty. *International Studies in Sociology of Education, 10,* 113-31.

Hood, C., and Scott, C. (2000). *Regulating government in a "managerial" age: Towards a cross-national perspective.* London: Discussion paper no. 1, Centre for Analysis of Risk and Regulation, London School of Economics and Political Science.

Maguire, M. (2000). Inside/outside the ivory tower: Teacher education in the English academy. *Teaching in Higher Education, 5,* 149-66.

Mahony, P., and Hextall, I. (1997). Sounds of silence: The social justice agenda of the teacher training agency. *International Studies in Sociology of Education, 7,* 137-56.

McCulloch, G. (1997). Privatising the past: History and education policy in the 1990s. *British Journal of Educational Studies, 45,* 69-82.

Mohanty, C. (1997). Women workers and capitalist scripts: Ideologies of domination, common interests, and the politics of solidarity. In M.J. Alexander and C.T. Mohanty (Eds.), *Feminist genealogies, colonial legacies, democratic futures* (pp. 3-29). New York: Routledge.

Morley, L. (1999). *Organizing feminisms: The micropolitics of the academy.* London: Macmillan.

–. (2004). *Theorising quality in higher education.* London: Institute of Education, University of London.

Nixon, J., Marks, A., Rowland, S., and Walker, M. (2001). Towards a new academic professionalism: A manifesto of hope. *British Journal of Sociology of Education, 22,* 227-44.

Openshaw, R. (1999). Forward to the past in New Zealand teacher education. *Journal of Education for Teaching, 25*(2), 111-12.

Ozga, J., and Deem, R. (2000). Carrying the burden of transformation: The experiences of women managers in UK higher and further education. *Discourse: Studies in the Cultural Politics of Education, 21,* 141-53.

Reay, D. (2000). "Dim dross": Marginalised women both inside and outside the academy. *Women's Studies International Forum, 23,* 13-21.

Rich, E. (2001). Gendered positioning in teacher education in England: New rhetoric, old realities. *International Studies in Sociology of Education, 11*(2), 131-56.

Robbins, D. (1998). The need for an epistemological "break." In M. Grenfell and D. James (Eds.), *Bourdieu in education: Acts of practical theory* (pp. 27-52). London: Falmer.

Robertson, S. (2000). Teachers' labour, class, and the politics of exchange. *International Studies in Sociology of Education, 10,* 285-302.

Rose, N. (1999). *The powers of freedom: Reframing political thought.* Cambridge, UK: Cambridge University Press.

Sassen, S. (1998). *Globalization and its discontents: Essays on the new mobility of people and money.* New York: New Press.

Skeggs, B. (1995). Women's studies in Britain in the 1990s: Entitlement cultures and institutional constraints. *Women's Studies International Forum, 18,* 475-85.

Smyth, J., Dow, A., Hattam, R., Reid, A., and Shacklock, G. (2000). *Teachers' work in a globalizing economy.* London: RoutledgeFalmer.

Steedman, C. (1986). *Landscape for a good woman.* New Brunswick, NJ: Rutgers University Press.

Wyn, J., Acker, S., and Richards, L. (2000). Making a difference: Women in management in Australian and Canadian faculties of education. *Gender and Education, 12,* 435-44.

8
The Political Economy of Legal Scholarship: A Case Study of the University of British Columbia Law School

Theresa Shanahan

In the past two decades, Canadian universities have gone through a period of considerable change as Canadian social policy has shifted away from a Keynesian welfare state toward global capitalism. During this period, there has been a rise in neoliberal economic policies that champion the principles of market primacy, free trade, privatization, deregulation, and decreased government intervention in the economy and social welfare. At the same time, there has been an intensification of globalization. In this political economic environment, there have been drastic cuts in public expenditures and the emergence of an evaluative movement reflected in a discourse of accountability and efficiency. Government fiscal policies have, in turn, influenced postsecondary policy, pushing economic objectives to the centre of the university. Free-market forces have been promoted at the same time that public expenditures on higher education have been cut (Arthurs, 1997, 2001; Brodie, 1994, 1995; Brown and Lauder, 1996; Buchbinder, 1993; Fisher and Rubenson, 1998; Magnusson, 2000, 2001; Rice and Prince, 2000; Teeple, 1995).

The economic imperative in higher education encourages the expansion of the private sector and an increase in the number of degree-granting institutions, thereby increasing competition in postsecondary education. We see a greater emphasis on meeting labour market needs through skills-oriented programs and curricula and through research and development. We see a shift in government funding for higher education toward the use of tied, targeted, and matching private sector funding mechanisms alongside a concomitant shift in student tuition and assistance policy in some Canadian provinces. The intention is to download the cost of postsecondary education to the private sector and the student "consumer." To balance their budgets, postsecondary institutions place more emphasis on university-industry partnerships, fundraising, and profit-producing activities, and they increase their engagement at the professorial level in entrepreneurial, revenue-generating, and grant-winning activities (Bruneau and Savage, 2002; Currie and Newson, 1998; Fisher and Rubenson, 1998; Magnusson, 2000; Polster, 1996; Slaughter, 1998; Slaughter and Leslie, 1997).

The political economy of Canadian postsecondary education raises concerns for academic freedom and autonomy (Buchbinder, 1993, 1995; Newson, 1992; Newson and Buchbinder, 1988, 1990; Polster, 1996). Critical scholars have drawn attention to the influence of economic objectives on the fundamental role of the university in society. They have argued that the academic world is being overtaken with business values and infused with a market culture that fundamentally compromises the critical function of the university in society (Polster, 1996; Saul, 1995). Some scholars have suggested that in this environment market principles are replacing educational values, private interest is supplanting public interest, and the academic culture of the university is being shaped in accordance with principles and priorities of the market. As a result, professional autonomy, participation in decision making, and academic freedom are diminished as academic culture and scholarship become skewed toward the market (Axelrod, 1986, 1998, 2002; Buchbinder, 1993, 1995; Currie, 1998a, b, c; Fisher and Rubenson, 1998; Kelsey, 1998; Magnusson, 2000, 2001; Newson and Buchbinder, 1988; Polster 1996; Polster and Newson, 1998; Thornton, 2001a, b). While this presents concerns for all disciplines in the academy, it is compounded for professional disciplines already externally regulated by professional organizations. Autonomy and control over their knowledge base and work are essential for professional status in society (Abel, 1997; Arthurs, 1995, 1998; Eraut, 1994; Freidson, 1986, 1994; Johnson, 1972; Larson, 1977; McGuire, 1993).

This chapter presents data from one component of a program of research that considers the relationship between political economic change and legal scholarship in Canadian law schools.[1] It focuses on findings from the case study of the Faculty of Law at the University of British Columbia (UBC). The impact of market-driven pressures on academic culture and legal scholarship in Canadian law schools is unclear and raises the questions central to this chapter. Have changes in political economy had an impact on scholarship and academic culture in law schools? What are the implications for professional autonomy and academic freedom?

Context: Legal Scholarship and Academic Culture at Canadian Law Schools

The influence of neoliberal restructuring on the academic culture of law schools and legal scholarship has received very little attention in Canadian higher education literature or legal education literature in terms of a critical, empirical analysis. This may be understandable given the relatively young tradition of scholarly research in Canadian law schools. This is attributed by some scholars to the relatively late evolution of law schools into the university in Canada compared to Britain, the United States, and other commonwealth jurisdictions (Consultative Group on Research and Education in Law, 1983; Shanahan, 2002). In fact, the importance of legal scholarship only began to emerge in the 1980s, as evidenced by one of the most extensive examinations of legal education and research in Canada, entitled *Law and Learning Report to the Social Sciences and Humanities Research Council of Canada* by the Consultative Group on Research and Education in Law (1983). This national study, also known as the Law and Learning Report, was first conceived by SSHRCC in 1978 after only two research grants in law were awarded that year. Concerns were raised about the strikingly low participation of academic lawyers in research grant competitions, and the council wanted to understand why applications from the legal academic community did not conform to the patterns in other disciplines (Law and Learning Report, 1983). The report commented that "scholarly or intellectual legal study is diluted and marginalized by the predominance of professional concerns. The non-vocational study of law as one of the humanities or social sciences is seldom undertaken" (p. 153).

In the past two decades, critical scholarly literature has emerged from law faculties across North America. This literature reflects on many dimensions of legal education and the legal profession from a variety of theoretical frameworks. However, many of the analyses of legal scholarship in the literature emanate from the United States (e.g., Beazley and Edwards, 1998; Ellickson, 2000; Jones, 1998). Some current American scholarly efforts attempt to understand broader trends in legal scholarship by simply using citation analysis of published works that counts references to scholars, faculties, or journals.[2] Recent literature from Australia provides a foundation for a critique of the emerging neoliberal legal academy (see Kelsey, 1998; Thornton, 2001a, b). While these studies show important trends in legal scholarship, it is unclear if the findings accurately reflect the Canadian landscape of academic legal scholarship.

This gap and the pressing need for analytical research were recognized by Canadian legal educators at the Legal Research Institute at the University of Manitoba when they hosted the Workshop on the Future of Canadian Legal Education: Excellence, Competition, and Hierarchy (May 1999) and the follow-up Conference on the Future of Legal Education held in Ottawa (September 2000). The initiatives sought to identify the main factors provoking change in Canadian legal education. On behalf of the workshop, Backhouse (1999) summarized fifteen transformative factors in Canadian legal education, including reductions in university budgets; government demands for accountability; privatization of funding; marketing and competitiveness; internationalization; technological change; demographic change; inclusion in the university academy; increased pace of academic work; tension between law faculty members; leadership; tensions between law schools and university administrators; and local factors unique to each law school. The factors identified by Backhouse (1999) clearly mirror trends in the larger university and have been associated in the higher education and legal education literature with economic restructuring, neoliberal policies, and globalization (Arthurs, 1997, 1998, 2001; Buchbinder, 1993; Currie, 1998a, b, c; Kelsey, 1998; Pue, 2001).

Method, Data Sources, and Data Analysis

The purpose of the larger study upon which this chapter is based was to determine the factors that shape the scholarship, employment environment, and culture of law schools in western Canada.[3] This project utilized survey, interview, and case study methodologies as well as the collection and analysis of public domain and archival documents (Merriam, 1998; Yin, 1984). The researcher spent one year physically at the UBC campus collecting data. Data collection for the UBC case study took place between January 2002 and June 2003, with follow-up in May 2004.

The research project involved two phases. The first phase included the pilot testing of the survey instrument by a small sample of law professors to determine the reliability and validity of the questions. This was followed by a mailed questionnaire sent to all full-time faculty at the western Canadian law schools. The questionnaire included demographic questions (e.g., age, gender, educational background, academic experience, rank, and appointment information) but also asked faculty questions about their teaching, research, and practical work activities. In addition, the questionnaire included questions about the factors that are shaping law professors' scholarship, employment environment, and law school culture. Finally, the questionnaire included a question asking participants to indicate their willingness to be interviewed for the study and to provide contact information if they agreed. The overall response rate to the survey across the six western Canadian law schools was 41 percent. The response rate from the University of British Columbia law school was 45 percent. The demographic data from the survey were analyzed using simple descriptive statistics, including frequencies and cross-tabulations. The open-ended questions were coded and analyzed across themes that emerged from the evidence and the literature.

Following the survey, case studies of the law schools commenced. Case studies were chosen on the basis of provincial representation, size and age of the law school and university, presence of the law school in a research intensive university, and extent of the law school's research profile. This second phase of the project involved interviews of faculty, administrators, and staff and included archival searches and document collection and analysis. The interviews focused on the culture of scholarship and work environment at each law school and the factors that influence them. Fifteen interviews were done at UBC law school between November 2002 and January 2003.

This number represented 50 percent of the full-time faculty physically present at the school during data collection. The interviews were semi-structured and lasted between sixty and ninety minutes. To achieve a representative sample, the following criteria were used to select interviewees: age, rank, disciplinary background, and gender. Faculty in senior administrative positions within the law schools were also selected for interviews. Interview data were transcribed, coded, and analyzed against the themes in the literature review on the political economy of Canadian higher education.

In addition, searches were conducted of university, law school, and government reports and the university archives. Documents examined included annual reports of the law school; academic plans of the law school and university; the law school's calendars over the past two decades; curriculum and program information; the law school mission statements; charter legislation of the university; university and SSHRCC research-funding information; archival documents on the history of the university and the law school; and histories of professional legal education in the province. Document and content analysis were used to develop descriptive profiles of the law school and the university within the context of the legal profession's history in the province.[4] This chapter presents findings from the UBC interviews and document analyses related to the impact of the political economy on academic culture at the law school.

Academic Culture at the Faculty of Law, University of British Columbia

The University of British Columbia (hereinafter UBC) is currently categorized as a medical-doctoral university having a broad range of PhD programs and research as well as a medical school. It houses twelve faculties, including commerce and business administration; law; medicine; dentistry; and arts and science. UBC researchers are members of twenty-one Canadian Networks of Centres of Excellence. The university is characterized by its commitment to research and interdisciplinary studies.[5] At the same time, it has recently committed itself to a millennium vision that includes nurturing close connections with the off-campus community.[6]

At the time of data collection (2002-3), the Faculty of Law had a complement of forty full-time faculty.[7] Nine of the forty faculty members (or 23 percent) held a PhD as their highest degree. Twenty-nine of the forty faculty members (or 73 percent) held a LL.M. as their highest degree. One hundred and ten adjunct faculty from the practising profession teach courses in the law school. The school offers the LL.B. program. This degree is the educational requirement for admission to the bar of the province and provides the point of regulation by the Law Society of British Columbia. The school also offers graduate degrees: a LL.M. and a PhD in law. A joint LL.B./MBA program is offered with the business school at the university. In 2000-1, the school enrolment in the LL.B. program totalled 617 full- and part-time students, not including additional exchange students. The incoming class enrolment was 213. Enrolment in the graduate programs for the 2000-1 year stood at 68 in the LL.M. program and 16 in the PhD program (*Dean's Report,* 2000-1). Tuition at the university had recently been deregulated after a six-year freeze. Tuition figures were under adjustment at the time of data collection.[8]

The Faculty of Law at the University of British Columbia houses the Centre for Asian Legal Studies, the Centre for Feminist Legal Studies, and is annexed to the International Centre for Criminal Law Reform and Criminal Justice Policy, an independent, non-profit institute affiliated with the United Nations. The law school offers unique programs such as First Nations Legal Studies; Environment, Sustainable Development, and Law; and the Alternative Dispute Resolution Program. The teaching program includes a Clinical Teaching Program and a Legal Research and Writing Program. The law school was awarded a Tier 2 Canada Research Chair (CRC) starting 1 July 2002. This is the first CRC for the law school. In addition, there are two Visiting Chairs established from private endowments to the law school. Two Permanent Chairs in Feminist Legal Studies (the first of its kind in Canada) and the Nemetz Chair in Legal History were made possible by private and public donations and the Province of British Columbia as part of the World of Opportunity Campaign. The Faculty of Law also publishes two student-run legal journals: The *UBC Law Review* and the *Canadian Journal of Family Law.* In addition, a number of faculty members co-edit the *Canadian Journal of Women and the Law* (*Dean's Report,* 2000-1, pp. 1-12).

Scholarship at the Faculty of Law

The data from this component of the study suggest that legal scholarship has flourished over the past twenty years and that legal knowledge has exploded in terms of subject areas and specializations. Academic legal scholarship has changed in its conceptual difficulty, complexity, and interdisciplinary character. While doctrinal scholarship still has a presence in the law school, the proliferation of theoretical and critical scholarship has been evident in the doctoral program as well as other new programs over the past two decades: "There is still a strong core of basic doctrinal analysis in the legal academy. We haven't abandoned doctrinal scholarship because [that is] basic legal analysis especially regarding new areas. Law is highly mobile because decisions are made all the time, so just understanding and grappling with the effects and meanings of new laws is a major job in itself. We have just combined critical [components] with it" (UBC: 2).[9]

Doctoral studies began at UBC in 1993 and have grown steadily from just a few students to nineteen continuing in September 2003 (Faculty of Law, 2004, p. 2). New faculty, hired in the past decade (1992-2002), were described as having stronger academic credentials coming into positions at the faculty than in the past. Whereas in the past most incoming faculty had a master of law degree (LL.M.) and had few publications, today doctorates in hand or in progress as well as publications are common. This ratcheting-up of credentials and publications was attributed in part to the tight and competitive market for positions in law schools across Canada in the 1990s. As a consequence, new faculty are entering law schools with greater research training and a research agenda heightening the research mission of the law schools, which was once almost predominantly focused on teaching. Additionally, with advanced graduate degrees, new faculty typically have had exposure to various academic research traditions and disciplines, and thus they have an understanding and appreciation of scholarship from other disciplines that may influence their own work. In part a consequence of law professors' increased research training, and in part a response to heightened publication expectations for tenure and promotion, law professors were described as more productive in their scholarship than in the past.

Interdisciplinary scholarship by law professors at the faculty, while on the rise, was described as a "minority trend" (UBC: 7). Multi-disciplinary work was described as difficult to engage in successfully. Few law professors worked across disciplines, but they were more likely to cite scholarship in other disciplines in their work than in the past, revealing an increasing awareness of trends outside their discipline. Similarly, while collaborative research is increasing, especially for younger law faculty and for law faculty engaged in social science-type research, the predominant mode of research was individual and solitary for most law professors. The trend toward collaborative research centres was noted to be increasing at the law school not just between full-time academics but also within the international community of scholars, government, and practising lawyers (UBC: 1). However, this trend was not considered a systemic change by the professors; rather, the data suggest that research centres are established on an ad hoc basis by faculty and that there is little external pressure from the university, government, or funders of research to organize scholarship along these lines.

A generational divide emerged as a distinct pattern in faculty scholarship. Older faculty were more likely to engage in doctrinal work, whereas new, younger faculty hired in the past decade were more likely to engage in critical theory or empirical or social science research, often with an interdisciplinary element. The generational divide extended to funding, with older faculty less likely to seek funding for their research, while younger faculty were more likely to seek funding. This pattern was explained in terms of the type of research being undertaken. Doctrinal work requires little or no funding, whereas empirical and social science-type research costs more to undertake. Exceptions to this finding were found primarily among experienced faculty who had worked in other disciplines or in the social sciences, who carried this interdisciplinary experience into their scholarship, and who were familiar with the process and expectation of obtaining research grants. Of this exceptional group, it was said that they had been "immersed in a funding culture for some time" (UBC: 2).

The law professors in this study suggested that most academic legal research requires little if any funding and thus typically is unfunded or funded internally by the law school with small amounts of money. Moreover, by their own account, law professors are well resourced for their research compared to other faculty in other parts of the university. Consequently, they tend not to look outside the school or university for research funds. Funds internal to the law school are readily available to provide research assistance. At the time of data collection, this source of funding was underutilized.[10]

Professors suggested that typically little or no large funding existed for research in law, no industry funding and no direct funding from the private sector, and very little indirect funding for research from the profession through endowment funds or endowed chairs at the law school.[11] The absence of private foundations that support legal research in Canada was also noted (in contrast to legal education in the United States). Funds supporting faculty research came primarily from the public sector – the Law Commission of Canada or government justice departments or the Social Sciences and Humanities Research Council of Canada (henceforth SSHRCC). SSHRCC grants, held by a few faculty at UBC's law school, were considered uncommon in law, cumbersome to apply for, and unnecessary for most research projects conducted by law faculty. The lack of SSHRCC funds was attributed in part to the lack of applications by law professors and in part to the constitution of the SSHRCC adjudication committees, which some faculty believed did not appreciate the nature of legal research, its methods, theory, and analysis (UBC: 7, 10, 12).

Information from SSHRCC's awards database confirmed these findings. Between 1998 and 2003, UBC received 1,269 SSHRCC awards[12] (grouped across SSHRCC programs, including doctoral fellowships, Standard Research Grants [SRG], Major Collaborative Research Initiatives [MCRI], and Community-University Research Alliances [CURA]). In the same time period, the law school received twenty-two of these awards, representing 1.7 percent of the university's total SSHRCC award base. This included two doctoral fellowships, a Canada Research Chair, two multi-year MCRI, and two CURAs as well as SRGs. The Canada Research Chair at the law school is one of twenty-five awarded to the university since 2001. No law faculty were involved in Networks of Centres of Excellence, although twenty-one faculty across the university are connected with NCEs.[13] Table 8.1 shows that the majority of SSHRCC-funded money awarded to UBC law school in the past four years has come from the MCRI and CURA programs. Standard Research Grants awarded to individual faculty represent a very small percentage (6.75 percent) of the total money awarded to the law school. Five faculty held SRGs. These

Table 8.1

SSHRCC awards, Faculty of Law, UBC, 1998-2002

Program		Amount ($)	Average award ($)
Research base:	Major Collaborative Research Initiatives (MCRI) Program	145,000.00 *31.79%*	72,500.00
	Standard Research Grants (SRG)	30,787.00 *6.75%*	30,797.00
Strategics:	Community-University Research Alliance (CURA)	280,250.00 *61.45%*	140,125.00
Total		456,037.00	91,209.40

Source: SSHRCC program statistics, http://www.outil.ost.uqam.ca/CRSH.

findings reflect the lack of individual grant funding received by law faculty from SSHRCC through Standard Research Grants, but they also suggest a promising trend toward funding of interdisciplinary scholarship through MCRIs and CURAs. Table 8.1 also shows that the total amount of SSHRCC funding across funding programs to the Faculty of Law (1998-2002) is surprisingly low, amounting to less than $500,000 over four years.

Professors expressed ambivalence in their accounts of pressure to attract research funds to the law faculty. Some felt little or no pressure to obtain research grants and no pressure to establish a track record of obtaining grants.[14] While some tenure-stream faculty felt pressure to produce that in some cases included the need to obtain funds, faculty did not connect these pressures with the market; rather, they connected them to the tenure and promotion structure at the university. However, funded research was valued by the university administration even for graduate students, as evidenced by the university's decision to link funding for graduate students in the law school to the number of SSHRCC awards they obtained.[15]

For another professor, seeking research funds was part of the job description and a reasonable expectation: "We are expected to seek funds outside the university because we are linked to a very influential and rich community, and our graduates, like medicine, will make big money" (UBC: 8). Another faculty member understood the necessity of bringing in research dollars as a response to the changing context within the discipline: "Other colleagues who have operated for many years in an unfunded context now feel pressure [to obtain research funding]. As an academic, that is one of the things you do: you get support for research. Now there is pressure to get external funding especially from SSHRCC. A lot of faculty feel their research doesn't appeal to SSHRCC committees, and a lot of them feel aggrieved by that expectation"

(UBC: 7). Some believed that this revenue-generating priority had crept into the criteria for the search for a new dean under way when the interviews were conducted. Some faculty suggested that the ability to raise money for the school was a desirable characteristic sought in the new dean (UBC: 1, 5, 7, 10).

The Commercialization of Knowledge

The literature critically analyzing the impact of economic restructuring on universities suggests a trend toward entrepreneurialism on the part of individual faculty (Slaughter and Leslie, 1997). This is reflected in efforts to commercialize knowledge, technology transfer, and university partnerships with industry. In the legal world, this trend looks different than it does in the sciences and other professions because law professors have a "marketable skill but not a marketable product" (UBC: 6).

> From the point of view of the faculty member, at no point do you create something that you can turn into a commercial thing. What you have got is a skill that you can exercise commercially for yourself – and some do a certain amount of practice, or you can exercise it in a pro bono capacity. Or you can spend time doing teaching and research. Law is not like engineering and science, where you can develop something you can commercialize. Law doesn't have new discoveries or inventions or processes. You become a skilled expert at some area of law that allows you to practise if you want. There is an entrepreneurial temptation like doctors or dentists who practise on the side. Not that you are developing something commercially that you created at UBC. You are just exploiting your knowledge and professional capacities. (UBC: 6)

Commercialization of knowledge occurs in the sale of services by law professors. Many law professors are licensed to practise law, and the law profession has traditionally been entrepreneurial.[16] This kind of extracurricular activity is neither new nor exceptional and is understood by study participants as engaging in professional practice rather than as the commercialization of knowledge.

Often law professors' sale of services takes the form of consulting for law firms on cases. A difference of opinion exists in the accounts of consulting because, as one professor suggested, people have been quite secretive about it (UBC: 7). A tension between faculty members appeared in the various accounts as to the appropriateness of law professors engaging in this kind of activity because it takes them away from their work with students. Given the heavy work demands and expectations for publishing, some professors wondered aloud how time could be found for such extracurricular activities: "At every law school, some full-time faculty have been entrepreneurs, running a part-time law practice out of their office ... To the extent that people are entrepreneurs here, it's more their private practice activities. We could have a debate as to whether that's appropriate in academic studies, but it does happen, and it's a sale of services as opposed to developing a product" (UBC: 7).

Perceptions of the pervasiveness of and the remuneration received from consulting and private practice activities also varied. Some suggested that much of the professional practice work by law professors was limited and had a large public service orientation, such as working on cutting-edge cases before the Supreme Court. In this respect, this work was viewed as informing their teaching, benefiting the school and the larger community, and not inconsistent with their vocation as law professors – not to mention raising the profile of the university, which "would be viewed as a good thing for the university" (UBC: 7). The findings indicate that some professors were "making equal to their salary" (UBC: 7) through this work. They were spending parts of the week at their law firm offices or working out of their law school offices doing work on retainers as consultants for law firms.[17]

The Culture of the Law School

A recurring theme throughout the accounts of the faculty regarding the culture of the law school related to its dual mission. A tension exists in the law school (and in the broader legal world) between its training and education missions. It must train for employment (because the LL.B. is the educational prerequisite for admission to the bar), and it must provide a broader academic, intellectual, postsecondary education. One professor summed up the tensions: "There are those that think law schools should provide more training, and there are those that think law schools should do what universities do best: [that is,] bombard students with interesting ideas, engage them, teach them to think critically, teach them core legal concepts within this, as part of a larger critical engagement in the larger intellectual enterprise which is the university" (UBC: 5). The tension has a history in Canadian law schools and was connected by one professor to the tension between theory and practice in professional schools and the debate over whether professional schools should be technical schools or provide a more academic intellectual education (UBC: 11; see also Bourdieu, 1988; Schon, 1995; and Veblen, 1957).

The dual mission of the law school also emerged in the professors' comments regarding the teaching and research agenda of the law school. Professors agreed that historically the teaching mission drives the law school. They suggested that teaching and student demands would become more prominent in the law school with the recent tuition increases. However, some professors argued that research was becoming increasingly important in the law school, while others said that teaching and research were mutually supported. The importance of research was reflected in the criterion of strong research agendas for new hires and in the number of faculty who had strong reputations for scholarship. One professor observed that the law school was known for its "amazing scholars," but it did not have the same reputation as an excellent teaching school (UBC: 10). The research culture as reflected in the graduate program at the UBC Faculty of Law was described by professors as strong, innovative, and an important part of the milieu in the school. The recent growth in the graduate program to include a doctoral program had enhanced the research agenda of the law school. It had also increased the school's international and interdisciplinary character (UBC: 11).

The culture of the school was defined as being progressive, as noted through the commitment to issues of social justice and social policy. According to faculty, this priority was reflected in the scholarship of recently hired professors. One professor suggested that the law school was known for its "left law" and went so far as to say that junior faculty held "contempt" for professional, corporate, doctrinal scholarship (UBC: 4). The faculty was not perceived to be overwhelmingly focused on the practice of law, and the concerns of the private-practising profession were not perceived as being central to the faculty. In fact, some worried that the concerns of the profession had become irrelevant to most faculty.

Although underfunding was an issue from years of budget cuts to universities in the province, the data suggest that the law school had not turned to the private sector to make up the shortfall. However, it did enjoy the support of the practising law profession. Significantly, not a single faculty respondent described a move toward privatization, a trend they observed in Ontario law schools. Faculty were clear that trends associated with neoliberal restructuring that had manifested in other jurisdictions, such as Australia, the United Kingdom, and the United States, had not (yet) reached the law school at UBC. "We are massively underfunded here. We don't have resources, we don't have time, we don't have staff, and we don't have all the things you need to manage big research projects. But we have not moved down the privatization route like Ontario" (UBC: 1). At the same time, faculty were aware of the dramatic changes taking place in legal education across Canada but concluded that it was too soon to tell if these changes would make their way into their law school. Moreover, when asked about the influences on the academic culture of the school, one professor described the pervasive role of the market in shaping the academic culture of the school: "More than political it [the culture of the law school] is market driven, and there is no collegiality because it's a profession. You are competing for funds all the time. You are competing in [tenure and promotion] review; that [review] process is a sort of competition as well. Students are evaluating you; that's a sort of competition as well. You are competing to publish ... If you are working in an area of international law, you are competing internationally with people from other parts of the world to publish in the *Harvard Law*

Review" (UBC: 8). While some professors were clear that law school culture was becoming more competitive and market oriented, several noted that students, not professors, were the most vulnerable to the economic changes. Market-like behaviour translated into "fierce" competition among students (UBC: 1, 7, 8, 10).

Autonomy and Academic Freedom

The faculty described high levels of institutional and individual autonomy for the law school and the professors. The school was described as "an anomalous creature" curiously independent from both the university and the profession (UBC: 6, 11, 12). Institutional autonomy has been historically strong at the law school, notwithstanding recent incursions and potential challenges from the various constituencies having vested interests in the law school, such as the law profession, the university, and the students.[18] The Law Society of British Columbia's limited regulatory relationship to the school was described and accepted as one of the few "constraints" on the law school. Faculty noted that any discussion of autonomy must be seen within the context of the Law Society's mandatory requirements on the curriculum (UBC: 8, 12). Ironically, the law school's relationship to the practising profession was described as an integral part of their history and essential to their autonomy within the university. The law school has had a history of professional support. Faculty described the relationship with the profession as "important," "good," and "close" (UBC: 1, 2, 3, 6). "The relationship between the law school and the profession has always been very supportive. That's partly because this law school started because the profession demanded it and backed it and has always seen itself as part of the law school. Their crest is over our entrance to the library since the early days of the law school. The Law Society sees itself as a stakeholder in the law faculty, and we respect that" (UBC: 6).

The school has enjoyed generous support from the legal profession within the province. This support includes financial and human resources. The profession provides numerous scholarships, bursaries, and awards for law students. It has contributed to an endowment fund that directly supports students and indirectly supports faculty research through the provision of research assistant jobs given to students. In the past, the profession has contributed capital toward the building of the law school. It has extensive involvement in the school through adjunct professors. The adjuncts are much needed because the law school does not have adequate full-time faculty to teach all the students. Adjuncts' salaries are minimal, and many contribute their salaries back to the law school (UBC: 1, 7, 10). However, there was concern over the law school's increasing reliance on adjunct professors from the practising profession required because of cutbacks that had affected faculty hiring (UBC: 7). Faculty suggested that the law school's dependence on the profession for money and support compromised its ability to make independent decisions. Even adjuncts who were poor teachers could not be turned away for concern over offending the law firms from whence they came (UBC: 7, 8).

The law school's relationship with the university was also canvassed, and faculty commented that the law school was "self-contained," even "isolated," and enjoyed a high level of independence within the university, especially regarding the setting of standards. They attributed this to the regulatory relationship with the practising legal profession (UBC: 4, 6, 12). One professor suggested that the law school demonstrated "very little accountability" to the university (UBC: 4): "There is a tradition of treating us independently and with quite a lot of respect because we are a professional school. And we have clout with the profession and government. And I would say the university doesn't realize a lot of that has disappeared. And we don't have as much influence and connection with those people we once did. We are protected by our history" (UBC: 4). While individual professors were becoming increasingly integrated into the university, the law school was less connected. One sensed that it was on the margins of the university compared to other disciplines: "Traditionally, there has been the view that the university has been gentle with the law school because we are a professional school with connections to downtown. We can pretty much do as we like, set our own standards, and the university is not going to interfere as they would in the arts and maybe even the sciences" (UBC: 4). Others suggested that the central administration of the university left the law school alone because it did not make too many demands on university resources (UBC: 7, 12). At the same time, faculty acknowledged that the law school had strong links to central university governance and decision making as many law faculty were often called upon to serve on university governance committees (UBC: 6, 12).

The law professors in this study consistently described high levels of academic freedom in their scholarship. Funding of research, where it did take place, was largely untied. Scholarship was overwhelmingly described as directed by "faculty's research interests" (UBC: 1, 5, 11) or "faculty curiosity' (UBC: 4, 2, 3) and was "unconstrained" (UBC: 2, 5). Faculty were described as having "a lot of control" over their scholarship (UBC: 3, 12). One professor summed it up: "I've had a lot of control over what I do. I'll often say to people 'will you look at this?' before it goes out. But I've never had anyone try to steer it" (UBC: 3). Influences on the direction of scholarship were described as "opportunity" to do certain work, available financing for costly research (UBC: 3), and "judgment of peers" (UBC: 4, 7).

While faculty were aware of various pressures and changes in the higher education environment, there was a consensus that law faculty experienced high levels of individual autonomy and that there were few if any constraints on their research.

> There is an incredible amount of freedom to pursue one's own research agenda within the university and within this corner of the university. And by and large, faculty still set their own research projects. It is the incredible luxury of an academic job. It also raises an important function of the university setting – space to allow people to pursue things that are important to them but also socially, culturally, and politically [important] ... There is a large measure of academic freedom. I don't feel constrained in my research agenda. (UBC: 5)

Conclusion

The findings suggest that at the time of data collection the changing political economy had not [yet] affected the law school at the University of British Columbia in the same way, or to the same extent, as in other jurisdictions and disciplines, as described in the literature. The law professors in this study of the UBC Faculty of Law did experience challenges associated with increased workloads accompanied by a serious scarcity of basic human and financial resources. They described changing expectations for research production and grant winning (especially for young untenured professors who participated in the study). They noted pressure on their intellectual scholarship and an increasing emphasis on research and revenue generation. However, they also described high levels of academic freedom and professional autonomy. Moreover, they insisted that they were largely immune to the imperatives of scientism and commercialism, funders' agendas, and the university's ties to industry. The participants attributed their immunity to their professional status and their connection to a wealthy, supportive profession. The participants in this study did not equate the sale of legal services (undertaken by some professors in the form of consulting) with the commodification or commercialization of their academic research and knowledge. Rather, they understood it as engaging in the private practice of law, not a new trend and consistent with the historical entrepreneurial nature of the law profession.

The findings suggest that, while the law school has moved into the university, it still lacks overall integration into the university academic culture. As a consequence, there is little influence, for good or ill, on the culture of the law school by other disciplines in the university. Moreover, the nature and degree of the influence of postsecondary policies on the law school is markedly different from other disciplines in the university. At the same time, the law school has a supportive relationship of relative independence and light regulation with the profession's regulatory body. Academic law has considerable autonomy from its practising profession, which may explain why market pressures associated with the practice of law have not overwhelmed the academic arm of the profession. The law school's relationship with the private practising profession secures, if not strengthens, the law school's position within the university. The relationship is encouraged by the university as it provides a source of capital for the law school and minimizes the law school's drain on the university's scarce resources.

The faculty at UBC law school did not see neoliberal restructuring playing out in their law school as it had in other provinces (e.g., Ontario). Similarly, they distinguished their academic context from trends occurring in the United States, the United Kingdom, and Australia. One faculty member insisted that British Columbia was not a comparable political environment and that there had never been anything like neoliberal micro-management of curriculum and scholarship in the law schools in British Columbia, stating that "it just hasn't happened here" (UBC: 1). However, economic priorities, market principles, and increasing competition were acknowledged to be influencing students and, by extension, the curriculum through students' choices. One professor suggested that the corporatization of the law school would occur through the students' choices as "consumers" and not through faculty choices regarding their scholarship (UBC: 10). Moreover, legal education was described as on the cusp of significant changes due to tuition deregulation. One professor suggested that change in tuition policy was "the most significant change in legal education in half a century" (UBC: 6). The potential implications of tuition deregulation were perceived as enormous. Faculty argued that it could change the landscape of legal education, leading to stratification, privatization, and accreditation, which would ultimately increase professional and external regulation of the law school and decrease its autonomy (UBC: 2, 6). In the area of the law school's teaching mission, and especially tuition policy (as opposed to law professors' scholarship), one currently finds the most pressing evidence of the influence of the political economy at the law school.

This study clearly captures the academic culture of the law school at the University of British Columbia at a moment in time. Follow-up one year after data collection suggested the faculty were already experiencing changes, including more pressure to obtain funding for their research and to increase research productivity. In this respect, this case study provides a useful benchmark upon which to capture change over time at the law school. The findings of this study also contribute to our understanding of changes that are occurring in academic culture in the current policy environment and illustrate one discipline's response to those changes. The findings of this study suggest that the impacts of national and global factors on academic culture vary across disciplines (and perhaps professions) within the university. Issues surrounding the transformation of academic culture associated with capital accumulation and international competitiveness manifest in ways that are specific to each discipline in the university, making cross-disciplinary analyses essential to a meaningful understanding of this phenomenon.

Notes

An earlier version of this chapter was published as "Creeping capitalism and academic culture at a Canadian law school" in the *Windsor Yearbook of Access to Justice*, 26(1) (2008), 123-63.

1 The first component of the study focused on the six law schools in Ontario. The second component, currently under way, focuses on law schools in western Canada. This program of research has been supported by a SSHRCC Doctoral Fellowship and a SSHRCC Postdoctoral Fellowship.

2 For several American examples, see the works published in Delgado (1997-98); Interpreting Legal Citations: A Symposium Sponsored by the West Group (2000); and Symposium on Trends in Legal Scholarship (1996).

3 These included Faculties of Law at the University of British Columbia, the University of Manitoba, and the University of Alberta.

4 The findings of the case study of the Faculty of Law at the University of British Columbia relate to the time period during which the data were collected. Shortly after the data were collected, the administration of the law school changed. Follow-up communication with faculty confirmed that aspects of the research culture had changed at the law school with the new administration. I have endeavoured to make a note of this where relevant in presenting the data.

5 The *Maclean's Guide to Canadian Universities and Colleges* (2003) reports that UBC has the highest percentage of full-time faculty with PhDs of the fifteen medical-doctoral Canadian universities (p. 38). UBC ranks second after the University of Toronto for the biggest average size and number of peer-reviewed research grants for both the Social Sciences and Humanities Research Council of Canada and the Canada Council for the Arts (p. 39). It ranks third after the University of Toronto and McGill University in the size and number of peer-reviewed research grants from both the National Sciences and Engineering Research Council and the Canadian Institutes of Health Research (p. 39).

6 See UBC (2000, 2002).

7 This number included faculty on sabbatical and other leaves as well as faculty who had been seconded to other parts of the university. The actual number of full-time faculty physically present at the law school during data collection was thirty.

8 The *Dean's Report* did not provide tuition figures. The law school website updated March 2001 cited (now out-of-date figures) \$5,000 for the first year and \$4,042 for the second and third years for the LL.B. Non-Canadian citizens and non-permanent residents had to pay \$461 per credit. The average year consists of thirty to thirty-two credits. Additionally, all students paid \$2,300 in various fees. Subsequently, the law school website updated to 2004 listed tuition for Canadian and landed immigrant students at \$9,000 for the first year. International students' tuition was listed at \$16,928 for the first year.

9 To protect confidentiality, each participant in the interviews was assigned a number. References from interview transcripts are indicated in the text with the notation "UBC" followed by the number corresponding to the participant.

10 Support for research internal to the law school comes primarily from a "law endowment fund" created by a fundraiser in past years through donations from the practising legal profession. To this is added other "soft money" from sabbatical leaves, unfilled positions, and other donations from individuals or classes. The money has few ties but must be used to benefit students. It allows law professors research assistance in the form of graduate student salaries but does not allow for other research expenses, such as travel expenses associated with research or attending conferences. At the time of this interview, it was reported that \$50,000 was available in the last round of applications for assistance by law faculty, and only half of that was actually allocated (UBC: 4).

11 This does not include consulting done by professors. Also, professors noted the tremendous support for the profession by way of human and financial resources for areas other than faculty research (e.g., adjunct professors and money for scholarships and bursaries for students, major donors to fundraising campaigns in the past, and contributions to build the law school in the 1970s). However, it was noted that the profession does not directly fund

faculty research, but indirectly some of its contributions support the scholarship of faculty, as in the case of the above-noted endowment fund.

12 Each year of the award appeared to be counted in the database separately. Therefore, the actual number of multi-year awards received is lower than the database would suggest.

13 See SSHRCC Awards Engine under "Detailed Lists of Projects." Search parameters: Institution-UBC, Discipline-Law, Fiscal Year-1998/1999-2001/2002, at http://www.outil.ost.uqam.ca/CRSH/.

14 This finding changed with the new administration. Follow-up in May 2004 revealed increased encouragement to attract research funds to the law school.

15 The absurdity of this action taken by the university administration was noted by faculty, who pointed out that most of their graduate students were enrolled in one-year LL.M. programs and would finish their studies by the time SSHRCC sent them the results of their applications.

16 See Rice and Richlin (1993). The "entrepreneurial professions" are business, journalism, and law. The "helping professions" are dentistry, medicine, ministry, nursing, pharmacy, social work, and teaching. The "technical professions" are architecture, engineering, and the military. This classification is based on Stark, Lowther, and Hagerty's (1986) work on the primary missions of each field.

17 UBC has guidelines that address integrity and ethical consideration of consulting and private practice activities: Conflict of Interest and Conflict of Commitment (Policy 97). Activities outside the university must not conflict with commitments within the university or adversely affect the individual's ability to remain responsible to his or her work within the university. University faculty and staff are expected to disclose any activities that might be a potential conflict of interest or commitment.

18 The Law Society's recent unsuccessful attempts to shape the curriculum of the law school by introducing Bar Admission Entrance Exams were seen by most faculty as an unacceptable incursion on the law school's autonomy. Although this effort by the profession was perceived by faculty as an "intrusion" into the law school (UBC: 7), professors explained that the law school was perceived by the practising profession as "unresponsive" and increasingly "irrelevant" to the profession's curricular needs (UBC: 3, 8).

References

Abel, R. (Ed.). (1997). *Lawyers: A critical reader.* New York: New Press.

Arthurs, H. (1995). A lot of knowledge is a dangerous thing: Will the legal profession survive the knowledge explosion? *Dalhousie Law Journal, 18*(2), 295-309.

–. (1997). Globalization of the mind: Canadian elites and the restructuring of legal fields. *Canadian Journal of Law and Society, 12*(2), 219-46.

–. (1998). The political economy of Canadian legal education. *Journal of Law and Society, 25*(1), 14-32.

–. (2001). Poor Canadian legal education: So near to Wall St., so far from God. *Osgoode Hall Law Journal, 38*(3), 381-408.

Axelrod, P. (1986). Service or captivity? Business-University relations in the twentieth century. In W. Neilson and Chad Gaffield (Eds.), *Universities in crisis: A medieval institution in the twenty-first century* (pp.45-68). Montreal: Institute for Policy Analysis.

–. (1998). Challenges to liberal education in an age of uncertainty. *Historical Studies in Education, 10,* 1-19.

–. (2002). *Values in conflict: The university, the marketplace, and the trials of liberal education.* Montreal: McGill-Queen's University Press.

Backhouse, C. (1999). *The changing landscape of Canadian legal education.* http://www.umanitoba.ca/faculties/law/LRI/Legal_education.htm.

Beazley, M., and Edwards, L. (1998). The process and the product: A bibliography of scholarship about legal scholarship. *Mercer Law Review, 49*(3), 741-71.

Bourdieu, P. (1988). *Homo academicus.* Stanford: Stanford University Press.

Brodie, J. (1994). Shifting the boundaries: Gender and the politics of restructuring. In I. Bakker (Ed.), *The strategic silence: Gender and economic policy* (pp. 46-61). London: Zed Books.

–. (1995). *Politics on the margins: Restructuring and the Canadian women's movement.* Halifax: Fernwood Publishing.

Brown, P., and Lauder, H. (1996). Education, globalization, and economic development. *Journal of Educational Policy, 11*(1), 1-25.

Bruneau, B., and Savage, D. (2002). *Counting out the scholars: The case against performance indicators in higher education.* Toronto: Lorimer.

Buchbinder, H. (1993). The market oriented university and the changing role of knowledge. *Higher Education, 26,* 331-47.

–. (1995). Globalization, deficit reduction, and Canadian universities: Considering the contradictions. *Higher Education Policy, 8*(3), 23-26.

Consultative Group on Research and Education in Law. (1983). *Law and learning report to the Social Sciences and Humanities Research Council of Canada.* Ottawa: SSHRCC.

Currie, J. (1998a). Globalization practices and the professoriate in Anglo-Pacific and North American universities. *Comparative Education Review, 42*(1), 15-29.

–. (1998b). Introduction. In J. Currie and J. Newson (Eds.), *Universities and globalization: Critical perspectives* (pp. 1-13). Thousand Oaks, CA: Sage.

–. (1998c). Globalization as an analytical concept and local policy responses. In J. Currie and J. Newson (Eds.), *Universities and globalization: Critical perspectives* (pp. 15-20). Thousand Oaks, CA: Sage.

Currie, J., and Newson, J. (1998). *Universities and globalization: Critical perspectives.* Thousand Oaks, CA: Sage.

Dean's Report. (2000-1). Faculty of Law, University of British Columbia.

Ellickson, R. (2000). Trends in legal scholarship: A statistical study. *Journal of Legal Studies, 29*(1) (Part 2), 517-55.

Eraut, M. (1994). *Developing professional knowledge and competence.* London: Falmer Press.

Faculty of Law, University of British Columbia. (2004). *Report of the Graduate Committee for the Academic Year, 2003-2004.*

Fisher, D., and Rubenson, K. (1998). The changing political economy: The public and private lives of Canadian universities. In J. Currie and J. Newson (Eds.), *Universities and globalization: Critical perspectives* (pp. 77-98). Thousand Oaks, CA: Sage.

Freidson, E. (1986). *Professional powers.* Chicago: University of Chicago Press.

–. (1994). *Professionalism reborn: Theory, prophecy, and policy.* Chicago: University of Chicago Press.

Interpreting legal citations: A symposium sponsored by the West Group. (2000). *Journal of Legal Studies, 29.*

Johnson, T. (1972). *Professions and power.* London: Macmillan Press.

Jones, D. (1998). Research and teaching on law faculties: An empirical exploration. *Chicago-Kent Law Review, 73*(3), 765-821.

Kelsey, J. (1998). Privatizing the universities. *Journal of Law and Society, 25*(1), 51-70.

Larson, M. (1977). *The rise of professionalism: A sociological analysis.* Berkeley: University of California Press.

Maclean's Guide to Canadian Universities and Colleges, 2003. (2003). Toronto: Rogers Media.

Magnusson, J. (2000). Examining higher education and citizenship in a global context of neo-liberal restructuring. *Canadian Ethnic Studies Journal* (March) 72-88.

–. (2001). Canadian higher education and citizenship in the context of state restructuring and globalization. *Encounters,* 107-23.

McGuire, C.H. (1993). Sociocultural changes affecting the professions. In L. Curry and J. Wergin (Eds.), *Educating professionals: Responding to new expectations for competence and accountability* (pp. 3-16). San Francisco: Jossey-Bass.

Merriam, S. (1998). *Qualitative research and case study applications in education.* San Francisco: Jossey-Bass.

Newson, J. (1992). The decline of faculty influence: Confronting the effects of the corporate agenda. In C. Williams, L.C. Ruffman, R. Currie, and D. Harrison (Eds.), *Fragile truths: Twenty-five years of sociology and anthropology in Canada* (pp. 227-46). Ottawa: Carleton University Press.

Newson, J., and Buchbinder, H. (1988). *University means business: Universities, corporations, and academic work.* Toronto: Garamond Press.

–. (1990). Corporate-university linkages in Canada: Transforming a public institution. *Higher Education, 20,* 355-79.

Polster, C. (1996). Dismantling the liberal university: The state's new approach to academic research. In R. Brecher, Q. Fleischmann, and J. Halliday (Eds.), *The university in a liberal state* (pp. 106-22). Aldershot, UK: Avebury.

Polster, C., and Newson, J. (1998). Don't count your blessings: The social accomplishments of performance indicators. In J. Currie and J. Newson (Eds.), *Universities and globalization: Critical perspectives* (pp. 173-92). Thousand Oaks, CA: Sage.

Pue, W. (2001). Globalisation and legal education: Views from the outside-in. *International Journal of the Legal Profession, 8*(1), 87-102.

Rice, J., and Prince, M. (2000). *Changing politics of Canadian social policy.* Toronto: University of Toronto Press.

Rice, E.J., and Richlin, L. (1993). Broadening the concept of scholarship in the professions. In L. Curry and J. Wergin (Eds.), *Educating professionals: Responding to new expectations for competence and accountability* (pp. 279-315). San Francisco: Jossey-Bass.

Saul, J.R. (1995). *The unconscious civilization.* CBC Massey Lecture Series. Concord, ON: Anansi Press.

Schon, D. (1995). Educating the reflective legal practitioner. *Clinical Law Review, 2,* 231-50.

Shanahan, T. (2002). *Legal scholarship: An analysis of law professors' research activities in Ontario's English-speaking common law schools.* Unpublished doctoral dissertation, University of Toronto.

Slaughter, S. (1998). National higher education policies in a global economy. In J. Currie and J. Newson (Eds.), *Universities and globalization: Critical perspectives* (pp. 45-70). Thousand Oaks, CA: Sage.

Slaughter, S., and Leslie, L. (1997). *Academic capitalism: Politics, policies, and the entrepreneurial university.* Baltimore: Johns Hopkins University Press.

Stark, J.S., Lowther, M.A., and Hagerty, B.M.K. (1986). *Responsive professional education: Balancing outcomes and opportunities.* ASHE-ERIC Higher Education Reports 3. Washington, DC: Association for the Study of Higher Education.

Symposium on Trends in Legal Scholarship. (1996). *Chicago-Kent Law Review, 70.*

Teeple, G. (1995). *Globalization and the decline of social reform.* Toronto: Garamond Press.

Thornton, M. (2001a). Among the ruins: Law in the neo-liberal academy. *Windsor Yearbook of Access to Justice, 20,* 3-25.

–. (2001b). The demise of diversity in legal education: Globalization and the new knowledge economy. *International Journal of the Legal Profession, 8*(1), 237-57.

UBC. (2000). *TREK 2000: UBC's vision.* Vancouver: UBC.

–. (2001). *Calendar, 2001-2002.* Vancouver: UBC.

–. (2002). *The University of British Columbia strategic plan: Summary.* Vancouver: UBC.

Veblen, T. (1957). *Higher learning in America.* New York: Hill and Wang.

Yin, R. (1984). *Case study research: Design and methods.* London: Sage.

9 Keeping the Commons in Academic Culture: Protecting the Knowledge Commons from the Enclosure of the Knowledge Economy

Jennifer Sumner

> The commons – a material and symbolic reality, always changing, never purely local or global, traditional or modern, and always reflecting the vibrant colours of its ecological, political, cultural, scientific and social character – is not at all disappearing into the dustbin of history. To the contrary, we find that the commons are increasingly becoming a site for robust and tangible struggles over class, gender, nation/ethnicity, knowledge, power and, of course, nature. (Goldman, 1998, p. 14)

We are all familiar with the concept of the commons – naturally occurring resources held in common that provide a subsistence living to various communities of people – and the enclosure of the commons by powerful, private interests. We are less familiar with the concept of the civil commons – co-operative arrangements among people that ensure universal access to the means of life. A recognition of the civil commons helps us to understand its long-standing, but unrecognized, role in our lives and the importance of protecting it against modern forms of enclosure. One subset of the civil commons, the knowledge commons, is under threat from the enclosure demands of the knowledge economy. Global, corporate pressures to accumulate capital by competing internationally are forcing hard choices within academic culture: to be agents of the enclosure or guardians of the public good.

This chapter begins with the concept of the commons before moving to the civil commons and one of its subsets, the knowledge commons. Then it discusses modern forms of enclosure, with reference to the privatization of knowledge within the academy. Finally, it explores various ways that academics have been resisting enclosure of the knowledge commons and reaching out to other knowledge communities.

The Commons

An inclusionary term, the commons represents "the shared heritage of us all, for which we all serve as trustees" (Rowe, 2002, p. 28). This Trojan horse concept injects the idea of collective sharing into what is becoming a largely individualistic, commodified, and privatized society. Indeed, Bollier (2002a, p. 3) maintains that "the commons is arguably the default mode of economic organization around the world and throughout history, even though, of course, market exchange has always existed." This default mode of economic organization has taken on a number of forms, from common grazing land to acacia trees and public forests.

Historically, the commons or common property regimes, controlled by local communities, have given sustenance to the poor (Tammilehto, 2003, p. 49). Gary Snyder (2001, p. 475) points out that the word *commons* has an instructive history: it is formed of *ko,* "together," with (Greek) *moin,* "held in common." The Indo-European root *mei* had a special meaning of "exchange of goods and services within a society as regulated by custom or law," which he links to the principle of gift economies. Snyder adds that the root comes into Latin as *munus,* meaning "service performed for the community." The commons became part of Roman law, reflecting the Roman belief that some forms of property, by their very nature, should not be subject to individual ownership and control (Bollier, 2002b, p. 176).

The commons was first used in the English language in singular form – "the common" – and appeared in print as far back as the late 1500s (*Oxford English Dictionary,* 1989, p. 567). Bocking (2003, p. 26) explains how it was used to describe parcels of land that were used "in common" by peasant farmers, very few of whom possessed enough land to survive. Although probably owned by titled notables, the commons were protected by strict rules, recognized by the courts, that assured their availability to peasant farmers. Bocking goes on to outline how landowners began removing "the commoners" by planting hedges or otherwise barring their access from land that had been used in common for centuries.

This exclusionary process of barring access to the commons has long been referred to as enclosure, understood as "extinction, with or without a physical fencing of land, of common and customary use rights on which many people depended for their livelihood" (Wood, 1999, p. 83). Tammilehto (2003, p. 50) describes how the enclosure process started during feudalism and other precapitalistic regimes, with the first legal act to enforce enclosure of the common lands being passed in Britain in 1235. However, it was during the rise of capitalism that the seizure of the commons became a prevailing historical process. In Britain, for example, between the fifteenth and nineteenth centuries, most of the commons were privatized so that, by 1876, a mere 0.6 percent of the population owned 98.5 percent of the agricultural land in

England and Wales. Through the enclosure process, Tammilehto explains, "the poor have lost their independent livelihood in a power struggle where the commons have been privatised or destroyed. In this process, small holders have been driven into a corner so that they have sold their land, and the communal and cultural structures and technological practices supporting autonomous means of livelihood have been destroyed" (p. 49).

While some argue that the enclosures helped lead to the creation of modern industrial markets, they also inflicted "devastating social, environmental and human costs on once-stable rural communities" (Bollier, 2002b, p. 5). Starvation, forced migration, vagrancy, and destitution faced those people whose common resources were stripped away for private profit, with no avenue of legal or local recourse. "The law itself becomes now the instrument of the theft of the people's land, although the large farmers make use of their little independent methods as well" (Marx, 1965, p. 724). Resistance was met with official suppression, and thousands of peasants lost their lives. So powerful were the forces that supported the enclosure process that few people in high places spoke against them. One who did, Lord Protector Somerset, lost his life after giving "encouragement to the rebellious peasants by his staunch denunciation of enclosures" (Polanyi, 1957, p. 35).

Although various forms of enclosure have been carried out for centuries, the concept of the commons and its enclosure again became the centre of debate with the publication of Garett Hardin's paper "The Tragedy of the Commons" in 1968. Hardin argued that the commons could not work as a concept because of human greed. After projecting the self-maximizing principle of neoclassical economics onto others who do not operate out of that value system, he advocated that "the tragedy of the commons as a food basket is averted by private property, or something formally like it" (p. 1245).

Hardin's work has been criticized from a number of perspectives, but one of the main critiques, which Hardin himself later came to agree with, argued that he was describing an open-access domain, not a commons. In spite of this counterargument, however, his paper "provided an academic rationale for the privatization of land and resources. It encouraged such things as the transfer of land from tribal peoples to the state or to corporations or individuals; it was used to justify the industrial exploitation of the fisheries, and the privatization of water. Neoconservatives cited it in support of the private takeover of many things long considered to be public assets or part of the commons" (Bocking, 2003, p. 28).

The rise of corporate globalization over the past twenty-five years has been accompanied by intensifying forms of enclosure on a global scale. The whole range of public goods such as fresh water, the atmosphere, genetic structures, and wilderness areas – in short, our common wealth – are becoming candidates for enclosure. This drive for enclosure is promoted by transnational corporations, facilitated by complicit governments, and enabled by supranational, unelected institutions such as the World Bank and the International Monetary Fund. The sadly ironic outcome of this modern enclosure movement is that it is turning all forms of the commons into open-access domains for the self-maximizing use of transnational corporations, setting the stage for a real tragedy of the commons of global proportions. Without the values that support the commons – community, co-operation, and respect for the rights of others – it becomes decimated by the values of enclosure – exclusion, private ownership, monopoly control, and personal or corporate gain.

Overall, the commons can be understood as our common property, a source of well-being that we all share (Rowe, 2002, p. 29). Enclosure of the commons harms us all, preventing access to life-giving resources that maintain or increase our well-being. "For human beings, as for the biosphere, the tragedy of the commons is not the tragedy of their existence but the tragedy of their disappearance" (Monbiot, 1998, p. 362). The growing body of rules and regulations that strip the commons must be challenged and replaced by an alternative vision. And that vision begins with the concept of the civil commons.

The Civil Commons

While the commons represents the naturally occurring resources that maintain and increase our well-being, the civil commons represents the formal and informal rules and regulations that govern commons development and usage for the common good. A concept put forward by philosopher John McMurtry (1999a, p. 1), the civil commons is "any co-operative human construction that protects and/or enables the universal access to life goods." As such, the civil commons is *co-operatively built* through human agency at many levels: the local, the provincial, the national, and the international. It *protects* both the individual and society through binding social rules such as regulatory systems for clean air, water, foodstuffs, and safe working conditions; it *enables* both the individual and society through opening up public spaces that provide the opportunity for development (e.g., universal education, public art and architecture, and open environmental space) (McMurtry, 2002, p. 835). The civil commons ensures *universal access,* not just access for those with the money to buy their way in. And it provides the key to *life goods,* or the means of life, which enable life to be preserved or extended on the three vital domains of thought, feeling, and action. In sum, the civil commons is "society's organized and community-funded capacity of universally accessible resources to provide for the life preservation and growth of society's members and their environmental life-host" (McMurtry, 1998, p. 24).

Examples of the civil commons abound at many levels: internationally through agreements like the Amsterdam Treaty on dumping, the Kyoto

Agreement on climate change, the European Union (in its aspects that protect or enable universal access to life goods, such as minimum wages and free movement of labour), the United Nations Convention on the Rights of the Child, and the United Nations Universal Declaration of Human Rights; nationally through social assistance, the Canada Health Act, Banff National Park, the CBC, and the Charter of Rights and Freedoms; provincially through water and power installations, public education, highways, bridges, and public libraries; locally through bylaws prohibiting the cosmetic use of pesticides or the arrival of "big-box" stores and promoting neighbourhood care teams for the terminally ill. Multi-scalar in its web of interactions, the civil commons is "the vast social fabric of unpriced goods, protecting and enabling life in a wide and deep seamless web of historical evolution that sustains society and civilization" (McMurtry, 1998, p. 25).

McMurtry (1999b, p. 205) is careful to distinguish between the traditional commons and his concept of the civil commons: "It is important to distinguish between 'the commons' as nature-given land or resource and 'the civil commons' which effectively protects it, and ensures access of all members of the community to its continuing means of existence." In this way, the civil commons is "civil" insofar as "the common life-good it embodies is protected by conscious and co-operative human agency" (1999a, p. 205).

The civil commons has been with us for thousands of years but below the level of consciousness. Faced with threats of enclosure, it is time to acknowledge its nurturance and inclusionary power. As McMurtry (1999b) points out, "where there is an evolved civil commons sensibility, its concerns for fellow members of the community extend wider as it develops, past the family or the region to the nation and outwards to the civil commons of the world as it might be. The civil commons is an open possibility" (p. 215). Part of that open possibility is the academy itself. When understood as a co-operative human construction that protects and/or enables universal access to the lifegood of education, universities are part of the civil commons. This understanding has its roots in the academy of the ancient Greeks, with its practice of open dialogue. As far back as the 1300s, thesis defences were public events, when the candidate was required to stand in the courtyard for three days and take on all comers in public debate. While the modern defence lasts only about three hours, the same spirit remains. In essence, "the idea of the commons lies at the heart of academe. It informs the very identity and mission of the university, and accurately describes why its work is so valuable. Academia *is* a commons" (Bollier, 2003, p. 2). Canadian universities can be seen as examples of the civil commons in action. As publicly funded institutions, they have a mandate to serve the public interest, which can be found in their mission statements. For example, the "objects and purposes" of the University of Guelph, as laid down in the University of Guelph Act, are "the advancement of learning and the dissemination of knowledge." On its website, the university "invites public scrutiny of the fulfillment of its mission, especially by the people of Ontario, to whom it is accountable." Central to this mission is the complex question of knowledge.

Knowledge and the Knowledge Commons

Knowledge, though intangible, is a life good that contributes to increased well-being. It can be understood as a set of shared, subjective, often taken-for-granted meanings and assumptions that are socially and historically constructed (Mezirow, 1995, p. 52). These meanings and assumptions are neither static nor bounded but fluid and changing. In effect, "knowledge is not a final perception, but an evolving conception, no more immutable than the environment in which it makes sense" (Allen, 1996, p. 298).

In his *Knowledge and Human Interests*, Habermas (1978) argues that humans are interested in three kinds of knowledge: empirical-analytic knowledge, historical-hermeneutic knowledge, and critical-emancipatory knowledge. Following his framework, Morrow and Torres (1995, p. 23) contend that the diversity of the human interest in knowing must be recognized. They propose that empirical-analytic knowledge provides the kind of knowledge associated with the natural sciences, that historical-hermeneutic knowledge provides the kind of knowledge associated with the human sciences, and that critical-emancipatory knowledge provides the kind of knowledge associated with critical thought. In other words, "knowledge ... is based upon a desire potentially to control through the analysis of objective determinants, to understand through the interpretation of meanings, and to transform reality through the demystification of falsifying forms of consciousness" (p. 24). All three kinds of knowledge contribute to what has come to be known as the knowledge commons. A subset of the civil commons, the knowledge commons involves co-operative human constructions that protect and/or enable universal access to the life good of knowledge. Co-operative constructions such as public education, learning circles, rural extension, and kitchen table meetings all ensure universal access to knowledge. This knowledge is shared, not privatized, packaged, priced, and profited from. As such, it forms part of the common wealth that sustains individuals and communities around the world. But the knowledge commons and its ethic of sharing, like other forms of the civil commons, is under siege from the privatizing demands of the global corporate market. This unrelenting process provides a modern example of the historical enclosure of the commons.

The Knowledge Economy as a Modern Form of Enclosure

Karl Polanyi (1957, p. 35) has argued that "enclosures have appropriately been called a revolution of the rich against the poor." This revolution is being waged with as much ferocity today as in medieval England, with many of the same consequences. Just as the traditional commons were cleared by acts of enclosure to make way for private profit, so too the civil commons is currently being cleared by the policies of corporate globalization to make way for private profit. "There is now no place in the world, indigenous or industrialized, in which the civil commons is safe from corporate market invasion" (McMurtry, 1998, p. 372). Around the world, long-evolved institutions of the civil commons, such as education and health care, are under assault. The shared resource of the knowledge commons is under similar threat, and the vehicle for this expropriation is the knowledge economy.

A search of the Internet reveals an avalanche of sites dealing with the knowledge economy but few that explain what it really means. Most of the definitions are tied, in one way or another, to economic development, a euphemism for prioritizing private, for-profit enterprise. If knowledge is produced by millions of people around the world every day, and economies are supposed to be concerned with the production and distribution of goods otherwise in short supply, then the knowledge economy seems to be a contradiction in terms.

The oxymoronic meaninglessness of the knowledge economy, however, has not prevented the phrase from catching on. Institutions such as the World Bank, the Social Sciences and Humanities Research Council of Canada, and universities have eagerly adopted it as the celebratory buzzword for the shotgun marriage between the academy and transnational corporations. The enclosure of knowledge did not begin with the knowledge economy, however. It has been with us for millennia in the form of expert, or official, knowledge.

In spite of the fact that "the human interest in knowledge is a plural one" (Morrow and Torres, 1995, p. 23), certain restrictive forms of knowledge have dominated human existence, taking on the mantle of "expert knowledge." This expert knowledge has, in turn, been understood as a kind of official knowledge that supports the dominant groups in society. Cunningham (1988) explains the role of such official knowledge from a Gramscian perspective: "All bodies of knowledge are not equal. The knowledge that supports the dominant paradigms in a culture is systematically produced, disseminated, and reified so as to become common sense to the average citizen" (p. 137). One of the ways that official knowledge supports the dominant paradigms in a culture involves either the co-option or the dismissal of knowledge that does not conform to this notion of "common sense." All forms of knowledge can be co-opted into maintaining the status quo, and knowledge that cannot be co-opted is ignored, marginalized, or criminalized.

Official knowledge has excluded other kinds of knowledge throughout history. Forms of common knowledge, such as indigenous knowledge, women's knowledge, experiential knowledge, transformative knowledge, situated knowledge, and local knowledge, have all experienced the exclusionary power of the official knowledge regime. What is unprecedented, however, is the range and power of current forms of official knowledge. Their breadth of reach and depth of penetration have been made possible by the commodification of knowledge on a global scale and the creation of the knowledge economy. Within the knowledge economy, knowledge is being transferred from the public realm to a "corporate sector that views knowledge merely as another commodity to be bartered in the marketplace" (Berman, 1998, p. 230).

Universities and the Enclosure of Knowledge

Universities, in many countries, have traditionally been one of the sources of the knowledge commons: "One of the purposes of a public system of higher education is to provide a haven where the exchange of ideas may flow, not only between teacher and student, but also among peers ... The knowledge created is shared freely for the benefit of all society" (Doherty-Delorme, 1999, p. xi). But this time-honoured source of common knowledge is drying up as defunding increases under neoliberal pressures. For this reason, universities provide a microcosm for investigating the enclosure of knowledge: "The idea that universities can enter into partnerships in which knowledge is traded off for money implies that 'knowledge' can be bundled up into neat packages and a precise monetary value can be attached to them. To accomplish this end, knowledge needs to be quantified and measured in terms of its economic 'exchange' value" (Newson, 1998, p. 116). This packaging and pricing of knowledge go against the vision many people have of universities. Instead of pressing the boundaries of knowledge and inspiring student questioning (Chomsky as cited in Shaker, 1999, p. x), universities today are producing knowledge that Polster (1996, p. 109) describes as "increasingly narrow and oriented to serving the needs of industry."

One of the reasons for this altered purpose is that universities, like other parts of the public sector, are targets for privatization. The first step in this privatization process involves the reduction of public funding for higher education. Strategies such as lowering taxes, diverting public money to service deliberately created debts, and discrediting public service can virtually bankrupt higher education, thus eliminating the competition of low-priced or free public knowledge. Facing insolvency, universities have been forced not only to restructure but also to forge alliances with transnational corporations, euphemistically known as the private sector. In the wake of this corporatization of higher education, the major product of the university – knowledge – becomes ripe for enclosure.

In *Silent Theft: The Private Plunder of Our Common Wealth*, Bollier (2002b, p. 40) discusses gift economies, which are "a powerful force in creating and sustaining the commons." He defines a gift economy as "a web of enduring moral and social commitments within a defined community sustained through the giving of gifts (of goods, services, and courtesies) without any assurance of personal return" (p. 31). Bollier goes on to describe the academy as a flourishing gift culture, "which presumed (and still presumes, for the most part) that data, research tools and other scholarly resources should be widely shared and openly scrutinized" (p. 137). While knowledge has been one of the gifts freely given in academic culture, the drive to privatize knowledge means that "proprietary knowledge aspires to neuter and replace common knowledge" (p. 141). In spite of a proud history of contributing to public knowledge, it is clear that, "nowadays, the gift culture in academia is under siege. Smart money wants to make darn sure that its precious knowledge is locked up in equity shares" (p. 146).

Opting Out by Not Buying In to the Knowledge Economy

While academics must often work within the bounds of the knowledge economy, there are still a number of ways they can refuse to buy in to it. Both within the academy and outside its walls, academics can participate in building and maintaining the knowledge commons.

Resisting Enclosure within the Academy

Academics can resist the enclosure of the knowledge commons within the academy itself. Brown (2000) offers a rationale for academic resistance when he raises the question of accountability: "I do not for a moment believe we should be living in an ivory tower, indifferent to the world outside. The question is to whom we should be accountable – to use a favourite term of the privatizers. The answer is simple: the public. We owe it to them to keep knowledge free for all" (p. 1702). Brown advises that, within the university, "regular academics must take up the cudgels" (p. 1702): at the individual level, academics can refuse to do contract research that requires non-disclosure and insist on keeping knowledge public; at the university level, academics can put pressure on their leading administrators to take decision-making power out of the hands of private interests, corporate or philanthropic; at the political level, academics can pressure government leaders to keep research and education as part of the public good.

Polster (1996, p. 118) also provides suggestions for action by academics, along with relevant community groups. At the level of the state, they can work to reform, if not abolish, unelected and unaccountable advisory bodies as well as a host of federal programs, policies, and regulations that put control over university resources into private hands; they can also press for a range of new federal programs and policies that would promote closer research and other links between the university and a broad range of social groups. At the level of the institution, they can wage campaigns against particular university/industry research initiatives; they can oppose new decision-making procedures that marginalize community participation; and they can demand greater accountability and improved representation from the leaders of their institutions who sit on the various politically incorporated advisory boards and other bodies that are gaining greater influence over higher educational policy making.

The Massachusetts Institute of Technology (MIT) provides a path-breaking example of resistance to the enclosure of the knowledge commons. By announcing in April 2001 that it was making most of its course materials available for free to the public through the Internet, MIT "swims against the current that sees knowledge as private property and the Internet as a way to make money by attracting on-line, fee-paying students" (Fine, 2001, p. A1). In a move intended to counter the privatization of knowledge, MIT sees itself as sharing its knowledge, especially with Third World countries that want to use its courses as templates for starting up their own. Based on a belief that access to knowledge is a right that should be available to everyone, MIT's refusal to join the enclosure movement represents a watershed in the knowledge wars.

Lowering tuition fees is also a form of resistance because it broadens the base of knowledge production within the academy. In the face of escalating tuition fees in countries like Canada, which increasingly ensure that only the children of the elite can afford higher education, both Ireland and Scotland have recently reversed the trend, making university tuition free of charge. The issue of tuition fees and enrolments is extremely complicated. There is a positive correlation between increasing fees and increasing university enrolments; however, this is entangled with both economic and social factors. Despite an opening up of entry to universities in the 1960s and in the 1980s and 1990s, there is a disproportionately high enrolment of middle- and upper-class students and a disproportionately low enrolment for students from lower-class backgrounds and, in particular, for Aboriginal students (Conway, 2004; McKenzie, 2007).

As a primary source of knowledge production within higher education, research can become a site of resistance. While some research has always served private interests, there has been a seismic change in university research priorities as a result of the enclosure of the knowledge commons. Corporate funds and a patenting frenzy have turned the traditional commons of shared knowledge into a petri dish of secrecy and paranoia (Rowe, 2002, p. 30). One indicator of this massive change in research is intellectual property, which involves the privatization of formerly public knowledge. Intellectual property embodies the idea that knowledge can be "commodified and thus offered for sale and appropriated as the protected (even private) property of an owner" (Newson, 1998, p. 117). Polster (2000) describes how groups opposed to the development and extension of intellectual property regimes (IPRs) currently advocate two strategies of resistance. The first involves claims that some forms of knowledge, such as information about the human genome, should be declared unprivatizable because they belong to the common heritage of humanity. The second involves arguments for various forms of exemptions from IPRs in the name of the public interest. Polster advocates including academics in these exemptions, arguing that such an exemption is crucial to the survival of the liberal university and hence vital to the public interest. She also suggests additional measures, such as trying to change government policies that promote the commercialization of university knowledge and launching campaigns to get academics to voluntarily sign over to the public the IP rights to their work.

Thesis defences also provide sites for resisting the commodification of knowledge. One of the spin-offs of the corporate research agenda now controlling universities is closed thesis defences. Traditionally open to the public as part of the pursuit of common knowledge, some thesis defences are now closed to everyone except those who are willing to sign a document promising they will not reveal what they have heard behind closed doors without the expressed permission of the researcher. This abrogation of the defining tradition of the academy – shared knowledge and open debate – has been permitted because "from time to time a student will develop significant intellectual property in the course of his or her research and wishes, legitimately, to protect that property until it can be patented or published in a particular format" (Heathcote, 2000). And while some may find it "legitimate" to privatize knowledge produced at publicly funded institutions, academics should make it clear that such privatization not only contravenes the mission of many institutions of higher learning but also contributes to the destruction of public education and undermines the public good.

Academic knowledge sharing in the form of colloquia, seminars, and informal talks also provides a means to resist the enclosure of the knowledge commons. With cutbacks and downsizing, overworked faculty may find that they no longer have the time for such endeavours. But making the time to share research results, explore new lines of thinking, and report on collaborative ventures helps to create a nurturing climate in which the knowledge commons can thrive. From here, academics can develop what Polster (2000, p. 36) refers to as "knowledge collectives," in which various academics pool their intellectual capital and use it as a lever to free up even more knowledge. She suggests that anyone wanting to use the collective's knowledge would have to share his or her own knowledge in return, thus reversing the progressively limited access to knowledge while protecting and enlarging the knowledge commons.

Resisting Enclosure outside the Academy

Another route to overcoming the enclosure of the knowledge commons involves building new relations of knowledge production. To say that knowledge is produced suggests "an active process of creative construction 'on site' according to specific local rules and conditions. Specifically, producing knowledge entails a confluence of the right conditions of production: people, places, ideas and material artifacts" (Barnes, 2000, p. 452). One of the ways of achieving that confluence of conditions is to reach out to other knowledge producers to build the knowledge commons. A form of resistance in itself, reaching out begins with the understanding that knowledge is socially produced and can be produced by any group of people.

Understanding that knowledge is socially produced changes the way people relate to it and changes the way they relate to those who have the power to control it. No longer merely the purview of experts (including academics) or the private property of transnational corporations, knowledge can emerge from many locations. Reaching out and forming alliances with the larger community makes the knowledge that is produced rich and varied, creating a kind of epistemic diversity that challenges the packaged homogeneity of commodified knowledge.

Progressive social movements provide an opportunity for reaching out and building the knowledge commons. While social movements have long been known as sites of knowledge production, academics have traditionally shied away from associations with them. This aversion to dealing with issues affecting the public good and building alliances with groups that pursue these issues must be overcome if we are going to change the relations of knowledge production in the academy and in society at large.

Another opportunity for reaching out involves universities sponsoring working groups, community forums, and conferences that promote alternative visions of society. Such forums create spaces where different kinds of knowledge can be shared, which mirrors the commitment to the dissemination of knowledge that has historically been the mandate of publicly funded universities. For this reason, reaching out to such alternative venues helps to build the knowledge commons.

One more example of reaching out involves the establishment of free universities. Free universities are part of a long line of common-knowledge institutions such as mechanics' institutes, agricultural extension, educational associations, and various forms of lifelong learning. According to Brians (1999), the first free universities were born in the radical context of the late 1960s. The model was the alternative college at San Francisco State, where courses were offered in a host of subjects not covered (or covered in a limited way) in the conventional curriculum. When establishing the Community Free University in Pullman, Washington, Brians recalled how members set up a vision that has been largely adhered to over thirty years: "We would let anyone teach anything to anyone so long as the content wasn't positively illegal. The fee for a course would be a minimal one dollar. No exams, no requirements, and – most significant of all – no pay for the teachers. This was to be a strictly volunteer effort."

A twenty-first-century version of the free university can be found in the People's Free University of Saskatchewan (Woodhouse, 2003). Working from the idea that "everyone can teach, everyone can learn," it opened its doors in the fall of 2002 with six courses offered in different locations in Saskatoon. Retired professors and members of the community gave their services for free to almost 200 students. Upon completion of the course, these students could obtain a certificate of learning. The People's Free University was created because of opposition among faculty, staff, and students to the privatization of the University of Saskatchewan, including a doubling of tuition fees and funding for research that increasingly serves the corporate market.

Reaching out could also involve appointing a community activist in residence. While many universities feature an entrepreneur in residence or a CEO in residence, such a choice does little to prevent enclosure of the commons. Inviting a community activist to be a vital part of academic life legitimizes alternative ways of viewing communities and builds alliances with community groups, not corporate "partners" who use the university affiliation as an opportunity for brand exposure.

Using Our Commons Sense

The social construction of knowledge reminds us that knowledge cannot be locked away by the privatization restrictions of the knowledge economy. It blooms at every opportunity that people come together to talk and share and learn. The question for academics is whether they want to be gatekeepers for the knowledge economy or participants in the knowledge society, whether they want to be agents of enclosure or agents of enablement. To become part of the co-operative human agency of the civil commons, we need to start using our "commons sense" – that is, reorienting ourselves to affirming the civil commons in our thoughts, feelings, and actions. Using our commons sense not only challenges the "corporate turn" in education but also affirms the core values of education itself.

Academic culture does not transform itself. It is transformed by decisions and choices from without and from within the academy. The demand for international competitiveness to promote capital accumulation for transnational corporations can be countered by the reality of local, national, and international co-operation to enable knowledge sharing for society at large. This is the dream of educators around the world and the promise of the knowledge commons.

References

Allen, B. (1996). Forbidding knowledge. *The Monist, 79*(2), 294-310.

Barnes, T. (2000). Local knowledge. In R.J. Johnston, D. Gregory, G. Pratt, and M. Watts (Eds.), *The dictionary of human geography* (4th ed., pp. 452-53). Malden, MA: Blackwell.

Berman, E.H. (1998). The entrepreneurial university: Macro and micro perspectives from the United States. In J. Currie and J. Newson (Eds.), *Universities and globalization: Critical perspectives* (pp. 225-49). Thousand Oaks, CA: Sage.

Bocking, R. (2003). Reclaiming the commons: Corporatism, privatization drive enclosure of the commons. *CCPA Monitor, 10*(5), 26-28.

Bollier, D. (2002a, 21-24 November). The commons as an emerging model for knowledge creation and governance. Remarks at the Rockefeller Foundation's conference Collective Management of Intellectual Property: Tackling the Anti-Commons, Bellagio, Italy. http://www.bollier.org/pdf/Bellagio_remarks11_21_02.pdf.

–. (2002b). *Silent theft: The private plunder of our common wealth.* New York: Routledge.

–. (2003, 13 June). Preserving the academic commons. Paper presented at the Eighty-Ninth Annual Meeting of the American Association of University Professors, Washington, DC. www.learcenter.org/pdf/BollierAAUP.pdf.

Brians, P. (1999). History of the community free university. http://www.wsu.edu/~brians/cfu.html.

Brown, J.R. (2000). Privatizing the university: The new tragedy of the commons. *Science, 290,* 1701-2.

Conway, J. (2004). The arithmetic of tuition fees. *On Campus News* [University of Saskatchewan], *12*(8). http://www.usask.ca/communications/ocn/04-dec-03/viewpoint3.shtml.

Cunningham, P.M. (1988). The adult educator and social responsibility. In R.G. Brockett (Ed.), *Ethical issues in adult education* (pp. 133-45). New York: Teachers College Press.

Doherty-Delorme, D. (1999). The corporate takeover of our universities and colleges. *Education, Limited* [Canadian Centre for Policy Alternatives, Ottawa], *1*(4), 11-19.

Fine, S. (2001, 5 April). The tuition's okay, but don't expect a prof. *Globe and Mail,* pp. A1, A12.

Goldman, M. (1998). Introduction: The political resurgence of the commons. In M. Goldman (Ed.), *Privatizing nature: Political struggles for the global commons* (pp. 1-19). New Brunswick, NJ: Rutgers University Press.

Habermas, J. (1978). *Knowledge and human interests* (J.J. Shapiro, Trans.). Boston: Beacon Press. (Original work published 1968)

Hardin, G. (1968, 13 December). The tragedy of the commons. *Science, 162,* 1243-48.

Heathcote, I.W. (2000). Private correspondence to author from dean of the Faculty of Graduate Studies, University of Guelph.

Marx, K. (1965). *Capital* (vol. 1). Moscow: Progress Publishers.

McKenzie, H. (2007). Debunking a neoliberal education myth: It's tuition fees that are regressive, not public funding. *CCPA Monitor 14*(1) [Canadian Centre for Policy Alternatives, Ottawa]. http://www.policyalternatives.ca/MonitorIssues/2007/06/MonitorIssue1695/index.cfm?pa=DDC3F905.

McMurtry, J. (1998). *Unequal freedoms: The global market as an ethical system.* Toronto: Garamond.

–. (1999a, 7 June). The life-ground, the civil commons, and global development. Paper presented at the annual meeting of the Canadian Association for Studies in International Development, Congress of the Social Sciences and Humanities, Sherbrooke, Quebec.

–. (1999b). *The cancer stage of capitalism.* London: Pluto Press.

–. (2002). The life-ground, the civil commons, and the corporate male gang. *Canadian Journal of Development Studies, 22,* 819-54.

Mezirow, J. (1995). Transformation theory of adult learning. In M. Welton (Ed.), *In defense of the lifeworld: Critical perspectives on adult learning* (pp. 39-70). Albany: SUNY Press.

Monbiot, G. (1998). The tragedy of enclosure. In D. VanDeVeer and C. Pierce (Eds.), *The environmental ethics and policy book: Philosophy, ecology, economics* (pp. 360-62). Toronto: Wadsworth.

Morrow, R.A., and Torres, C.A. (1995). *Social theory and education: A critique of theories of social and cultural reproduction.* Albany: SUNY Press.

Newson, J. (1998). The corporate-linked university: From social project to market force. *Canadian Journal of Communications, 23,* 107-24.

Oxford English Dictionary (2nd ed.). (1989). Oxford: Oxford University Press.

Polanyi, K. (1957). *The great transformation: The political and economic origins of our time.* Boston: Beacon Press.

Polster, C. (1996). Dismantling the liberal university: The state's new approach to academic research. In B. Brecher, O. Fleischmann, and J. Halliday (Eds.), *The university in a liberal state* (pp. 106-21). Brookfield, VT: Avebury.

–. (2000). The future of the liberal university in the era of the global knowledge grab. *Higher Education, 39,* 19-41.

Rowe, J. (2002). The promise of the commons. *Earth Island Journal, 7*(3), 28-30.

Shaker, E. (1999). *Higher education, limited: Private money, private agendas* [Canadian Centre for Policy Alternatives, Ottawa], *1*(4).

Snyder, G. (2001). The place, the region, and the commons. In M.E. Zimmerman, J.B. Callicott, G. Sessions, K.J. Warren, and J. Clark (Eds.), *Environmental philosophy: From animal rights to radical ecology* (3rd ed., pp. 471-86). Upper Saddle River, NJ: Prentice-Hall.

Tammilehto, O. (2003). *Globalisation and dimensions of poverty.* Helsinki: Ministry for Foreign Affairs of Finland, Department for International Development Co-Operation. http://global.finland.fi/english/publications/pdf/tammilehto_globalisation.pdf.

University of Guelph. 2008. New faculty survival guide: Mission statement. http://www.uoguelph.ca/facultyjobs/join/fsg_intro.shtml.

University of Guelph Act. 1964. Statutes of Ontario, c. 120, Province of Ontario.

Wood, E.M. (1999). *The origin of capitalism.* New York: Monthly Review Press.

Woodhouse, H. (2003). Strengthening Saskatchewan communities through education. *Saskatchewan Notes* [Canadian Centre for Policy Alternatives, SK], *2*(3), 1-4.

Conclusion

Adrienne S. Chan and Donald Fisher

Our aim in this book, and in the conference from which it sprang, has been to reveal how academic culture in Canadian universities changed during the 1990s. Discussion in the preceding chapters has been framed by what we take to be the two most important structural trends: commercialization and marketization. Authors have utilized the work of Slaughter and Rhoades (Chapter 1) on the "academic capitalist knowledge/learning regime" as well as the concept of "quasi-market" developed by Marginson (1997). At the same time, we have been conscious of accountability in the setting and implementation of educational policy. The authors in this book generally agree that Canada is following in the footsteps of American postsecondary educational systems and that this is a negative trend. While globalization and the emergence of the knowledge society are not the focus of this book, inevitably the changes described are contained within and contribute to these larger developments.

We have been particularly concerned with the connection between public universities and the private sector. We have attempted to document in this book how and why the contours of this territory have been changing and the impacts of these changes on universities' internal life. Both the public space and the activities within that space have been redefined. New circuits of knowledge connect the state, postsecondary education, and the market. Research becomes the watchword for progress and for increasing institutional status. Individual students are forced to assume more of the financial burden for their education through higher fees and more loans. As the content of academic work changes, the burden falls most heavily on women and minority faculty in the gendered professional schools. Dominance of an economic imperative in educational policy coupled with the structural trends described above creates the conditions for the emergence of what we have described as the "exchange university."

Effects and Consequences

A central aspect of adoption of the academic capitalist knowledge/learning regime has been elevation of research to be the most important function and defining characteristic of our public universities. Slaughter and Rhoades discuss the traditional tripartite role of teaching, research, and service and the imbalance that occurs when the state and university administrators put research first. In the case of the University of Ottawa (Chan and Fisher), changes in academic culture were housed in the motivation and determination of administrators to become a research intensive university and for the university to redefine the relationship between itself and the private sector. The University of Ottawa has moved closer to the market and competes fiercely with other universities for available funding. Yet privatization occurs more at the level of rhetoric than substantively at the level of research funding. The increase in research funding has come primarily from the state as public space has been transformed into a quasi-market. For Muzzin, traditional "white men" are still entrenched in the dwindling number of existing tenured positions, and new women and minority faculty must struggle harder to get tenured jobs (if they are even available) and funding. Similarly, in the professional schools (Dillabough and Acker), the rise of research culture is a central aspect of how women are gendered and marginalized in a globalized, market-oriented academy. Finally, we note the general trend toward Mode 2 knowledge production, which means research done in context of application. We (Chan and Fisher) note this change at the institutional level and Gemme and Gingras in the education and training of new researchers.

The tension between teaching and research demands in higher education institutions becomes more apparent when seen through the lens of gender. Women, especially new faculty and contingent faculty, often take teaching jobs that may possess less managerial, decision-making power. While universities are changing, their faculties are still "heteropatriarchal." Dillabough and Acker observe that older "white" "straight" men may be retiring but that their positions are not being renewed; they are instead being changed to part-time or adjunct positions (increasingly with regularized benefits but often with less privilege and power in decision making).

Universities grapple with finding tools and systems that allow for new technologies to co-exist with individual/collective autonomy in ideas and practices (collegiality) as the centre of institutional life (Chan and Fisher, Gemme and Gingras, Muzzin, Newson and Polster). These struggles are instead characterized by a great deal of ambivalence and sometimes a degree of "apparent" indifference. However, taking up the struggle may be precarious in the academy as individuals face issues of tenure, funding, and collaboration with colleagues in other institutions. While the term "ambivalence" is not used in this book, it characterizes a broad range of discussion running through it. For example, according to Slaughter and Rhoades, universities "want the best of both worlds – the protection and continued subsidies of the public sector, and the flexibility, opportunities, and potential revenue streams of the private sector." The tension between what is private, what is public, and how universities find a balance between public (intellectual) interests/practices and private (corporate) interests/practices is constant.

Ambivalence is also manifested in the themes of the "privilege" and "merit" tenure system versus the emergence of cadres of contingent/functional faculty. Privilege/merit is being redefined in terms of the success that faculty display as academic capitalists. Such academic capitalism erodes the "political mind" of faculty as a collective and their collective autonomy in deciding what is worthwhile public knowledge. Newson and Polster suggest that the interests of faculty are mediated by funding and subordinated to corporate agendas. Such agendas influence the work available and the work that students choose to do, or are encouraged to do, within universities. Ambivalence exists between what seems to be a "romantic" notion of an unencumbered, curiosity-driven, autonomous pursuit of knowledge and the far more complex current system of pressures and expectations that faculty face when making professional and scholarly choices.

Redefining Public and Private

Within this overall tension between what is public and what is private, there is an additional question of how it is being redefined at the individual level as well as at the systemic/structural level in universities. A number of themes are considered here: globalization and commercialization, circuits of knowledge, and entrenchment of gendered education. Each theme has a particular impact on the academy.

Globalization and Commercialization

Globalization and commercialization are evidenced by the research intellectual/technical product in the form of patents, copyrights, and consultation outside the institution. Faculty face increasing pressure to acquire external revenue sources and to focus on knowledge production. In this sense, the collegial ethos is undermined and to some extent replaced by individual entrepreneurial activities. Newson and Polster refer to this situation as the "displacement of collegial self-governance by managerialism in universities."

According to Shanahan, tenure and promotion increasingly depend on both knowledge production and the ability to raise research funds. Indirectly, commercialization may guide the recruitment of members and sponsors for university advisory boards from the private sector. This trend reinforces the tension between private and public knowledge interests/investments. New faculty are more likely to be influenced by university corporate agendas.

Adoption of capitalistic market structures, systems, strategies, and discourses such as the "accounting logic" (the "logic model") and the risk of privatization of education are suggested by Chan and Fisher, Muzzin, Newson and Polster, Shanahan, and Axelrod. Quantification of tasks, numbers of students, "outputs," and "outcomes" eclipse a number of reasons why some faculty seem to do better than others.

Most ethnocultural minority and female faculty in the social sciences, liberal arts, and humanities are less likely to excel in this "accounting logic" in their fields due to historically entrenched inequities and emerging inequities (e.g., women working as part-timers and contingent faculty at great cost to their personal lives) and due to different knowledge paradigms and practices. Measuring "inputs" and "performance indicators" and linking motivation to concrete rewards (outcomes/outputs) suggest that academics are not trustworthy ("deadwood") unless they continually account for what they do. This erodes not only individual autonomy but also, by virtue of fragmenting the constituency, collective autonomy (Newson and Polster). Axelrod reinforces this theme by identifying "conditional grants," which are given according to how universities meet government-prescribed goals.

Privatization of higher education, flooding of the market with a range of applied credentials, and accreditation of many semi-private educational institutions may diminish the value and perceived distinctiveness of a degree from a traditional university. Such apparent choices and "democratization" processes in the education system conceal the marketization of education. On the one hand, flooding of the market may counteract elitism; on the other hand, it saturates workplace markets. Often this phenomenon is depicted in connection with specific fields, such as social sciences, liberal arts, "public welfare," and "social work" (Dillabough and Acker), which traditionally have enrolled women and less privileged minority groups. Ironically, these fields have often been considered to be engaged in public dialogue and public critique of the establishment. Thus, the market value of liberal arts is diminished and progressive intellectual work further eroded.

We are forced to redefine "the student" as a consumer of educational products. The joint pressure of marketization and internationalization creates quasi-markets within which students choose on the basis of cost, prestige, and access. The reregulation of tuition fees so that universities have more control is a relatively recent phenomenon in Canada. Similarly, the significance of international markets for students has become far more pronounced in recent years.

The emergence of a new regulated market economy of labour in universities is the result of privatization and commercialization. This economy of labour is a counterpoint to a traditional economy of knowledge that is public and energized by the collective autonomy of the academy. What emerges are new circuits/systems of knowledge such as the new cadre of nomadic temporary academic workers who have no specific allegiance or political or intellectual relationship to a particular university/college.

New but Fragmented Circuits of Knowledge

Interstitial organizations function as new networks of knowledge. For example, a cadre of managers oversees, promotes, and regulates distance education programs that depend on information technology and business owners, managers, and technicians of those (often separate) organizations that support/service universities. Intermediating organizations exist with, for example, networks of administrators and trustee networks. Trustee networks are individuals from the corporate sector, donors, and sponsors. Axelrod provides the example of OCUA in Ontario, which has centralized power to regulate the formulas by which universities are allocated funding and authority to approve new institutions.

These networks have led to an accumulation of power that runs parallel to faculty networks of knowledge. Networks may have competing interests that influence traditional networks of intellectual knowledge, such as the accrual of wealth for universities through grants and private funding. A positive influence may include the pressure to compete in an open market system. This open market system pressures "non-productive" academics and challenges the traditional male white hierarchy. Another effect may be the restructuring of power in intermediating organizations. Women (largely in the social sciences, humanities and arts, and social/public welfare work) and minorities may not be hired for those positions. However, they often become contingent workers or new faculty overloaded with additional expectations of management and co-ordinating roles.

Members of *intermediating* organizations are unlikely to consult with internal constituencies in universities (faculty and student associations) and may erode democratic decision making. For Newson and Polster, "the most that is granted to the academic or public constituency is 'input' into decision making. Control over the parameters of the debate, the attention given to particular inputs, and the final resolution all rest in the hands of a small, less accessible group of decision makers comprised mostly if not wholly of institutional managers."

Often the emergence of new programs is aimed at expanding the economic reach of universities. For example, the new "terminal master programs" and online and distance education courses require expanded management and cadres of temporary, itinerant, highly skilled workers at the expense of tenure positions. These programs promote academic life as functional and with the purpose of providing skilled workers. Private sector and academic partnerships are encouraged with the expansion of "linking mechanisms such as industrial liaison offices," whose role is to attract and sustain industrial partnerships (Newson and Polster).

These trends contribute to erosion of the collective and private "autonomy" of teachers and students and the emergence of what we call the "exchange university." Knowledge is pursued and accrued in the interest of what the capitalist workplace requires. The work of faculty and part-time intellectual workers is focused on these new purposes; the knowledge required is specific and predetermined. These new networks of knowledge circulate fragmented knowledge (which is not necessarily linked to political/power-brokering processes within universities). There is a more explicit link to private sector interests and corporate visions and disinterested, marginalized workers (e.g., nomadic, contingent faculty). These emerging networks of knowledge may erode the power of members of traditional intellectual networks (faculty cadres, professional associations, unions) to influence the agenda and the collective autonomy of universities.

According to Shanahan, the emergence of a number of interdisciplinary studies programs is suggested as one protective reaction against fragmentation and commercialization of the aims of higher education. However, the caveat is that this is a "minority trend" and difficult to pursue. For Shanahan, the dominant trend is diminishment of public discussion, debate, commentary, and critique within our universities.

New technologies mediate lives and functions in the institution. Faculty practice and student activities are part of the application of new technologies. For example, the application of information technology to academic work erodes autonomy in the sense that it pressures academics to make themselves available to students online and reduces their ability to organize and control their working lives. A number of minority and women teachers might fall within this category because they are likely to be in the contingent cadre and willing or needing to compromise labour conditions.

Further Entrenchment of Gendered Education

The issue of gender in relation to globalization emerges strongly in Dillabough and Acker's, Shanahan's, and Muzzin's chapters. The historical antecedents of well-entrenched power imbalance and inequities are often associated with racism and ethnocentrism. Dillabough and Acker document the devaluation of feminized academic fields and practices (e.g., the social sciences, humanities, and liberal arts). Corporatization of the institution is resisted in these enclaves but is felt in the pressure for production, particularly among new faculty and female contingent faculty. Female work (particularly teaching) seems to be rendered even more invisible by new technologies, new managerial systems (e.g., accounting logic), the increase in part-time, nomadic, and detached contingent faculty, and the commercialization of education.

Minoritization of the university population (faculty and students) and migratory work suggests themes about employment and workloads and intersects with the issues of historical gendering and racializing of various academic fields and academic labour (Muzzin). Prestigious universities market themselves to students and compete for students who score high in standardized tests (and who may be interested in target fields); this marketing determines that traditionally disadvantaged minority students attend community colleges (Slaughter and Rhoades). International students are viewed as an important new target market.

The book ends on a more positive note – Sumner pushes us to focus on how we might resist the dominance of the academic capitalist knowledge/learning regime and marketization. She emphasizes the enclosure of knowledge to illustrate the change in academic culture. As education is increasingly defined as a private good, so our universities become places of exchange. In response, Sumner holds up the examples of "free universities" and open access to knowledge initiatives as ways for us to confront the invasion of capital. We need to re-create our universities as common public spaces that are accessible to everyone.

Reference

Marginson, S. (1997). *Markets in education.* St. Leonards, UK: Allen and Unwin.

Contributors

Sandra Acker is a professor in the Department of Sociology and Equity Studies in Education, Ontario Institute for Studies in Education, University of Toronto. She has worked in the United States, Britain, and Canada. She is a sociologist of education, with interests in gender and education, teachers' work, and higher education. Book publications include *Gendered Education* (Open University Press, 1994), *The Realities of Teachers' Work: Never a Dull Moment* (Continuum, 1999), and, co-edited with Elizabeth Smyth and others, *Challenging Professions: Historical and Contemporary Perspectives on Women's Professional Work* (University of Toronto Press, 1999).

Paul Axelrod is a professor and the former dean of the Faculty of Education at York University (2001-8). He has published widely on the history and politics of schooling and higher education. His publications include *Values in Conflict: The University, the Marketplace, and the Trials of Liberal Education*; *Making a Middle Class: Student Life in English Canada during the Thirties; The Promise of Schooling: Education in Canada, 1800-1914;* and *Scholars and Dollars: Politics, Economics, and the Universities of Ontario, 1945-1980.*

Adrienne S. Chan is on faculty at the School of Social Work and Human Services at University of the Fraser Valley and is an adjunct professor at the Centre for Policy Studies in Higher Education and Training at the University of British Columbia, Department of Educational Studies. Her interests include diversity (race, gender, class, dis/ability, and sexual orientation), policy studies, social justice, child welfare, anti-racism and anti-oppression, institutional change, academic culture, research ethics, and research culture. Recent publications include "Policy Discourses and Changing Practice: Diversity and the University-College" *(Higher Education,* 2005); *Diversity and Change in Institutions of Higher Learning* (Edwin Mellen Press, 2007); and *The Evolution of Professionalism,* co-edited with Donald Fisher and Kjell Rubenson (Centre for Policy Studies in Higher Education and Training, 2007). She holds a SSHRCC Standard Research Grant (2006-9), and she is the principal investigator of a study examining social justice in the context of Canadian universities.

Jo-Anne Dillabough holds the position of reader in the Faculty of Education, Cambridge University (appointed September 2007). She retains her position as an associate professor in the Department of Educational Studies, University of British Columbia; a faculty associate (2005-6) at the Peter Wall Institute for Advanced Studies, University of British Columbia; and a Spencer Research Fellow. Her recent publications include *Challenging Democracy: International Perspectives on Gender, Education, and Citizenship,* co-edited with Madeleine Arnot (Routledge Falmer, 2000). She is also a co-editor, with A. Halsey, H. Lauder, and P. Brown, of *Globalisation, Education, and Social Change* (Oxford University Press, 2006). Her forthcoming books include *Lost Youth in the Global City,* with J. Kennelly (Taylor and Francis, 2008); *Troubling Gender Theory in Education,* co-edited with Martin Mills and Julie McLeod (Open University Press, 2008); and *Cultural Identities and Political Community: An Ethnographic Study of the Representation of "Indigenous Culture" in Canadian Schools* (UBC Press, forthcoming). She is currently the holder of two major SSHRCC grants and a Spencer Foundation grant. She also holds a UBC Killam Junior Research Fellowship for the 2007-8 academic year.

Donald Fisher is a professor and the co-director at the Centre for Policy Studies in Higher Education and Training, Department of Educational Studies, University of British Columbia. He has had a long and distinguished career in the sociology of education and public policy analysis. His interests include academic industry and the culture of universities, privatization, the state and educational policy, the history and sociology of the social sciences, and changing conceptions of academic culture in Canada. One of his early notable works was *The Social Sciences in Canada: 50 Years of National Activity by the Social Science Federation of Canada* (Wilfrid Laurier University Press, 1991). Recent works include "Brokers on the Boundary: Academy-Industry Liaison in Canadian Universities" (*Higher Education,* 2002), with J. Atkinson-Grosjean; and "Changes in Academy/Industry/State Relations in Canada: The Creation and Development of the Networks of Centres of Excellence" *(Minerva,* 2001), with J. Atkinson-Grosjean and D. House. His most recent book (co-authored) is *Canadian Federal Policy and Post Secondary Education* (Centre for Policy Studies in Higher Education and Training, 2006). Dr. Fisher is the past president of the Canadian Federation of the Humanities and Social Sciences.

Brigitte Gemme holds a BA in science, technology, and society and an MA in sociology, both from Université du Québec à Montréal. She is a PhD student (educational studies) at the University of British Columbia and a research associate at the Centre interuniversitaire de recherche sur la science et la technologie (CIRST). Her work focuses on the research education of graduate students in the context of university-industry and university-community partnerships.

Yves Gingras is a professor in the Department of History, University of Quebec at Montreal (UQAM), the former director of the Centre interuniversitaire de recherche sur la science et la technologie (CIRST), and a Canada Research Chair in History and Sociology of Science. His research covers the formation of scientific disciplines, the transformation of universities, and the effects of the mathematization of the sciences. He has recently edited an issue of the French journal *Actes de la recherche en sciences sociales* on *Academic entreprises* (June 2003). This issue is devoted to the transformation of universities in relation to industry over the past thirty years. His most recent book is *Éloge de l'homo techno-logicus* (Fides, 2005).

Linda Muzzin is an associate professor at the Ontario Institute for the Study of Education, University of Toronto, and is cross-appointed to the Faculty of Pharmacy and to Public Health Sciences in the Faculty of Medicine. Her most recent publication is a co-edited book with Peggy Tripp entitled *Teaching as Activism: Equity Meets Environmentalism* (McGill-Queen's University Press, 2005). Her other research and publications focus on academic capitalism and the pharmaceutical sciences, feminist and anti-racist approaches to professional education, and the chilly climate for minoritized faculty in the academy.

Janice Newson is a sociologist who critically examines the emergence over the past three decades of the corporate-linked university. She has been on the faculty at York University in the Department of Sociology since 1971. Among other things, her research analyzes the political implications of changes in funding policies, critically assesses technology-mediated teaching, and traces the development of mechanisms that allow particular economic, political, and intellectual agents to more effectively manage and shape the objectives and content of knowledge and to control its accessibility. In addition to her research and writing, she has been politically active in promoting an awareness of how the increasing business orientation of contemporary universities undermines their public-serving mission.

Claire Polster is an associate professor in the Department of Sociology and Social Studies at the University of Regina. She has published widely on the transformation of higher education in Canada, addressing issues such as the commercialization of academic research, the growing importance of research grants in Canadian universities, the erosion of university autonomy, the transformation of public policy and policy making for Canadian universities, and the implications of these changes for the public interest. Recent publications include "The Nature and Implications of the Growing Importance of Research Grants to Canadian Universities and Academics" (*Journal of Higher Education*, 2007) and "Private Interests at Public Expense: Transforming Higher Education in Canada" (in *Power and Resistance* [Samuelson and Antony (Eds.)], 2007). She has also been involved in a number of organizations and campaigns aimed at resisting the corporatization of Canada's universities.

Gary Rhoades is a professor and the director of the University of Arizona's Center for the Study of Higher Education. His research focuses on the restructuring of higher education organizations and of academic professions. His recent books are *Managed Professionals* (SUNY Press, 1998) and, with Sheila Slaughter, *Academic Capitalism and the New Economy* (Johns Hopkins University Press, 2004).

Theresa Shanahan is an assistant professor in the Faculty of Education and the co-ordinator of the Graduate Diploma in Postsecondary Education in the Faculties of Education and Graduate Studies, York University. She is a lawyer called to the Bar of Ontario in 1990. Her research interests include education law and policy, the political economy of postsecondary education, university governance, professional education/governance/ethics, human rights, and access and equity issues in education (especially for women, minorities, "at-risk" groups, immigrants, and foreign-trained persons). She is currently involved in higher education policy research, including the project Alliance for International Higher Education Policy Studies (AIHEPS), sponsored by the Ford Foundation. Theresa is the principal investigator for the case study of Ontario's higher education policy. Some recent publications include "Shifting Roles and Approaches: Government Co-Ordination of Post-Secondary Education in Canada, 1995-2006" (*Higher Education Research and Development,* 2007), and, with Glen Jones, "Legal Scholarship in Ontario's English-Speaking Law Schools" (*Canadian Journal of Law and Society,* 2007).

Sheila Slaughter is the Louise McBee Professor of Higher Education, Institute of Higher Education, University of Georgia. Her research areas are the political economy of higher education; science and technology policy; academic freedom; and women in higher education. Her most recent book, co-authored with Gary Rhoades, is *Academic Capitalism and the New Economy* (Johns Hopkins University Press, 2004). Her most recent book chapters are, with Amy Metcalfe, "Can Women Survive Academic Capitalism?" in *Unfinished Business: Women, Gender, and the New Challenges of Higher Education* (J. Glazer-Raymo [Ed.], Johns Hopkins University Press, 2007); and, with Gary Rhoades, "Academic Capitalism and the New Economy: Privatization as Shifting the Target of Public Subsidy in Higher Education," in *Globalization and Higher Education in the Americas* (C.A. Torres and R.A. Rhoads [Eds.], Stanford University Press, 2006). Dr. Slaughter received the Association for the Study of Higher Education Research Achievement Award in 1998 and the American Educational Research Association Career Research Achievement Award in 2000.

Jennifer Sumner is an assistant professor in the Department of Adult Education and Counselling Psychology at the Ontario Institute for Studies in Education, University of Toronto. Her research interests include adult education, knowledge production, sustainability, globalization, and critical pedagogy. She is the author of *Sustainability and the Civil Commons: Rural Communities in the Age of Globalization* (University of Toronto Press, 2005).

Index

Printed and bound in Canada by Friesens

Set in Stone by Artegraphica Design Co. Ltd.

Copy editor: Dallas Harrison

Proofreader: Sarah Munro

Indexer: Lillian Ashworth